T0287622

A MUSEUM AT WAR

Snapshots of life at the Natural History Museum
during World War One

Karolyn Shindler

Published by the Natural History Museum, London

First published by the Natural History Museum,
Cromwell Road, London SW7 5BD
© The Trustees of the Natural History Museum,
London, 2018

The Author has asserted her right to be identified
as the Author of this work under the Copyright,
Designs and Patents Act 1988

ISBN 978 0 565 09461 4

A catalogue record for this book is available from
the British Library

10 9 8 7 6 5 4 3 2 1

Reproduction by Saxon Digital Services
Printed by Toppan Leefung Printing Limited

Front cover & back cover images: © The Trustees
of the Natural History Museum, London

Contents

Introduction

'War is a great readjuster of values. Already its distant blaze throws into relief the vanities of life... And now even we museum curators may experience searchings of heart as we continue to enter our quiet halls to settle down to our accustomed routine'. Dr Francis Bather, Assistant Keeper, Geology Department.

August 4 1914. No one has any idea of what the scale of the war might be. The Foreign Secretary, Sir Edward Grey, has warned a few days earlier of the 'risk of a catastrophe of which it is impossible to measure either the dimensions or the effects', but even he cannot have imagined that so many millions will be killed or wounded, so many lives destroyed.

For the first time ever, bombs fall from the sky on to Great Britain. No-one has considered how to warn whole towns and cities of air attacks, protect people and buildings, conceal essential lights, and preserve the country's heritage and its future: priceless works of art, irreplaceable scientific specimens, books and manuscripts.

There are so many unknowns. With hundreds of thousands of men in the battlefield, how do you combat the hell of cold, wet, mud-filled trenches, where lice, frostbite, ticks, trench foot, rats and trench fever thrive? Where a wound infected by bacteria from the devastated farmland of the Western Front is almost invariably, in the first years of the war, fatal? Or where, in the extremes of parched heat and cold, sodden winters in Salonika and Gallipoli, malaria, dysentery and tick-born diseases kill and disable more men than battle?

At sea, where the sinking of merchant ships and submarine blockades threaten the country with starvation, what sort of instruments are needed to warn of the enemy's approach underwater? How can the design and speed of airships and submarines be improved? What – if anything – can be learned from fish, whales and dolphins, and what is the best wood for airship construction? How can the new allotments now taking over golf courses, parks and back gardens – so essential in their contribution to the country's diminishing food supplies – be kept free from pests and fungi? And can a sceptical population really be persuaded to eat porpoises and puffins?

How can adapting the protective coloration of insects, mammals and birds make gun emplacements and soldiers disappear? How do you educate and inform the military and the civilian population of the devastating danger of flies, lice and fleas – and show them how personal and domestic hygiene can literally save lives? And how, in 1914, do you target thousands of key people in neutral countries and persuade them of the righteousness of your cause?

All these, and many more, are the questions which government departments, the military and the public send to the Natural History Museum in South Kensington during World War I. Their need is invariably desperate and always urgent but they trust that their problem will be resolved by the expertise of the Museum's scientists.

That these scientists, the Keepers and assistants of the departments of Zoology, Entomology, Geology, Botany and Mineralogy, can produce answers is because of the depth and breadth of the vast collections held in the Museum, and their experience and dedication. That they can produce as much work as they do is all the more extraordinary, as the war depletes the Museum of so many staff that it would have had grave difficulty in functioning at all without volunteers in all departments. Scarcely a month goes by without more and yet more demands for men 'to join the colours', as thousands are killed each week. And, throughout it all, the ordinary work of the Museum, the care and conservation of the collections, still has to be maintained.

Amongst the many enquiries are those which the Museum calls 'economic' – practical and applied science where organisms, including lice, flies and rodents, impact on humans and society. Exhibitions are mounted in the Central Hall, and what the Museum calls its 'economic series' of leaflets, posters and pamphlets which describe, warn and advise on the dangers of vermin of all kinds, are published in their tens of thousands. A poster describing the danger of houseflies is an instant bestseller and has to be reprinted immediately.

All this work has to be done without many of the attendants and boy-attendants – the departmental support staff whose essential role is dealing with correspondence as well as writing labels, arranging specimens and looking after departmental visitors. The majority of attendants have enlisted in the armed services or been sent to other government departments for vital clerical work connected with the war, particularly to the Ministry of Munitions.

And while the staff have been depleted, the flood of visitors flocking to the much-loved Museum hasn't. As well as civilians, soldiers – wounded or on leave – fill the galleries daily. The exhibits are viewed for pleasure but also for educating military men – their instructors find that teaching from the Museum's specimens is of enormous value in communicating information quickly and memorably.

The main burden of leading the Museum during the war years is carried by the Assistant Secretary, Charles Edward Fagan. He has been the pillar of the Museum since the 1890s, when the failing health of the then Director, Sir William Flower, meant he had increasingly to rely on Fagan's outstanding administrative abilities. The current Director, Lazarus Fletcher, also suffers from poor health, is frequently absent from the Museum and relies totally on Fagan's sure touch.

A few days before the outbreak of war, Fagan writes: 'The relations of the Museum to the Government and practical applications of Natural History in the country is a very big question…I have little doubt that there will be immense development in this direction in the future'.

These words have great prescience and Fagan is at the forefront of promoting the Museum's expertise in many fields, as well as being the driving force behind the Museum's significant role in disseminating British propaganda across the world.

At the beginning of the 20th century, the Museum was still part of the British Museum in Bloomsbury. The natural history departments of the British Museum, under their first superintendent, the great comparative anatomist Sir Richard Owen, had moved to their purpose built home in South Kensington in 1881. Its official title was British Museum (Natural History), but the new building instantly and popularly became known as the Natural History Museum.

Its governance still flowed down from Bloomsbury, with the same Board of Trustees for both institutions, whose approval was necessary for almost every action. The three Principal Trustees were the Archbishop of Canterbury, the Speaker of the House of Commons and the Lord Chancellor, men appointed by virtue of their offices. Just about everything that the Museum did was recorded in the minutes of the Trustees' meetings, the Keepers' monthly reports, and the vast correspondence that flowed into – and out of – the Director's Office and the individual departments.

All this has been preserved in the invaluable Archives of the Natural History Museum. In these records is the extraordinary story of how the Museum responded to the dislocation and tragedy of war, revealing in great detail the challenges and demands on its staff, its science – and on its very existence. It is this daily revelation of unceasing pressure, courage, persistence and applied expertise that inspired this book. It is told as it happened and much is in the words of the participants, through their letters, reports, notes and the all-important minutes and papers of the Trustees' meetings.

It is a series of snapshots of what happened between 1914 and 1918 in a Museum at war.

Special Meeting of Standing Committee,

British Museum, Bloomsbury,

Thursday, 20th August, 1914,

to consider circumstances

arising out of the war.

———————————

Natural History Museum business.

Notice of the Special Meeting of the Museum Trustees on 20 August 1914 'to consider circumstances arising out of the war' – which include the numbers of men enlisting in the military and the possible requisitioning of galleries for use by the Government.

Chapter 1
August–December 1914

On 3 August 1914, the eve of the declaration of war, *The Times* declares: 'The great catastrophe has come upon Europe'. And so it has. For the Natural History Museum – as with so many other organizations – these first months of war are full of uncertainty. By October, across Great Britain, more than 750,000 men have enlisted in Lord Kitchener's New Army. More than 30 of them are staff from the Natural History Museum. Six more Museum staff are loaned to the War Office and other government departments for essential clerical duties. What the role of the Museum and its remaining staff could or should be seems far from clear. Dr Francis Bather, Assistant Geology Keeper, reveals his colleagues' doubts and uncertainties – their 'searchings of heart' – over what their function should be when viewed against what he calls the 'distant blaze' of war. He does, however, suggest a solution, and that is in 'work of direct practical utility'. In these first months, the Admiralty seeks help on the physiology of whales in connection with the design of submarines, soldiers visit the Museum to learn about horse anatomy, and Museum staff enrol for Red Cross training. But as concerns over hostile air-raids mount, the opening hours of the Museum are curtailed and lights are dimmed or disconnected.

5 AUGUST 1914 It is the day after Britain declares war on Germany. The Museum's Assistant Secretary, Charles Fagan, writes to the most senior staff – the Keepers of Zoology, Geology, Mineralogy, Botany, Entomology, and the Museum librarian. His letter is marked 'IMMEDIATE'. He asks them to send him 'without delay', the names of any of their staff who have been 'summoned to serve in any capacity outside the Museum on account of the national emergency'. The total number of men in full time employment in the Museum – both permanent and temporary – is 186.

Fagan also asks 'in confidence', if there is anyone of German or Austrian nationality at work in their department – quite often there is. The Aliens Restrictions Bill 1914 is introduced into the House of Commons, passes all its Parliamentary stages, receives the Royal Assent and becomes law, all in one day. Germans and Austrians are now 'alien enemies'. The Act is 'to enable His Majesty in time of war or imminent national danger or great emergency by Order in Council to impose Restrictions on Aliens and make such provisions as appear necessary or expedient for carrying such restrictions into

Charles Edward Fagan (1855–1921) – Assistant Secretary of the Museum from 1889 to 1919, secretary from 1919 to 1921. A man of outstanding administrative abilities, he carried the main burden of leading the Museum throughout the war.

effect'. An Order in Council is immediately made, requiring aliens to register with the police and restricting their movements to and from Great Britain.

7 AUGUST 1914 Field Marshal Lord Kitchener, newly appointed Secretary of State for War, calls for an additional 100,000 men to join the regular army immediately, 'in this present grave national emergency'. In large, bold type in almost every newspaper is the appeal: 'Your King and Country need you. <u>A CALL TO ARMS</u>'.

8 AUGUST 1914 The uncertainty in the Museum is echoed nationwide. *The Times* asks the question it believes interests 'every soul' in Europe: 'How long will the war last?' and is astonished to see how wide apart are the different estimates. It finds that from three weeks to three years have been suggested, and it is evident, according to *The Times*, that 'few people have given the matter much serious thought'.

10 AUGUST 1914 The Secretary of the Civil Service Commission, LCH (Lawrence Cary Hampton) Weekes, writes to all government departments, including the Natural History Museum. He informs them that there is urgent demand for additional staff from any government department that can spare them to be loaned to departments 'directly concerned with business relating to the war'. These include the Admiralty and War Office and also possibly the Foreign, Home and India Offices. 'In view of the public emergency', Weekes suggests, non-essential work might be suspended or curtailed, 'and the staff engaged thereon either dispensed with or reduced'. He asks for names and status of any available staff as soon as possible and to be sent further names later of any more who can be spared. As for how long these officers may be needed, at present he can give 'no estimate'.

11 AUGUST 1914 Weekes's letter is reinforced by one from Sir Thomas Little Heath, joint Permanent Secretary at the Treasury. Heath writes to the Trustees of the British Museum – of which the Natural History Museum is a part – who include the Archbishop of Canterbury and the Speaker of the House of Commons. 'It is very desirable from the point of view of economy and efficiency', Sir Thomas writes, that the additional requirements for extra staff in the Admiralty and War Office should be met by the loan of experienced officers from other departments, rather than have to rely on 'new and untrained men' recruited from the lists of the various competitive examinations held by the civil service.

Charles Fagan circulates the request to the Keepers, asking for the names and status of the various grades of staff in their departments, including their qualifications such as languages or laboratory experience.

15 AUGUST 1914 The Botany department informs Fagan that they have no one who is 'highly skilled in languages or in laboratory work; but, if stringent need should arise, we might be able to help – & help right willingly – in some capacity'. Across the Museum, six attendants are selected as suitable for clerical work at the Admiralty and War Office.

17 AUGUST 1914 Charles Fagan writes to the first ten members of staff to enlist in the military. He informs them that their Museum posts will be kept open until their return from military service, which will count towards their civil pension and annual salary increments. It is a letter Fagan is to send many more times.

20 AUGUST 1914 The Museum's Trustees are not due to meet until 24 October. However, today they hold a 'Special' meeting, 'to consider circumstances arising out of the war'. They are told that

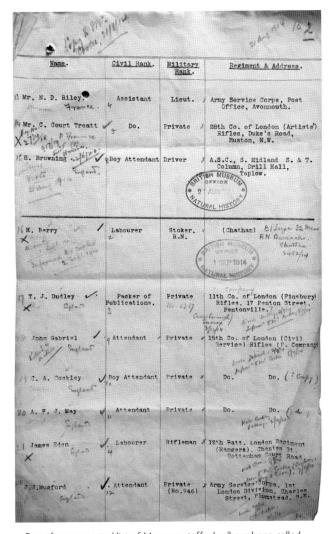

Name.	Civil Rank.	Military Rank.	Regiment & Address.
Mr. N. D. Riley.	Assistant	Lieut.	Army Service Corps, Post Office, Avonmouth.
Mr. C. Court Treatt	Do.	Private	28th Co. of London (Artists') Rifles, Duke's Road, Euston, N.W.
E. Browning	Boy Attendant	Driver	A.S.C., S. Midland S. & T. Column, Drill Hall, Taplow.
H. Berry	Labourer	Stoker, R.N.	(Chatham)
T. J. Dudley	Packer of Publications.	Private	11th Co. of London (Finsbury) Rifles, 17 Penton Street, Pentonville.
John Gabriel	Attendant	Private	15th Co. of London (Civil Service) Rifles (D. Company)
C. A. Cockley	Boy Attendant	Private	Do. Do.
A. F. J. May	Attendant	Private	Do. Do.
James Eden	Labourer	Rifleman	12th Batt. London Regiment (Rangers). Chenies St. Tottenham Court Road.
J. J. Mugford	Attendant	Private (No.946)	Army Service Corps, 1st London Division, Charles Street, Plumstead, S.E.

Part of an annotated list of Museum staff who 'have been called out or have enlisted for War Service' from August 1914. Key facts were added over the course of the war.

six assistants, seven attendants, one boy attendant, a taxidermist and a labourer have enlisted in the military. The Trustees sanction the loan of six attendants to assist clerical staff in government departments 'with business relating to the war' in answer to Weekes's and Heath's letters. They also sanction the loan of certain assistants with 'special qualifications', who may be required. The Trustees are informed that it is possible some of the Museum's galleries may be needed by the government to accommodate extra clerks, though not immediately. They are also told that the previous day, 19 August, Army officers inspected the Museum with a view to its possible use as military barracks.

The Trustees decide that Germans and Austrians – 'alien enemies' – working in the Museum who have complied with police regulations as to registration, 'should be granted the usual facilities' to continue their work.

26 AUGUST 1914 Charles Fagan replies to the Civil Service Commissioners' Secretary, Lawrence Weekes, regarding the loan of Museum staff. He informs him that although the Museum Trustees are ready to lend six attendants for clerical work in departments concerned with the war, the temporary loss of these men 'must necessarily cause a dislocation of the Museum service'. Furthermore, he writes, while the Trustees have shown their readiness to respond 'in view of the national emergency', they would have 'carefully to consider all the circumstances before giving their assent to deplete further the staff', in order to provide clerical assistance elsewhere. Fagan also tells Weekes that on the scientific staff of the Museum there are 'certain gentlemen whose expert knowledge may be of use to the Government in the present emergency'. There are five names. Their expertise includes languages, 'microscope analysis', medicine, pharmaceutical chemistry and chemical analysis. Among them is a botanist with expertise in French, Spanish and 'skill in organisation of postal services'. Another botanist 'might be useful in connection with medical supplies', while a 'native born Belgian' zoologist, now a naturalized British subject and fellow of the Royal Society, has an 'intimate knowledge of Belgium and its people', has French as his native language and reads and writes German.

By return, Weekes thanks Fagan for the offer of the six attendants, but tells him that 'at present' it is not expected that there will be 'occasion to take advantage of the kind offer of the gentlemen on the Staff'.

SEPTEMBER 1914 Dr Francis Bather, Assistant Geology Keeper, and an assistant in Entomology, Guy Coburn Robson, are keen to organise first-aid training under the auspices of the British Red Cross Society. The first course of emergency lectures in London for the public is already nearing completion and there is no indication

Dr Francis Bather (1863–1934), Assistant Keeper, Geology. In the war he was active in the Red Cross, allotments and propaganda work for the War Office. In 1924 he was appointed Geology Keeper.

of a new class starting soon. On the advice of the local Red Cross branch, it is decided the Museum should form its own class for the benefit of members of staff who are anxious to offer their services. Twenty Museum officials of all grades attend, and also four students and neighbourhood residents who are included by special invitation. Two lectures a week are held between 8 September and 13 October. Demonstrations are given on specimens and material in the Museum. An examination is held and among those who pass the training is the palaeontologist Dorothea Bate – an unofficial (temporary) scientific worker and one of the very few women then working in the Museum. In 1914 there are just nine women, all employed on a temporary basis.

5 SEPTEMBER 1914 The magazine *London Opinion* carries on its front cover an illustration of Lord Kitchener by Alfred Leete and the words 'Your country needs YOU'. It becomes an iconic image of the war. Around 10,000 posters based on the cover are printed privately – not by the government, which has its own recruiting posters. Six sets of these are sent to the Museum by Captain Thomas Whiffen, at the Chief Recruiting Depot, Great Scotland Yard. They are exhibited prominently in the Museum. Over the course of the war, the government issues millions of posters – 12.5 million in 1916 alone.

12 SEPTEMBER 1914 The Permanent Secretary of the Office of Works, Lionel Earle, writes to the Director. The letter is headed <u>IMMEDIATE AND CONFIDENTIAL</u>. Because of the possibility of attack from hostile aircraft, all 'Museums and Picture Galleries' are urged to close at dusk during the War, 'as it would otherwise be necessary to provide opaque blinds for masking the lights at night' at a cost of many thousands of pounds. He trusts closure at dusk of the Natural History Museum will be put into force at an early date. Where

Issued in 1914, this is probably the most famous recruiting poster of World War I. Based on Alfred Leete's *London Opinion* illustration, it is a direct appeal by the War Secretary, Lord Kitchener, for men to join the British army.

sections of the building have to be used during the evening, Earle requests that advice should be sought from the Controller of Supplies of the Office of Works for the best means of masking the lights.

The likelihood of attack from the air is recognized from the outset. Two days after war is declared, *The Times* publishes details of the different types of Zeppelin and other German airships. It gives the speed – between 35 and 50 mph, the distances they would have to travel from their bases to London – 300 miles from Hamburg and 400 miles from Cologne – and discusses how damaging their attack might be. What is unknown is the number of Zeppelins Germany may have. Estimates vary from a dozen to double that. What is certain is that more are being built and in all probability, according to *The Times*, 'it is quite likely that airships of other types will be employed'.

19 SEPTEMBER 1914 William Plane Pycraft is an assistant in Zoology. He is an osteologist, anatomist, ornithologist and whale expert, and one of the Museum's best-known scientists through his popular books and articles. He writes a regular column for *The Illustrated London News* and today his article is headed 'Khaki v Colour'. He writes about the concealing effect of what he calls obliterating 'countershading'. He describes how in many animals, the upper surface of their bodies is 'much darker than the under'. The effect when illuminated is for the dark upper body to appear light, while the white (or light-coloured) under-surface is shadowed, the result of which is 'generally held to confer on the wearer a sort of mantle of invisibility' – as long as they do not move. He describes how creatures in jungles or reed beds are often striped, and how in the 19th century it was realized that soldiers were far better protected in khaki uniforms than scarlet as previously, enabling them to blend with the background. What Pycraft is describing will, in the next year or so, be better known as camouflage, but today he does not use the word as it does not yet exist in the military sense. The word comes from the French verb camoufler, to disguise – the French are the first troops in the war to begin developing means to fool aerial surveillance and the *camoufleurs*, as they are known, first form a camouflage unit in 1915. Advising on how to adapt, for military use, the protective coloration of animals to hide from, observe unseen and deceive the enemy will become a key part of the Museum's war effort.

21 SEPTEMBER 1914 The Keeper of Entomology, Charles Gahan, reports that his department is so depleted by staff absent on war service – 12 men have already enlisted – that there are just three attendants (out of nine) remaining and no boy attendants – there were two. Just five months earlier, in May 1914, Gahan was asking for more accommodation as there were 41 people at work in his department – including volunteer and unofficial scientific workers – and the 'Keeper has no study'.

8 OCTOBER 1914 Charles Fagan writes to all the Keepers. So many men have joined Lord Kitchener's New Army that uniforms cannot immediately be provided for them all and a call for help has gone out to all government departments. As Fagan tells the Keepers, 'I have been asked to assist in supplying old clothes, especially <u>trousers</u> for recruits for Lord Kitchener's New Army, pending the issue of their uniforms'. Fagan asks them for help, and also to ask their staff for assistance. Any clothes should be sent to his office, as 'I am making up parcels daily'. He adds a PS: 'Underclothing is not required'.

12 OCTOBER 1914 Lieutenant Colonel E Lloyd Williams, the officer commanding depot medical units of the 2nd London Division, Territorial Force at the Duke of York's Headquarters in Chelsea, applies for permission for some of his men to visit the

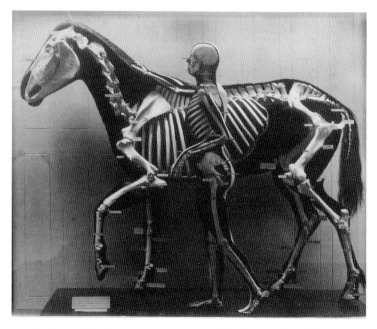

Soldiers training for transport duties visited the Museum from 1914 to study the anatomy of the horse from this model exhibited in the North Hall. Today it can be seen in the Mammals gallery.

Natural History Museum. They are training for transport duties and require instruction, by their own officers, on 'the points of the horse' and the 'anatomy of the horse', from specimens in the North Hall. Permission is granted for them to attend that week and for two days in November. The North Hall is temporarily closed to the public.

15 OCTOBER 1914 In response to the Office of Works' concerns about attack from hostile aircraft and the need for lights to be masked, the Keeper of Zoology, Dr Sidney Harmer, together with an electrician from the Office of Works, make an inspection at dusk of the western wing of the Museum to see whether lights are visible from the outside. Lights are turned on in a number of galleries, corridors, and two studies, including Harmer's. Where possible, blinds are drawn. They go up to the roof and Harmer is surprised by how much light from galleries comes through the skylights and windows of low buildings to the north of the main galleries. He notes that if those galleries 'were lighted they would certainly be conspicuous from the sky'. Black blinds fitted in some galleries, 'are remarkably effective', with no light visible from those windows. His own study, however, appears 'brightly lighted', even though the blinds are drawn – but they are yellow, not black. There are a number of rooms with the same blinds and Harmer notes that if they 'were fully lighted – even with drawn blinds – the outlines of a large tower would be clearly seen from the sky'.

The following day he reports his findings to the Director, Lazarus Fletcher, and makes recommendations on which lights can be used and which must be shaded – or not used at all. He also recommends that skylights and windows without blinds should be covered with brown paper.

Sir Lazarus Fletcher (1854–1921), Director of the Museum. His poor health throughout his term of office meant he had increasingly to rely on Charles Fagan.

17 OCTOBER 1914 The Office of Works sends a letter to the Museum marked 'Confidential'. It suggests that in view of the possibility of an attack on London by hostile aircraft, the Trustees might consider taking precautions to protect the most precious specimens, if they have not already done so. While it is hoped the danger is remote, in view of 'what has happened in France and Belgium' the danger cannot be disregarded. The newspapers have been reporting horrendous brutality by the invading German armies. The university city of Louvain had been sacked and burned – including its cathedral and world-famous library – in August and more than 200 civilians killed. German artillery shells in September had smashed through Reims and, 'the greatest iniquity of all', left the magnificent cathedral 'an empty shell of charred and blackened walls', according to the *Daily Mail*. Other Belgian and French towns had been attacked by air and land with shells and explosive and incendiary bombs.

22 OCTOBER 1914 The Office of Works writes again, this time the letter is from one of their architects, George John Thrift Reavell, with concerns about protecting the Museum's Spirit Building from fire. The building contains vast numbers of zoological specimens preserved in spirit in glass jars. In view of the possibility of attack by hostile aircraft, Reavell suggests that the building should be protected by a nine-inch (22.5 cm) layer of sand spread over its roof. Its windows should be protected by 'expanded metal' – strong wire-netting. If further protection is needed, then strong wire-netting 'could be strained all over the roof, about 3 feet above the sand'. However, Reavell notes, 'personally I do not think this necessary'.

24 OCTOBER 1914 At their regular meeting, the Trustees are informed that visitor numbers have dropped significantly. In August and September 1913, there were 96,410 visitors. In the same months this year, the numbers are down by more than 30,000 to 62,850. The

Trustees are also informed that a total of 31 members of staff have now enlisted. They are from all grades and departments across the Museum: assistants, attendants, two boy attendants, the packer of publications, labourers and commissionaires, including the head commissionaire who has been appointed a military instructor. With so many men absent on war service, there will be savings on the provision for wages and salaries in the Museum's estimates. The Director, Lazarus Fletcher, recommends to the Trustees that 'Treasury sanction be obtained' for these savings to be used to pay for outside temporary assistance so the 'service' of the Museum can be continued 'with a minimum of inconvenience'.

26 OCTOBER 1914 Concern over hostile air-raids increases. The Trustees order that the Museum is to be closed at 4 o'clock from 1 November, but that the studies should be kept open as far as possible by implementing precautionary measures for electric lights. Table lamps in studies must be 'properly masked', hanging lamps should be disconnected, and others are to be removed, painted black or darkened. All blinds must be drawn when lamps are lit. In the streets of London, lamps and shop lights are extinguished or obscured, advertisements switched off and, like the Museum, high windows and skylights covered. It takes time for people to become used to going home through darkened streets.

29 OCTOBER 1914 George Reavell of the Office of Works writes again about the safety of the Spirit Building. He has now made further enquiries and finds that 'the latest consensus of expert opinion is that no precautions (such as those proposed) would be really adequate'. In fact it has been calculated that the amount of sand suggested would be more likely to lead to the collapse of the roof than protect it. He therefore concludes, 'that the only thing to be done is to let the building take its chance'.

This whale, beached at Birchington in Kent, is a common rorqual, probably killed by a mine. It was mistaken for a crashed Zeppelin when first seen floating in the sea. It was examined by Zoology assistant, William Pycraft.

14 NOVEMBER 1914 William Pycraft, in his regular column in *The Illustrated London News*, 'Science Jottings', today reveals that he has been to Birchington in Kent. 'On Oct. 17 to be precise', Pycraft writes, 'the life-boat of Margate put off to rescue the possible survivors of a sinking Zeppelin! Eager crowds awaited the return of the rescuers with their "prisoners of war" and great was the disappointment when they learned that the supposed Zeppelin was nothing more than a dead whale'.

The mistake, Pycraft writes, 'was perfectly natural'. The whale was a common rorqual, *Balaenoptera physalis*, whose 'inflated throat and abdomen' were mistaken for the Zeppelin envelope. Since 1913, the Museum has had to be notified immediately of all stranded cetacea (whales, dolphins and porpoises) – as it still is – and it was 'speedily telegraphed'. The carcass had beached at Birchington and Pycraft was dispatched by the Museum to examine it.

Identifying it as a rorqual was simple, Pycraft writes. 'Taking its measurements was not'. He has to sprinkle sand on the slippery surface to obtain 'what was, at best, but an insecure foothold'. The animal was a female, 61 feet (18½ metres) long. Its death, Pycraft saw, had been caused by 'an enormous rent' in the abdomen, 'through which one might easily have dropped a large arm-chair'. The apparent violence of the injury, 'could only have been inflicted by some explosive action, such as by a mine'. Unfortunate though this was for the whale, Pycraft writes that the animal 'may all unwittingly have saved us another cruiser and hundreds of precious lives', and speculates on the possible number of mines 'that may thus fail of their purpose'.

18 NOVEMBER 1914 The Treasury responds to the Museum's proposal that any staff savings made in consequence of absences on war service should be devoted to payment of outside experts. The news is not good. The proposal cannot be sanctioned, the Museum is informed, 'In view of the paramount necessity for economy during the present emergency', and the Treasury hopes it 'will not be pressed'.

19 NOVEMBER 1914 Dr Francis Bather reports to the Trustees that the 17 members of staff who qualified as first aiders 'are anxious to turn the knowledge acquired to some account'. He proposes they form a unit of the Voluntary Aid Detachment under the British Red Cross Society. To ensure work in the Museum is disrupted as little as possible, he suggests that no more than six personnel on any one day should be on standby for emergency duty between 10am and 5pm. Any call for their service is to be reported at once to the Director. Bather also suggests that perhaps two members of staff should give 'not less than two hours' continuous service at a hospital daily...each taking duty once a week'. This means no one will be away from the Museum for more than about two hours once every 10 days. His proposals are accepted and the first aiders become the Natural History Museum Division of the 31st London Voluntary Aid Detachment. He proposes that they hold a series of drills in stretcher and ambulance work (this applies only to the men) and that they be allowed the use of the Museum or its grounds. The proposals are approved in principle by the Keepers of the departments affected and warmly received by the Red Cross Society.

In these first months as the wounded arrive in numbers no-one has prepared for, or imagined, they are transported from train station to hospital by delivery van, taxi, or motor car, loaned by businesses and individuals and manned by volunteers. The Museum men's role is assisting the wounded at stations and receiving and unloading ambulances at hospitals.

27 NOVEMBER 1914 Dr Sidney Harmer, Keeper of Zoology, reports to the Trustees that he has received an enquiry from Admiral Sir Percy Scott 'with regard to certain points connected with the physiology of whales'. Scott is a highly regarded – if controversial – naval officer, engineer and gunnery expert, brought out of retirement on the outbreak of war. Since June 1914, his views on the devastating impact of submarines and the need for Britain to develop her submarine rather than battleship fleet, have been much debated in Whitehall and the newspapers. In September three British warships were sunk in one day in the North Sea by a German submarine.

The Admiral's interest in whales is focused particularly on two questions. The first is the whales' maximum period of continuous immersion. The second is their vision, with special reference to the whales' powers of distinguishing distant objects. The shape and speed of the whale is also of interest in the design of submarines.

Dr Harmer tells him that his department has not been in a position to make observations on these subjects, and has had to rely entirely on the experience of whalers and those with knowledge of living whales. However, he is able to tell the Admiral that the period of immersion varies with the species and size of the animal, 'but may be prolonged exceptionally to one hour and twenty minutes'. With regard to their vision, Dr Harmer reports that their range of binocular vision is small, and an object some distance in front of the whale may not be seen distinctly. He informs the Admiral that experiments examining the penetration of light through sea-water 'indicate the probability' that a submerged whale could not see an object situated at a very great distance.

DECEMBER William Pycraft receives a phone call from a Major Leland in the Royal Army Medical Corps. Leland asks him whether he would help carry out urgent instructions which he has just received from the War Secretary, Lord Kitchener. He has been given just 48 hours to carry them out. The bitter weather on the Western Front has caused the army terrible hardship from frost-bite, incapacitating an unsustainable number of men. Conditions are appalling, with men immersed knee-deep in freezing mud and water. Feet become numb, then swell, and boots, once removed, cannot be replaced. Immersion in water for many days on end causes great, often irreparable, harm to feet. It has also been an abnormally wet autumn and trench foot and frostbite produces symptoms which at first seem the same.

Whale-oil, either in a pure state or mixed with other fats, has been suggested as protection, and given the number of men affected, 'a speedy decision' on whether this is right is vital. Leland comes to see Pycraft, who is able 'to afford him even more help than he had looked for'. Within the 48 hours allotted by Lord Kitchener, two tins of prepared oil are being sent to the front. Other remedies are developed over the course of the war and strict instructions issued on how to care for feet, but up to 10 gallons of whale oil a day are still issued to battalions at the front.

10 DECEMBER 1914 The Voluntary Aid Detachment of the Museum is given permission by the Director for stretcher drill to take place on Mondays, Wednesdays and Fridays at 2pm for about half an hour in the grounds of the Museum and, when wet, in the basement.

23 DECEMBER 1914 The Metropolitan Police at New Scotland Yard issue a warning to Londoners from the military authorities. It alerts them to the danger, when in the streets, of being hit by shell fragments and bullets from guns defending the capital against attack by hostile aircraft. It advises them to keep under cover, preferably in basements, as soon as they hear the sound of guns or explosives. Air-raid warnings have still to be invented. The following day, Dover is attacked from the air – one bomb is dropped, leaving a 10-foot hole in a garden. It is the first-ever aerial attack on Great Britain.

25 DECEMBER 1914 The Museum sends Christmas presents to members of staff who are serving in the military. Amongst the gifts the Museum sends are mittens, socks and cigarettes. Many of the men send back letters of thanks for the presents, which are 'very usefull [sic] and handy', 'most thoughtful', 'surprising and useful' and 'gratefully received'. One man also sends the address of his new posting as he 'would like to hear from work-mates'.

By the end of the year, across the UK, more than one million men have enlisted in the military. By the end of the war, more than eight million men from Britain and the Empire will have served. Of these, 888,000 will be killed.

Chapter 2
January–April 1915

By January 1915, the Natural History
Museum is striving to deal with the pressures
of war. Staff shortages, the vulnerability of the
collections and the constant need for vigilance, are
becoming oppressive. Visitors' bags are searched.
Coal is difficult to obtain, affecting the Museum's
heat and light. At its own suggestion, the Museum's
worldwide reach is utilised by the Foreign Office
to disseminate propaganda. A Volunteer Training
Corps is formed, and also a volunteer Anti-Aircraft
Observation Corps. The Museum joins those across
Great Britain who are making special collections of
essential items for the troops, and the military
seek advice on damage to an airship balloon. At
the front, nearly 140,000 allied troops have been
killed since August and efforts to urge more
men to enlist intensify. At Ypres, the Germans,
for the first time, launch a chlorine gas attack
on allied forces. In March the first
Museum man is killed in action.

5 JANUARY 1915 The threat of attack from the air is now acute. At the request of the Admiralty, London University has formed a Volunteer Anti-Aircraft Observation Corps. It is stationed at the top of the Imperial Institute Tower [now the Queen's Tower at Imperial College], just a few hundred yards north of the Museum. The Museum is asked for four or five volunteers 'from the Higher Staff' to join it. Sir Henry Miers, Principal of London University (and formerly a mineralogist at the Museum), requests that this is not included in the Museum's minutes, as it is 'inadvisable that any publicity should be given to the matter'. He hopes that the Museum will co-operate 'in this very useful piece of work,' which is under 'the direct control of the Admiralty'.

Five members of staff volunteer, including the Keeper of Zoology and future Museum Director, Dr Sidney Frederic Harmer. Each member of the corps is needed for duty 'not oftener' than one night a week, from 7.45pm to about 7.00am. The Watch consists of four men, two of whom are on guard at any one time. Exposure to the

Keeper of Zoology, Dr Sidney Frederic Harmer (1862–1950). Together with the Assistant Secretary Charles Fagan, Harmer was tireless in promoting the importance of the Museum's science to the war effort. In 1919 he was appointed Director.

January cold is not without consequences. The mineralogist, Dr George Frederick Herbert Smith, who 20 years later will be appointed Keeper of Mineralogy, is critical of the arrangements made for the observers. His health is not good and he is afflicted by 'Rheumatic neurotis'[sic] after his watch on the Tower on a particularly cold night.

10 JANUARY 1915 Sixteen German aircraft are seen crossing the English Channel, but have to turn back because of bad weather.

20 JANUARY 1915 The Museum's Assistant Secretary, Charles Fagan, writes to Dr Frederic Augustus Lucas, Director of the American Museum of Natural History in New York. He thanks the American for the 'kind expressions of sympathy you have used towards this country in this terrible war', and emphasizes how much 'we all value the friendship and sympathy of the people of the United States'. He tells Dr Lucas how the war has 'quite upset all our plans for the immediate future'. He touches on the enforced postponement of a projected Anglo-Swedish scientific station in the Antarctic and the investigation of whale fisheries in that part of the world, and adds: 'You no doubt noted that the Germans were very nearly taking the Falkland islands. It was fortunate that the British squadron arrived just in time to sink their ships'.

With its wide network of international correspondents – in universities and museums as well as private individuals – the Museum is in a position to utilize a critical weapon of war, propaganda. Charles Fagan realizes its potential almost at once. In December he sent Lucas copies of *Great Britain and the European Crisis*, a publication by the Foreign Office outlining the case for war. It consists of the correspondence, Parliamentary statements and 'introductory narrative of events' leading to the declaration of war. Dr Lucas has earlier told Fagan that copies have been placed 'where they will do most good', and Fagan now offers to send him 'as many copies as you may have use for'. To reinforce the message contained in the Foreign Office publication, Fagan tells Lucas he is also sending him the English translation of the French Government's *Yellow Book*, which gives the official French side of the negotiations that preceded the war. According to *The Spectator* magazine of 5 December 1914, the French *Yellow Book* 'adds some new information of extraordinary interest. It shows—what we all knew before—that Britain was ready to go to almost any lengths to avoid war... and that just when it seemed that the black cloud was lifting, Germany deliberately brought on the storm by declaring war on Russia and France'.

23 JANUARY 1915 At their regular meeting, the Trustees are informed that, subject to their approval, a Museum section of the Volunteer Corps for Home Defence has been formed. Also known as the Volunteer Training Corps, this is a home guard, set up in November in case of German invasion. The recruits are men over military age or who are medically unfit. They are taught the elements of military drill and rifle shooting. They are allowed to wear as a distinctive badge a red armband, with the royal cipher GR (Georgius Rex) inscribed on it. This quickly leads to volunteers being mockingly referred to by some as 'Gorgeous Wrecks'. It is proposed that the Museum Company should form a distinct unit affiliated to the Central Association of Volunteer Training Corps (VTC).

Between 70 and 80 members of staff have signified their intention of joining. It is expected that with the addition of recruits from the scientific institutions in the immediate neighbourhood, the numbers will be raised to a full company of 120 men. It is proposed that they should be allowed to practise military drill in the Museum grounds three evenings a week from 4.45pm to 5.45pm for the remainder of the winter months. The Trustees give their permission, on the understanding that the gardens at the front of the Museum, bordering Cromwell Road, will not be used for drilling. It is felt the grass will not stand up to such use. They also stipulate that if application is made for the Volunteer Corps to take part in active military service, they reserve the right to consider whether the Museum can spare their services.

The Trustees instruct the Director to prepare lists of those members of staff who are absent on naval or military service, for exhibition in the entrance hall of the Museum. A list is also compiled of sons of members of staff, or former members, who are serving in the military. Charles Fagan asks the Keepers to let him know about their staff as soon as possible. More than 30 have sons in the military, with more than 50 young men between them. Keepers Harmer, Rendle and Gahan all have sons in the army. So does Charles Fagan. Commissionaire Gamble has five sons, all enlisted. Just before Christmas he hears that one, Alfred, a private in the 13th Battalion, the London Regiment, has been killed in action.

Not least of all their concerns is the uncertainty, as Dr Harmer tells the zoologist Canon Alfred Norman: 'The War Office is not very communicative and I do not yet know when my son will go to the front. So far as I can ascertain it will probably be about April 10'. His son, Russell, a 2nd lieutenant in the Royal Engineers, is 18 years old.

1 FEBRUARY 1915 Captain HFM Warne of the 15th Battalion, London Regiment (Prince of Wales' Own Civil Service Rifles), sends a recruiting circular to government departments, including the Museum, asking for 300 recruits. Charles Fagan tells him he 'will do all he can to assist' him and asks for 30 more copies of the circular to be sent for distribution round the Museum. He advises Captain Warne, however, that 'a very good proportion of our men who are within the limits of age and physically fit have already joined the Civil Service Rifles and other regiments'. To help with his recruitment drive, staff contribute £3 [more than £200 today] to help meet the expenses of advertising for recruits.

3 FEBRUARY 1915 Charles Gahan, Keeper of Entomology, reports on the cause of damage to an airship balloon, sent to the Museum by Major Clive Maitland Waterlow, the Squadron Commander and Experimental Officer at the Royal Naval Airship Station, Farnborough. While the balloon shows evidence of a certain amount of mildew, Gahan reports that this does not appear to have been the cause of any appreciable damage to it. What he has found, however, is 'distinct evidence of injury by moths'. In three or four places 'at least, holes are present which undoubtedly were eaten through by larvae of moths'.

Gahan consults his department's moth specialist, John Hartley Durrant. He is unable to identify the species, but concludes that it was not 'one of the ordinary clothes moths'. Instead, Durrant thinks, it is a larger species 'whose larvae live in dust or rubbish of various kinds'. He believes the moths would not in the ordinary course attack the balloon, but it is possible that eggs or larvae in rubbish may have been enclosed in the folds of the balloon, and 'they naturally ate their way through its substance in order to make a passage for themselves'. To prevent further injury, Gahan recommends that care should be taken to keep the balloon clean when folding it, ensuring no extraneous matter is enclosed. 'I may mention', Gahan concludes, 'that when unfolding the balloon, a small piece of cork which had been attacked by moth, dropped out'.

This is the second time in a few months that Charles Gahan's department has been able to assist Major Waterlow. The previous summer, Waterlow sent 'considerable quantities' of beetles discovered in the envelope – the enormous outer-skin of the balloon – of HM Airship Eta. Waterlow wanted to know the species and habits of the beetle, whether it was likely to have damaged the envelope, and what

Army Airship "Eta".
MAys' Aldershot. 105.

HM Airship Eta, sometimes written as Aeta, over Colchester in 1913. 'Considerable quantities' of beetles (see p.36) were discovered in its envelope to the concern of the Royal Naval Airship Station, Farnborough, who sent specimens to the Entomology department.

was the best means of killing it. The huge, rubberized fabric envelope had been folded up for about six months.

Gahan told him that it was a species of ground beetle, *Nebria brevicollis*. They feed on the worms and larvae or grubs of other insects and were unlikely to have caused any damage to the fabric. Gahan thought they may possibly have been attracted by other insects, 'and in that case their presence would be beneficial rather than otherwise'. He advised Major Waterlow that 'They may quickly be killed by putting them in boiling water; but since they are beneficial rather than harmful it is not at all desirable to kill them.'

On the railways, priority is given to the movement of troops and other government requirements. This is causing delays in

Nebria brevicollis, the species of beetle that took up temporary residence in the Eta's envelope. The Keeper of Entomology, Dr Charles Gahan, reported that it was unlikely to have caused any damage.

transporting coal, with resulting shortages. Charles Fagan sends a memo to the Keepers and the librarian. 'In consequence of unavoidable delay in obtaining an adequate supply of coal', he writes, 'considerable difficulty is experienced in maintaining the heat of the Museum. The supply of electric light,' he adds, 'is also limited by the same conditions'. As the coal shortage intensifies, the Museum is instructed by the Office of Works to shut down 'the Steam Mains' at night. As a consequence, Fagan informs the Keepers, 'at the opening of the Museum at 10 am, it will not always be possible to bring the temperature up to the normal standard'. This will be a recurring theme throughout the war.

17 FEBRUARY 1915 For months now, the newspapers have been reporting allegations of horrendous atrocities in Belgium and France, perpetrated by the Germans. Pamphlets, cartoons and posters carry similar messages. *The Times* claims that the Germans have negated 'every human and international law', and brought back modern warfare 'to the methods of barbarian invasions'. The French government has published its own report into German outrages committed since the beginning of the war. It has been translated into English and published by the *Daily Chronicle* as 'a penny pamphlet'. Fagan requests 500 copies of the report 'for distribution among correspondents of the Museum in neutral countries' and receives an initial 150 copies from the Foreign Office. He also enquires whether Sir Edward Grey, the Foreign Secretary, 'has any objection to our circulating among the scientific correspondents of the Museum, many of whom have received German propaganda papers, the English translation of the Diplomatic Correspondence respecting the War published by the French Government'. This is the *Yellow Book* which Fagan has already been circulating.

One of those to whom he has sent it is the German-Brazilian Director of the Museu Paulista in San Paulo, the zoologist Dr Hermann von Ihering who has written to Fagan defending Germany's actions. In response, Fagan tells him that the French *Yellow Book*, 'gives further proof of the perfidy of Germany in bringing about this terrible war'. He also sends him extracts from the report 'giving an authentic account of the atrocities committed by the German troops in France'. Fagan enters into robust argument on the issue, addressing him in the third person: 'The statements contained in Dr von Ihering's letter have no value,' Fagan writes, 'as they have no foundation and are absolutely contradicted by the opinion held by the civilized world that Germany alone is responsible for bringing about this calamity. His allegations that the German prisoners of war in England are receiving ill-treatment are equally without foundation', and refers von Ihering to the report by the American consular agent appointed to investigate the matter.

In quite another tone, Fagan writes to Professor Edmond Perrier, Director of the Muséum National D'Histoire Naturelle in Paris, expressing the great 'indignation and horror' of all in the Museum, and expresses their 'earnest hope and belief that the magnificent efforts of the brave French Army will before long be successful in driving the barbarians from French soil'. To the Director of the Museum of Natural Sciences in Madrid, the entomologist Señor Ignacio Bolivar y Urrutia, Fagan writes: 'I beg on behalf of the officers of the British Museum of Natural History to express to you our warmest thanks for the kind expressions of sympathy towards this country contained in your letter', and sends him a copy of the French *Yellow Book*.

25 FEBRUARY 1915 Charles Fagan writes to the Keepers, asking them to inform their staff that he is collecting disused razors for the troops. These will be sent to the Master Cutler of Sheffield whose idea this is. So far 14,000 razors have been sent to Sheffield, but this response, 'though considerable', Fagan tells the Keepers, 'is insufficient and the Master Cutler begs that individuals who have disused razors will send them in.' The minimum quantity required, he writes, is about 100,000.

Fagan also receives a request from HM Stationery Office for literature which can be sent to troops at the front. Fagan writes that he will 'do all in my power to assist you', and says that members of staff are already contributing books 'which are at your disposal whenever you care to collect them'.

Throughout Britain, there are special appeals – enthusiastically answered – for a range of necessary items for the troops – from mufflers and mittens, to toothbrushes, handkerchiefs, fresh fruit and vegetables, and, of course, cigarettes.

27 FEBRUARY 1915 The Director informs the Trustees at their regular meeting that a letter has been received from the Office of Works. Marked 'Confidential', it states that attention has been directed to the danger, during the present crisis, 'of bombs being conveyed into Public Offices, Museums etc, for the purpose of destroying property of national value or interest'. It suggests that all visitors who seek admission to the Museum and who carry bags or parcels should leave them with the doorkeepers or show the contents if they have to be taken into the building for business purposes. The Director reports that immediate action has been taken to increase security. Instructions have been given to the police 'accordingly'.

The Trustees are also informed of security measures for the collections, 'in view of the possible risk from bombs of hostile aircraft'. The Keepers report that some objects of value have been removed from exhibition galleries 'to places of greater safety'. However, all have concerns about the danger and inconvenience of moving irreplaceable specimens.

Dr Sidney Harmer reports that zoological specimens of special rarity, including the great auk, the extinct starling of Mauritius and the dodo, have been placed in a steel case in the basement. A cabinet outside the mammal curator's study contains a number of types of small mammals – there are 191 of these at present. The most interesting, he writes, 'are perhaps Darwin's *Muridae* [rodents], collected during the voyage of the *Beagle*'. The cabinet however, 'stands in a place where it is protected by one of the Central Towers'. He acknowledges though, that the general collection of mammals is 'no doubt somewhat exposed' on the upper floor of the main building. Almost every drawer contains type specimens and to remove them, Dr Harmer argues, would mean all work 'would be dislocated and rendered impossible'. The danger from hostile aircraft, he believes, 'cannot be regarded as very serious'. And even if London were attacked, the chances are that the Mammal Gallery would escape injury. On the other hand, he argues, 'to remove priceless specimens to store-rooms not provided with suitable

The bones of two of the zoological specimens of great rarity – the extinct dodo (left) and the great auk – were placed in a steel cabinet in the basement for safety.

cabinets would be to expose them to the attack of Moths:- a danger which Dr Harmer considers a much more real one than the very problematical danger of hostile bombs'.

The two most important geological fossils, are, the Keeper Dr Arthur Smith Woodward reports, *Archaeopteryx* and the Piltdown skull. The first, the remarkable Jurassic fossil combining dinosaur and bird characteristics, is 'already beneath four floors in the South East Pavilion'. The second is 'in a fire-proof safe in the Keeper's room'. This, the famous Piltdown skull and part of a lower jaw, was discovered barely three years earlier in 1912 in a gravel pit near Piltdown Common in Sussex and hailed as the earliest known human fossil. (In 1953 it will be shown to be a malicious forgery.) Fossils housed in the back galleries, Smith Woodward admits, are more exposed to danger, 'but most of the thousands of unique

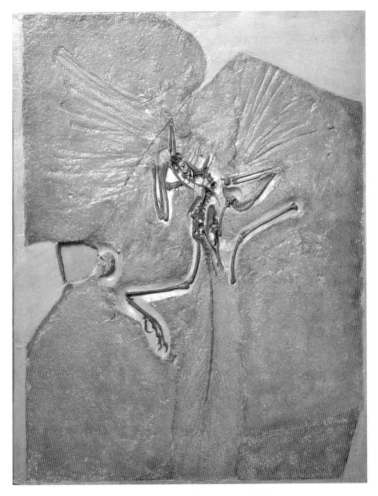

One of the most precious geological specimens, *Archaeopteryx* –
the Jurassic fossil combining dinosaur and bird characteristics – was
protected from air raids 'beneath four floors in the South East Pavilion'.

type-specimens kept there are so small, that their packing and removal would be an immense work and they would have to be stored in inaccessible packing-cases'. Furthermore, he is inclined to the opinion that these specimens would risk more harm from such packing and storage 'than they do at present from bombs'.

The Keeper of Mineralogy, George Thurland Prior, also subscribes to that view. So far he has refused to move anything, as he 'has not considered the danger as sufficiently imminent to justify him in running the risk of damage to delicate specimens by removing them to other parts of the building not under his control'. Furthermore, he writes that the Mineral Gallery 'is so situated as to be protected against the action of bombs falling on the roof or on the ground near the building'. However, in the event of the Mineral Gallery 'being considered by experts not sufficiently secure', he would place a selection of the rarest and most valuable specimens in a safe in a suitable part of the basement reserved specially for such specimens from all departments.

The vast and precious insect collection is already in the basement, the Keeper, Charles Gahan, reports, in cabinets in the Insect Room or in the South-West Basement Corridor. He considers that specimens there will be as secure from any danger arising from hostile aircraft as they would be in any other part of the Museum. The Insect Gallery, 'which is more exposed to danger', contains nothing that could not be replaced if destroyed, and Gahan does not consider it necessary to remove any of the specimens from the gallery to the basement rooms.

The Keeper of Botany Dr Rendle, reports that so far he has not removed any specimens in view of the possible danger. The 'objects which should be most considered in this respect', he writes, would seem to be 'portions' of the invaluable Sloane Herbarium 'and a few similar small pre-Linnaean collections'. However, these are housed in the departmental library, which is 'protected above by two floors'.

Happily for all these irreplaceable specimens, the Keepers' faith in the strength of the building is never put to the test.

10 MARCH 1915 The Museum gives permission for two attendants and the articulator in Zoology to join the Volunteer Ambulance Section of the Red Cross Society. Dr Harmer, the Zoology Keeper, tells the Director, 'if they can be useful, I raise no objection to their application being granted'. He adds that the department would undoubtedly miss them, 'if serious inroads were to be made on their time. But it seems to me that we must expect to be inconvenienced, from time to time, during the War'.

11 MARCH 1915 2nd Lieutenant Duncan Hepburn Gotch of the 1st Battalion the Worcestershire Regiment is, in civilian life, an assistant in the Imperial Bureau of Entomology which is based in the Entomology department of the Museum. He was appointed in 1913 on graduating in Natural Science at Cambridge. He has been at the front for barely two months and is fighting at Neuve Chapelle.

2nd Lieutenant Duncan Hepburn Gotch, an assistant in the Imperial Bureau of Entomology based in the Entomology department, killed at the battle of Neuve Chapelle, 11 March 1915.

His battalion is badly hit and Gotch is the last officer left in action with his company. He is leading the last remnants of his men to the charge, when he is killed by machine gun fire. Twelve thousand allied troops are killed in what the Museum's *War Memorial Record* calls the 'bloody' three-day battle. These heavy casualties, Field Marshal Sir John French says in his dispatch to the Secretary of State for War, 'are absolutely unavoidable'. German losses are 10,000 dead and nearly 2,000 taken prisoner. Gotch was, in the words of a fellow officer, 'a brave, cheery, kindly, popular officer and we can ill afford his loss'. For the Principal of the Imperial Bureau, Sir Guy Marshall, he was 'one of the keenest and most willing assistants I have ever had, and showed every promise of making a name for himself as a scientific worker... his place will be hard indeed to fill'. He is buried a mile from where he fell. He was 23 years old.

27 MARCH 1915 The Director informs the Trustees at their monthly meeting of Lt Gotch's death. Coincidentally, as it has been planned for some weeks, a Roll of Honour with the names of Museum staff serving in the 'naval or military forces of the Crown' is today fixed to a pillar in the entrance hall of the Museum.

30 MARCH 1915 The Permanent Secretary to the Admiralty sends a letter stating that the anti-aircraft defence of London has now reached the stage where it is no longer necessary for the volunteer look-out station on the top of the Imperial Institute Tower to be continued. The Lords Commissioners of the Admiralty thank the members of the Corps 'for their arduous services during the winter months'.

11–25 APRIL 1915 At the request of the War Office, a 'great recruiting campaign' is organised by the Parliamentary Recruiting Committee. It is to bring home to Londoners the necessity for every fit man to join the colours. Patriotic demonstrations are held in parks and open spaces, and lunchtime and evening meetings are organised throughout London.

22 APRIL 1915 At the front, at Ypres, the Germans for the first time release a cloud of chlorine gas. The French are the allied troops most affected.

23 APRIL 1915 The War Office takes a more direct role in the recruiting campaign. A circular letter is sent to all government departments including the Museum, suggesting that an appeal should be made by heads of departments to civil servants of recruitable age 'to join the colours'. This is on the proviso they can be spared 'consistent with the carrying on of the essential and pressing work of the Department'.

It suggests that their places could be taken by 'suitable substitutes'. The letter draws attention to the statement by the Secretary of State for War, Lord Kitchener, 'for the necessary permission to be given freely to their subordinates who are prepared to enlist. This is the form of military service of which the nation has the most pressing need'. Dr Harmer wants clarification of the circular, and enquires of Charles Fagan whether it means the Keepers are expected to take any new action, such as sending a letter 'urging every member of their Department who can be spared to enlist?' Fagan tells him that is 'not necessary at present'.

24 APRIL 1915 James Eden, a labourer at the Museum, is a sergeant in the 12th London Regiment (Rangers). They are fighting at Ypres. The regiment is ordered back from the trenches for a rest, but before they can get far they are called back into action for the 2nd Battle of Ypres. They suffer severe losses. After five days of continuous fighting, Eden is wounded. A finger of his right hand is smashed at the base by a bullet. He writes that his regiment 'went into action about 600 strong. Fourteen days later they were reduced to 35'. Eden is repatriated to England. In hospital his finger is amputated. He is there for six weeks. He then joins a reserve battalion, but has to return to hospital for a further operation. After that he is on clerical duty with a unit on Salisbury Plain.

In the House of Commons, the Government gives the latest total of reported war casualties as 139,347, up to 11 April. One of those is Lt Gotch. In the Museum there are now 45 members of staff on active service – nearly a quarter of the total staff. More than 80 who are physically unfit or over military age are in the Volunteer Training Corps, including unofficial workers and those from neighbouring museums. Twenty-four others are in the Museum Voluntary Aid Detachment of the Red Cross.

Chapter 3
May–August 1915

In the early summer of 1915 the threat of
air raids on London becomes a reality. The
east coast of England has already been bombed.
The Cunard liner Lusitania is torpedoed by a
German submarine off the Irish coast. A Ministry
of Munitions is created under David Lloyd George
to increase the desperately needed supply of
weapons, and Lord Kitchener calls for a further
300,000 recruits. A retired civil servant says a
million more men are needed. The Natural History
Museum, valiantly trying to maintain some
normality with a much-reduced staff, is providing a
valuable service to the military. Much of this work
falls to the Entomology department. Army biscuits
are exhibited in the Central Hall, war is waged
on the housefly and the weevil is washed out of
warehouses. By August, a year after the outbreak
of war, 52 members of the Museum's staff have
enlisted and many of those remaining have joined
the Museum's Volunteer Training Corps or the
Red Cross. In a welcome echo of normality,
a superb fossil elephant arrives in South
Kensington. The second Museum
man is killed in action.

7 MAY 1915 The Cunard liner *Lusitania* is torpedoed by a German submarine off the coast of southern Ireland. Nearly 1,200 lives are lost, including many women and children and 124 United States citizens. *The Times* describes how the news was received in America with a 'hush of horror'. In England, the sinking is described as 'heinous' and 'diabolical'.

12 MAY 1915 Frederick Wallace Edwards is a 27-year-old entomologist, enthusiastic for his subject and industrious. Quiet and unassuming, he has nevertheless aroused the ire of Charles Fagan. 'Dear Gahan', Fagan writes to the Entomology Keeper, 'Will you ask Mr FW Edwards to be good enough to wear a hat to and from the Museum. My attention has been called to the lack of respect to the Trustees and the Museum which a neglect of the conventions traditionally observed by members of the staff might seem to indicate'. Edwards is also a passionate pacifist, views that will cause him – and the Museum – more trouble in the coming year.

13 MAY 1915 Charles Fagan instructs the Museum's Chief Fireman, Sergeant of Police and the Messenger, that 'In the event of a Zeppelin raid over or near the Natural History Museum, day or night', Mr Fagan is to be informed immediately, 'and if he has left the building he must be fetched'.

19 MAY 1915 Part of the duties of the Museum attendants is clerical work. So many of them are now on military service, that there is an urgent need for replacements. In a break with tradition, it is suggested that *women* clerks should be employed. The Treasury sanctions this, but emphasizes that they 'may be assigned for <u>temporary</u> [underlined] service' only. Tens of thousands of women are taken on as clerks across all government departments. In fact the war presents women with many new opportunities, including work in munitions factories – which, over the next year employ more than half a million women – and as drivers, postal workers or in the police force.

21 MAY 1915 The Museum Trustees are informed that a warning has been received from the Engineering Division of the Office of Works, 'that an air raid on London was imminent'. The Trustees may already have been aware of this – in the preceding week *The Times* and other newspapers publish warnings of such an attack on London by a fleet of airships and other forms of aircraft. As protection, supplies of sand are laid in – 40 bins and 104 buckets. They are distributed throughout the Museum.

Police warn Londoners to keep doors and windows closed in the event of an air attack as it is thought some bombs may contain poisonous gas. Shops sell out of respirators.

26 MAY 1915 Fagan writes to the Chief Ordnance Officer, Royal Army Clothing Department. He asks whether it would be possible for the Museum to purchase 'four Smoke Helmets' for the use of the Museum's firemen. In fact the officer sends the Museum eight helmets, made of flannel with film eyepieces. They are issued to the Museum firemen and the police.

Fagan also writes to the Keepers and the general foreman. 'In view of future possibilities', he writes, 'I am directed to ask you to let me have a list of the men in your Department who would be prepared to offer themselves for naval or military service.' The list should state their ages, previous military experience (if any) and their marital status. Across the departments, a complex story emerges. In Botany, a 19-year-old would enlist, but his father works 'at all times in rifle manufacture' and he has to care for his invalid mother. Another man – aged 22 – has tried to join up but was rejected because of his eyesight. A 33-year-old attendant has a

Eight of these 'Smoke Helmets' were ordered from the Royal Army
Clothing Department for use by the Museum's firemen. At the front
they were first used in early summer 1915 as protection against
chlorine gas.

wife, a child 'and one expected', but would be prepared to go 'when
matters are more settled at home'. However, he objects to enlisting
'while unmarried men are free'. The Trustees are told that 'in general
the staff was reduced to such a level that very few men could now

be permitted to go, unless the facilities offered to the public for the use of the Museum are curtailed'. The Trustees do not think this necessary, and consider the record of both the British Museum and the Natural History Museum 'as highly satisfactory'.

28 MAY 1915 A letter from Sir Henry Arthur Blake, a highly regarded retired colonial governor, is published in *The Times*. In view of the memo he has just sent to the senior staff, it attracts the attention of Charles Fagan, who cuts it out of the paper. Blake is critical of the lack of progress in the war and the shortage of munitions, but it is his comments about the shortage of men enlisting that concerns Fagan. Blake writes that 'we shall require probably another million of men before this war can be brought to a triumphal ending'. He notes that fewer men are volunteering for service, and a disproportionate number are married. 'Every principle of justice', he writes, demands that the unmarried should be compelled to enlist. He refers to them as 'stalwart shirkers who now disgrace the country'. Fagan underlines in red Blake's call for 'compulsory service' to be introduced. He also underlines in red: 'The sooner then that it comes the better, but it may well be borne in mind that a conscript need not necessarily be entitled to the same pay as that offered to the volunteer'. Fagan sends the letter to all the Keepers, noting: 'I think the point marked in red in the enclosed cutting…should be carefully considered by those members of the staff of military age who have not yet joined the naval or military forces'.

29 MAY 1915 *The Illustrated London News* carries a full-page article on 'War: against barbarians – and flies!' It is by William Plane Pycraft, the Museum scientist who is known to the wider public through his popular books and articles. He is an osteologist, anthropologist and zoologist, and an expert on birds, whales and the Piltdown skull. His abilities have recently won him personal promotion to the grade of first-class assistant on the 'ground of unusual merit and promise'. As Dr Harmer, Zoology Keeper, reports to the Trustees, the aim of the promotion is to give him an income 'more in accordance with the value of his services'. To augment his £240 salary as a second-class assistant, Pycraft had become a regular contributor to the *ILN* and other newspapers. In his article on flies, Pycraft warns that 'unless we bestir ourselves, these apparently feeble creatures will slay more than shell and shrapnel among our countrymen who are fighting for us and more than Zeppelin raids and furtive bombardments at home'.

Concerns are frequently raised that in London and many towns and cities, the houses of the poor have no fires to burn rubbish, no disinfectants, and there is little understanding of basic hygiene.

The Illustrated London News article is part of an anti-housefly campaign. The Museum has just sent out a press release to national and regional newspapers. The title is 'War on the House-Fly. What the Natural History Museum is doing' – which, evidently, is a lot. The press release describes exhibits in the Central Hall illustrating how flies contaminate food, where they can breed in houses, and their life cycle. The exhibition labels list diseases spread by flies: 'typhoid, cholera, dysentery, infantile diarrhoea, etc'. There are similar exhibits at the Zoological Gardens in Regents Park in London. A Child Welfare and Mothercraft Exhibition, currently on in London, is intended as the nucleus of a travelling exhibition to go all round the country, informing and instructing mothers on the protection of their children against insect-borne diseases.

The Museum also has on sale a penny pamphlet, *The House-fly as a Danger to Health: its Life-history and How to Deal with it.* Fagan sends a copy to the booksellers WH Smith & Sons, writing: 'In connection with the campaign against these noisome pests', it would be a very useful public service if the pamphlets were available

BRITISH MUSEUM (NATURAL HISTORY)

Economic Series No. 1

THE HOUSE-FLY AS A DANGER TO HEALTH

ITS LIFE-HISTORY

AND

HOW TO DEAL WITH IT

BY

ERNEST E. AUSTEN

Assistant in the Department of Entomology
British Museum (Natural History)

LONDON
PRINTED BY ORDER OF THE TRUSTEES
OF THE BRITISH MUSEUM
1913

[Price One Penny]

The Museum published 15,000 copies of this pamphlet on the housefly in 1915. The threat of diseases spread by these insects was so great there was a nationwide campaign against 'these noisome pests', as Charles Fagan called them.

for sale at railway bookstalls and 'other places where they might be seen by large numbers of people'. Fagan offers a discount of 10 per cent 'on any number of copies you might desire to purchase with a view to placing them on your bookstalls throughout the country'. Fagan realizes how important these popular pamphlets can be in improving the health of the public and military, as he tells the banker and entomologist, (Nathanial) Charles Rothschild, 'I am very anxious to develop this side of the work of the museum'.

After the war, in the volumes on 'Diseases of the War' in *History of the Great War based on official documents* published by HMSO, it is calculated that illness from 'dirt diseases' accounted for nearly 50 per cent of the total sickness in an army. Men crowded together in trenches and cellars, rarely able to wash or change their clothes and eating in 'conditions which must convey infection if there is any infection to convey', must have a devastating effect. Lack of facilities for personal hygiene – and understanding of how disease can spread – also applies to many of the civilian population.

31 MAY 1915 An order is sent to the Museum's printers for 15,000 copies of the housefly pamphlet. It is marked <u>Urgent</u>, which is underlined twice.

German Zeppelins reach the outskirts of London during the night. An estimated 90 incendiary bombs are dropped from German airships. They hit outlying areas; none falls near the centre and casualties are mercifully few. No newspaper reveals the exact boroughs affected in case the information assists the enemy. The main armaments factories are housed in the outer suburbs of the capital.

1 JUNE 1915 Charles Fagan sends a memo to the Keepers regarding the sand bins and buckets placed throughout the Museum. He informs them that the Museum's 'Chief Fireman has been

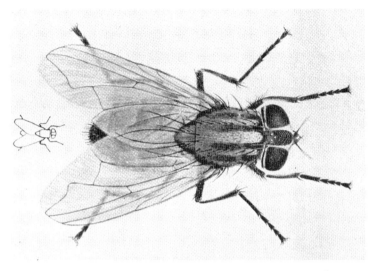

Illustration of the female housefly from the pamphlet, *The Housefly as a Danger to Health.*

instructed…to give you some explanation as to the using of the sand' in the event of fire caused by incendiary bombs.

Fagan also writes to Sir William Graham Greene, Permanent Secretary of the Admiralty. He tells him that a 'skilled taxidermist' in the Museum, Alfred Fieldsend, has brought to Fagan's attention an invention of his own 'for ensuring accurate aim from aeroplanes and a further invention of his for protection of seacraft against torpedo attack.' Fagan tells Sir William that Fieldsend will be writing to him directly.

3 JUNE 1915 The Museum receives an inquiry from the Naval Store Officer, HM Dockyard, Devonport. He wishes to know 'whether the common Weevil which infests grain, ship's biscuits etc., is likely to attack hemp'. He is concerned because he has been told that certain warehouses where it is proposed to store large

The two species of weevil which might have infested warehouses in which the Navy wished to store Italian hemp. The grain beetle (left), known in 1915 as *Calandra granaria*, now *Sitophilus granarius*, was unlikely to cause damage. The biscuit weevil, however, in 1915 *Anobium paniceum*, now *Stegobium paniceum*, was known to attack various substances and that could include hemp.

quantities of Italian hemp, 'are seriously infested with weevils'. Today the Keeper of Entomology, Charles Gahan, replies to him. The name 'weevil', he writes, is applied to more than one kind of insect, 'and it would be well to know for certain' whether the weevils infecting the warehouses are the common 'grain weevil' (*Calandra* [now *Sitophilus*] *granaria*) or the 'biscuit weevil' (*Anobium* [now *Stegobium*] *paniceum*). He asks for specimens to be sent to him for identification. While the grain weevil is not likely to attack hemp, he writes, the other species has been known to attack substances of various kinds. While he thinks it doubtful that it could feed on hemp, it 'may be capable' of damaging it to some extent. 'Would it not be advisable', he suggests, 'to have the warehouses steamed or washed out well with <u>hot</u> water, in order to destroy all the weevils, before storing the hemp?' The zoologist and Museum Trustee, Lord Rothschild, suggests fumigating the warehouses with formalin.

Charles Fagan writes to Harold John Tennant MP, Under Secretary of State for War. It is regarding the formation of a special section of the Army Sanitary Corps 'to deal with the fly peril'. He tells Mr Tennant that three members of the Entomology department are currently serving in the army and would be of use to the special section. Captain Ernest Edward Austen, serving with the 28th Battalion, London Regiment (Artists' Rifles), is a specialist on the Diptera (flies) and the author of the pamphlet *The House-Fly as a Danger to Health, its life-history and how to deal with it*, first published by the Museum in 1913. It is in great demand from the military and civilians. Lieutenant Norman Denbigh Riley is in the Army Service Corps, and Private Kenneth Gloyne Blair is in the 4th Battalion, Seaforth Highlanders. In addition to these men, Fagan also recommends Dr Cuthbert Christy, a naturalist, explorer and prolific collector for the Museum and someone who 'has had very great experience in dealing with insects injurious to man'. He is an assistant lecturer in Tropical Medicine at Liverpool University. Christy is prepared to go to France to help the Sanitary Corps should the government wish him to. He had been about to visit the Sudan to investigate sleeping sickness on behalf of the Sudan government, but would defer this, Fagan writes, if 'wanted by HM Government elsewhere'.

7 JUNE 1915 The Museum is due for its annual fire inspection by the London Fire Brigade. Charles Fagan asks the chief officer to give him two or three days' notice so the Museum's own fire officers can ensure the attendance of 'the Turncock [the official responsible for opening and closing the water supply], Police, Commissionaires, etc'.

8 JUNE 1915 With further indications of the concerns of potential damage from incendiary bombs, the Keepers are asked to examine their basement storerooms and dispose of any disused cases and other inflammable materials that are not absolutely essential.

9 JUNE 1915 The Keeper of Zoology, Dr Harmer, sends a detailed list of his staff of military age to Lazarus Fletcher, the Museum Director, giving the reasons why they are not prepared to enlist. The reasons are medical or family. Sir Henry Blake's letter in *The Times* on 28 May criticising those who have not yet volunteered, which Fagan sent to all the Keepers, causes Harmer to write in defence of his staff, 'that he thinks other members of the Department would not be found behindhand in patriotism if any means of making themselves of special service to the country, in the present emergency, were suggested to them'.

19 JUNE 1915 The Keeper of Entomology, Dr Gahan, reports to the Trustees that the Army is to make use of Captain Austen's expertise on flies. He is being transferred from the Artists' Rifles to the Army Sanitary Corps and is a member of the Special Commission appointed by the War Office to deal with the 'Fly danger' in France. The War Office has just requested 1,000 copies of his pamphlet for dispatch to the army in France. As the matter is urgent, they have been sent immediately. The Director authorises a further 7,000 copies to be reprinted.

24 JUNE 1915 Dr Gahan has asked another of his assistants, Bruce Cummings, to undertake a study of 'the Clothes (or body) Louse' for publication in the same series as *The House-Fly*. Dr Gahan reports to the Trustees that he has received several enquiries on lice from 'relatives and friends of men in camp and at the front', and he believes that the proposed pamphlet 'would be greatly appreciated'. As Cummings notes in his report, lice, under certain conditions, are 'a serious menace to the public health'. They not only irritate the skin, they cause trench fever – which has flu-like symptoms – and also typhus. The clothes louse, Cummings writes, 'always becomes abundant and troublesome' wherever human beings are gathered in large numbers with 'infrequent opportunities for changing their clothes and washing…it is notoriously present among the troops in the present war'.

Cummings has almost completed the manuscript, and has been in communication with Major Percy Samuel Lelean, Assistant Professor of Hygiene in the Royal Army Medical Corps, who has also been studying lice. Major Lelean has been sent to France to report on the efficiency of various suggested remedies. Cummings writes that 'the best preventative is strict personal cleanliness and the careful avoidance of those on whom the insects are likely to be found'. In wartime, as Cummings acknowledges, that is 'a counsel of perfection'. Frequent baths, and frequent changing of clothes, boiling garments or immersing them in gasoline, petrol or paraffin are all good remedial measures, Cummings writes, but all are almost impossible in war. Major Lelean experiments on groups of 25 men

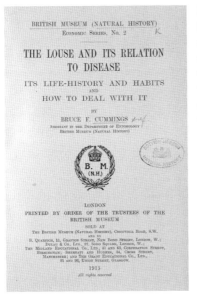

Lice were not just a skin irritant for both public and military. It had recently been shown that they were the cause of trench fever and typhus which severely affected the army. This popular pamphlet gave advice on how to avoid and deal with this 'serious menace' to public health.

Entomology assistant Bruce Frederick Cummings (1889–1919), is the author of the popular pamphlet on the louse. A talented but reluctant entomologist, he suffered from a devastating disease. His deeply moving diary, *The Journal of a Disappointed Man* which he wrote under the pseudonym WNP Barbellion, was published just after the war.

with a number of different chemical mixtures dusted on infected clothes. The measures recommended are a dusting of NCI powder – naphthalene, creosote and iodoform, or a proprietary substance based on a crude oil emulsion known as 'Vermijelli', used 'according to the instructions issued with each tin'. Major Lelean's remedies are included in the pamphlet.

Cummings' pamphlet is widely circulated and thousands of copies are printed. Expert though he is, Cummings is a reluctant entomologist. His passion is 'systematic zoology', but on joining the Museum he found himself, 'God save the mark – in the insect room!' His views on the Museum, his work and his tragically short life become known just after the War in his deeply moving diary, *The Journal of a Disappointed Man*, which he wrote under the pseudonym, WNP Barbellion. Cummings suffers from 'disseminated [multiple] sclerosis'.

26 JUNE 1915 The Trustees are told that so many members of staff are now on military service that, in order to keep the libraries functioning, a special rota has had to be arranged. Certain departmental attendants are now to be interchangeable between the General, Zoological, Entomological and Mineral Libraries.

28 JUNE 1915 The Board of Agriculture and Fisheries forwards to the Museum a letter from the London Chamber of Commerce, asking for the appointment of an expert to examine tins of 'Finest Pacific Lobsters', allegedly made from Japanese spider crabs. It is referred to the Keeper of Zoology, Dr Harmer, who consults his department's crustacea expert, Dr Calman. While they will do what they can, Dr Harmer tells the Director, it should be pointed out to the Board of Agriculture that while there would be little difficulty expressing an opinion with regard to a complete specimen of the crustacean in question, 'it may not be possible to come to a definite conclusion from an inspection of the edible parts of the animal preserved in tins'.

10 JULY 1915 Charles Fagan's letter of 1 June to the Admiralty on behalf of Alfred Fieldsend's proposed invention appears to have got nowhere. He now writes on Fieldsend's behalf to Major Clive Maitland Waterlow, the Squadron Commander and Experimental Officer at the Royal Naval Airship Station, Farnborough, who the Museum has helped on a number of occasions. Fagan tells Waterlow that Fieldsend is 'a mechanicus of considerable ingenuity'. While he is not able to say whether his bomb aiming invention 'has any serious merit,' he certainly thinks it is worthwhile sending Waterlow his brief description of it, and that Fieldsend would be 'glad to explain it to you personally'.

12 JULY 1915 The Museum sends out a press release to 24 national and regional newspapers about a new exhibit in the Central Hall. It illustrates the research done to determine the cause of insect damage to the staple of the military diet, the Army biscuit. The biscuits are part of the essential iron rations – together with 'bully beef', tea and sugar – carried by troops in battle. For some years, however, when the hermetically sealed biscuit tins were opened they were found to be quite inedible, riddled with holes and infested by moths and beetles. As Museum scientist William Pycraft describes them in his column in *The Illustrated London News* on 24 July, 'they might well have come from some witch's kitchen'. Pycraft also notes that these attacks 'on our army biscuits' have been going on for more than 100 years. To emphasise the food horrors soldiers have to put up with, he quotes a sergeant in the Gordon Highlanders in 1801: '...our biscuits were full of worms; MANY OF OUR MEN COULD ONLY EAT THEM IN THE DARK!'

The Museum entomologist, John Hartley Durrant and Colonel Wilfred William Ogilvy Beveridge of the Royal Army Medical Corps, have investigated how the biscuits became contaminated. Their report, known as the Army Biscuit Enquiry, was published in 1913. After exhaustive research, they concluded that the infestation occurred while the biscuits were cooling in the factory, an opportunity seized on by the moths to lay their eggs. They made recommendations to prevent another such attack recurring. These included ensuring that the temperature conditions during cooling were made 'as uncomfortable as possible for the moths' by 'introducing screened cooled air which should be continuously withdrawn by revolving fans, suction, or some similar contrivance'. This would more rapidly cool the biscuit 'and also render it practically impossible for the moth to oviposit on the biscuits'. They also suggest preventing access by the moth to where the biscuits are cooled or packed.

At the request of Major General Selden Long, Director General of Army Supplies, the Museum has mounted this exhibition, illustrating the new Army biscuit now being served to the troops, as well as showing examples of the old – literally moth-eaten – one.

This exhibit illustrating the successful research into the cause of insect damage to the staple of the military diet, the army biscuit, was in the Central Hall in July 1915.

The offending insects are also exhibited. John Hartley Durrant is commended to the Trustees. His research, the War Office tells him, 'has proved most valuable to the Army and deserves special acknowledgement.'

13 JULY 1915 A quiet day on the front at Vierstraat, Belgium. There is just the faint smell of gas. The men of the 2nd Battalion, East Surrey Regiment, are in their trenches. At about mid-morning, Ernest George Gentry, in civil life an attendant in the Museum's Botany Department, is changing guard. He is shot by a sniper, and killed instantly. He is buried where he lay. He had tried to enlist at the outbreak of war but was rejected as being too short. Earlier this year he reapplied, and this time was successful. In November 1914

Lance Corporal Ernest George Gentry, an attendant in the Botany Department, killed by a sniper in Vierstraat, Belgium, 13 July 1915.

the minimum height for volunteers was reduced to 5 feet 3 inches. He joined the East Surrey Regiment and was swiftly promoted to Lance Corporal. He had been with the Museum from the age of 15, when he joined as a boy-attendant. The Keeper of Botany, Alfred Barton Rendle, writes that 'we all liked him for his cheerful, willing disposition, and admired the persistence with which he tried to join up… He gave himself freely, and while deeply regretting his death we respect his patriotism and pluck'. He was 31 and left a wife and three children.

The Assistant Secretary Charles Fagan writes to his widow that he is 'very sorry indeed to hear of your husband's death while fighting for his country. It must be a great comfort to you to know that he was very much esteemed and liked here, and that he always performed his duties conscientiously and with complete satisfaction to his superiors. He will be much missed by all his colleagues in the Museum, and will always be remembered here as one of the staff who gave up his life for his country in this great war'. He ends 'with deep sympathy'.

In her reply, Mrs Gentry asks if there is any possibility of a gratuity, so she can 'start a shop'. She is told that an application on her behalf has been made to the Treasury and two months later, a gratuity is granted. Her husband's annual salary, with overtime, was £107.

20 JULY 1915 Charles Fagan writes to Captain TH Manners Howe at Cromwell Gardens barracks near the Museum. As requested, Fagan tells him, arrangements have been made for officers at the barracks to use the ground at the back of the Museum for cricket net practice.

24 JULY 1915 The Government has appointed a Retrenchment Committee to enquire and report on what public expenditure savings can be made in the civil service, 'in view of the necessities created by the war'. The Trustees authorize the Director to restrict expenditure throughout the Museum 'to such services as are absolutely necessary for the preservation and maintenance of the collections'. It effectively prohibits the purchase of most new specimens and severely restricts payments to temporary workers. Fagan tells the Keepers that 'all expenditure must be kept down to the lowest level compatible with the proper preservation of the collections and the keeping of them accessible for use by the public'. He also asks the Keepers for 'any suggestions tending to economy in the service of the Museum which you may care to put forward'. One of the first economies is the cancellation of the weekly delivery of ice to the Museum from Harrods.

The Museum's Red Cross Section is led by Guy Coburn Robson, an assistant in the Zoology Department. He reports that the section currently has 19 members and is attached to the London Ambulance Column. They have been principally employed in 'detraining the wounded at London termini and in receiving and unloading ambulances at hospitals etc'. Robson is 27 years old. He has told Dr Harmer that he has not enlisted in the military for domestic reasons. He is the only member of his family left to care for his father, whose health and business have been seriously affected by the war. The Red Cross occupies nearly all his non-official time. He is on duty several evenings a week and is often still on duty until 2 or 3am, helping some of the many thousands of wounded men who have been transported to London since the outbreak of the war.

11 AUGUST 1915 The Army Medical Service orders 2,000 copies of *The Louse and its Relation to Disease* for distribution to military medical officers. The Museum sends a further 500 to the medical service of the Canadian Contingents, Canadian Expeditionary Force. Charles Fagan also sends 100 copies of the housefly pamphlet 'for use in the Dardanelles and elsewhere' to the Medical Department of the Navy at the Admiralty.

15 AUGUST 1915 2nd Lieutenant Cyril Richard Lydekker of the Bedfordshire regiment is killed at Gallipoli. He was 25 years old. Cyril is listed on the Museum's roll of honour as the son of a member of staff. He was the younger son of Richard Lydekker, the acclaimed naturalist, geologist and unofficial scientific worker at the Museum for 30 years, who had himself died a few months earlier in April 1915. Cyril's elder brother Gerard is also killed – in France in 1917.

Temporary workers in the Museum who are serving with the armed forces are also listed on the roll of honour and their deaths recorded. In the first half of 1915, three of them are killed. Lieutenant Lewis Neil Griffitt Ramsay of the 3rd Battalion, Gordon Highlanders who was 25, was killed in France. A botanist and keen ornithologist in the Natural History Department of Aberdeen University, he had already published more than 10 papers and was working on the report of the 1910 British Antarctic (*Terra*

Nova) Expedition for the Museum. Lieutenant Richard Bowen Woosnam of the Worcestershire regiment died aged 34. A zoologist and traveller, he collected mammals and birds in Africa for the Museum. Like Cyril Lydekker, he was killed in action at Gallipoli. The natural history collector Captain SA Macmillan served with the 58 (Vaughan's) Rifles Indian Regiment. He was also killed in France.

16 AUGUST 1915 Dr Charles Andrews of the Geology department has been excavating the skeleton of a huge, straight-tusked elephant, *Elephas (Palaeoloxodon) antiquus*, discovered at Upnor in Kent in the grounds of the School of Military Engineering, Chatham. He has been working with Louis Emmanuel Parsons, Geology department preparator who lives near the site for the three months it takes to excavate it. Permission to excavate and take away the animal as a gift to the Museum has been given by the War Office. The Keeper of Geology, Dr Arthur Smith Woodward, reports to the Trustees

Geology department preparator Louis Emmanuel Parsons with the huge left femur from the Upnor elephant, *Elephas (Palaeoloxodon) antiquus*, which he excavated with Geology assistant Charles Andrews. The smaller left femur is probably from an Asian elephant for scale.

that this is the 'largest fossil elephant hitherto discovered in Britain', and also the first time in England that bones of this species have been found in direct association with the teeth. 'The discovery', he tells them, 'is of great importance' and will be 'a most valuable acquisition' for the Museum. However, due to the war – and the cost of reconstructing this enormous animal – the Upnor elephant does not go on display in the Museum until 1927, apart from one of its molars and a huge foot in 1916.

18 AUGUST 1915 Charles Fagan sends a copy of the *Louse* pamphlet to 70 newspapers and journals asking them to mention it in their columns. *The Graphic* calls it 'a most interesting little book. It should be sent to every soldier in the trenches'.

Chapter 4
September–December 1915

By the autumn of 1915, there are about
two million men of military age across the
UK who have yet to enlist. Twenty-eight of
them work in the Museum. The Government is
reluctant to introduce conscription, and instead a
scheme is devised which, it is hoped, will encourage
more men to join up. It is known as the Derby
Scheme. The constant pressure on the Museum for
staff to enlist is such that one Keeper warns that
work could stop altogether if he loses any more key
scientists to the war. In the Museum, the fight against
disease-spreading flies and lice continues, and
leeches are revealed as another enemy for soldiers.
The Keeper of Zoology suggests an insect-killing
apparatus for use by the military, and a lieutenant-
colonel asks the Museum's advice on explosive-
filled arrows. William Plane Pycraft, one of
the Museum's best-known scientists, is
arrested by the army.

1 SEPTEMBER 1915 Dr Sidney Harmer, Keeper of Zoology, writes to the Assistant Secretary, Charles Fagan, about an idea he thinks might be of interest to 'our own Army authorities' who are concerned with protecting the troops from vermin. It is an 'insect-killing apparatus', in use in some foreign museums. Harmer tells Fagan that with most methods in use, insects escape destruction by taking refuge 'in some crevice into which the poison will not penetrate'. He gives the minute burrows of furniture beetles as an example. This apparatus, he writes, 'is very simple, but it is thoroughly effective'. It encloses the infested 'furniture, fabric or whatever it is' in a metal cylinder, from which the air 'is exhausted until a fairly good vacuum is obtained', even in crevices and burrows. A poisonous gas is then introduced into the cylinder and 'it penetrates into the most protected situations. No films of air are left to shield the insect from destruction'.

Harmer has seen this in use in a museum in Stockholm. The cylinder, which is powered by a six horsepower engine, has a diameter of about 2.7 metres and its length is 4 metres. 'It is thus large enough to contain a very large number of clothes at one time'. Harmer tells Fagan that he would be 'only too glad' to show his notes and plans to a representative of the War Office, if they were interested.

6 SEPTEMBER 1915 Fagan sends Harmer's letter to Colonel Alfred Percy Blenkinsop, Assistant Director-General of the Army Medical Service. He asks that if he thinks Dr Harmer's suggestion is worth a trial, perhaps he would pass on the letter to the right quarter? Fagan concludes, 'I need scarcely add that we shall be only too glad to give any help in our power if the matter has any interest for the War Office'.

8 SEPTEMBER 1915 London is again attacked by Zeppelins – huge, tube-shaped balloons of menace at least 140 metres long, floating to their targets. A deep boom vibrates through the streets as a bomb hits. Bruce Frederick Cummings, Entomology assistant and author of *Journal of a Disappointed Man*, lives a quarter of a mile away from where the bombs fall. Shrapnel hits the roof and, terrified, he and his fiancée Eleanor run to a neighbour's house. They cower in 'absolute darkness' as the bombs explode and dogs bark. He records in the *Journal* that a great fire is burning in London. Deaths are officially given as 38, with more than 100 wounded. The Natural History Museum is not affected, but bombs fall around Bloomsbury, close to the British Museum. Five days later, Admiral Sir Percy Scott, whom the Museum advised in November 1914 on the physiology of whales, is placed in charge of the aerial defences of London.

15 SEPTEMBER 1915 The Keeper of Zoology, Dr Harmer, receives a letter from Dr VJ Woolley of the Military Hospital in Tooting, south London, concerning a large leech removed from the nose of a soldier invalided home from Gallipoli. Private Frederick Bunn, who is 28, of the 6th Battalion, York and Lancaster Regiment, is originally treated in Gallipoli for shrapnel wounds to his fingers in August. He then develops symptoms similar to those of enteric or typhoid fever. When he arrives in Tooting on 10 September, he is found to be suffering from malaria. Three days later, a nurse discovers the leech and removes it. Private Bunn states that the wells and springs he drank from were 'clear and good and passed by the medical officers'.

Zoology assistant Harry Arnold Baylis is asked by Harmer to examine the leech, and before the end of the day he reports that it is *Limnatis nilotica*, common in most of the warm countries around the Mediterranean. It is well known to give trouble to humans and mammals, 'being introduced either when swallowing water or crawling into the nostrils' when it is 'young and small'. It grows rapidly. Several fatal cases are on record, but the symptoms 'are said

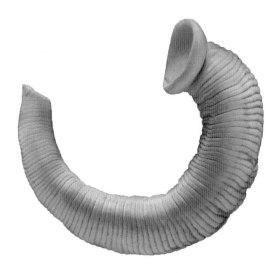

Limnatis nilotica, the species of leech removed from the nose of a soldier invalided home from Gallipoli. It was identified by Zoology assistant Harry Baylis.

to disappear rapidly on the removal of the leech'. Baylis also sends a newspaper photograph to Harmer of soldiers lowering each other head first into a river to drink, commenting 'if this is the kind of way the men drink, no wonder they get leeches!'

17 SEPTEMBER 1915 Dr Woolley returns Baylis's report which Harmer has sent him. He tells Harmer that 'it seems likely that the beast got into his [Private Bunn's] nose while he was asleep, as he had of course to sleep in the open'. The commanding officer of the hospital has no objection to the Museum retaining the leech, 'if you want to', Woolley writes, and tells Harmer that it was 'put into chloroform water for 24 hours and then into the spirit in which it was sent to you'.

Shearborn 523

180°

Leech

Military Hosp
Tooting
S.W.
[Sept. 17, 1915]

ackd 20.ix/15
S.F.H

Dear Harmer

Very many thanks for the information about the leech. I return you Mr Bayliss' report with a detailed statement about the man.
It seems likely that the beast got into his nose while he was asleep, as he

had of course to sleep in the open.
The O.C. thinks that there is no objection to your retaining the leech if you care to. It was put into chloroform water for 24 hours & then into the spirit in which it was sent to you.
With many thanks
yours sincerely
V.J. Woolley.

Dr VJ Woolley of the Military Hospital in Tooting who sent the leech wrote this letter of thanks to Dr Harmer. He tells him, 'it seems likely that the beast got into [the soldier's] nose while he was asleep...'

20 SEPTEMBER 1915 Dr Harmer sends a detailed report on the case to the Museum's Director Lazarus Fletcher and suggests that it indicates that the troops in Gallipoli 'may be exposed to a danger' unknown to army doctors. He recommends that the Director should contact the War Office.

The Director General of the Army Medical Service thanks Fletcher for alerting him, and states that the Mediterranean Expeditionary Force has been notified so that 'the necessary precautions may be taken'. Harmer recommends that boiling water or straining it through mesh with small holes 'seems to be indicated in doubtful cases'. The Director General of the Naval Medical Service has also been alerted, and asks permission to report the Museum's findings in the next issue of the *Naval Medical Journal*, under Dr Harmer's name. The *Journal's* joint editor, Fleet-Surgeon WL Martin, tells

R.J.

Capt. A. Northcott
    E Company, 1st Kent Cyclists Batt:
        Head Quarters,
            Birchington.   Sept. 22, 1915.

Dear Sir,

        Mr W. P. Pycraft has informed me that he has
been getting into trouble with the military authorities
by taking photographs in forbidden places ; and he
asks me to write to you to confirm the statements
he has made about himself.

        Mr Pycraft is a member of the scientific
staff of this Museum, and he occupies a
position of responsibility here. He is a well
known writer on scientific subjects. I have
not the slightest doubt that the photographs
he was taking, without being aware of the
fact that he was infringing regulations,
were taken with a scientific object, as
I understand he has informed you. You may
have every confidence in Mr Pycraft's
good faith in this matter.

                I remain,
                    Your obedient servant
                        S. F. Harmer
                        (Keeper of Zoology).

Dr Harmer, as well as Charles Fagan, wrote to Captain Northcott in
Birchington to try to secure Zoology assistant William Pycraft's release.
'I have not the slightest doubt', Harmer wrote, that Pycraft was unaware
that he 'was infringing regulations' by taking photographs.

Harmer that medical officers who have served in the Levant know of the leech danger from drinking by mouth from streams and wells, 'but there must be many now in our Service who have not heard of such a danger'.

22 SEPTEMBER 1915 Charles Fagan writes a most unusual – and awkward – letter to Major Bennett at the War Office. 'Dear Sir', he begins, 'Mr WP Pycraft who is spending his vacation in Birchington, writes to me that he has been placed under "open arrest" for taking photographs of the cliffs and that his camera and films and prints have been provisionally confiscated'. William Plane Pycraft, the Zoology assistant who is well known through his science articles, has visited Birchington before – in October 1914 he was sent there to work on a whale killed by a mine. Fagan tells Major Bennett that Pycraft occupies a position of responsibility in the Museum, and 'I feel sure that he unwittingly infringed the War Office regulations'. He has for some time been interested in coastal erosion, Fagan writes, and he took the photographs to show the erosion of the chalk. Fagan hopes that 'under the circumstances', Pycraft, his camera and photographs will be released, and he sends the letter to the War Office by hand. The authority for Pycraft's release however, rests with Captain Northcott of the 1st Kent Cyclist Battalion in Birchington. Fagan writes to him at once, and this time he also makes clear his irritation with Pycraft. 'I feel bound to say', he tells Captain Northcott, 'that I consider that Mr Pycraft was, to say the least, very indiscreet in doing what he did in face of the notices that are placed about in the Isle of Thanet prohibiting the taking of photographs. May I add', he ends, 'that I was glad to hear that your men were so vigilant in doing their duty'. Pycraft is released.

26 SEPTEMBER 1915 Lieutenant-Colonel Auberon Arthur Howell, 1st Battalion Cambridgeshire Regiment, writes to Dr Sidney Harmer, his brother-in-law: 'My dear Sidney, For some time I have been thinking that cross bows might well be used for throwing arrows filled with a high explosive to act like bombs'. He asks Harmer if he could introduce him to 'some person having charge of an armoury of medieval or uncivilised arms', and wonders if there might be such a collection in the British Museum – of which the Natural History Museum is still formally a part. Aerial darts, known as 'flechettes', are already in use on both sides. They are not shot from bows, but dropped from aircraft – about 100 at a time – onto troops below. *The Illustrated War News* reports that from an altitude of 4,000 feet, a dart 'falls with sufficient force to pierce right through a mounted man and his horse'.

Dr Harmer immediately makes enquiries, and tells Colonel Howell that he should see Sir Charles Hercules Read, Keeper of British and Mediaeval Antiquities and Ethnography at the British Museum. He hopes 'that your idea may prove of real practical service'.

Howell is a career soldier, and is now training recruits. In his letter he tells Harmer, 'This month I have sent 100 men and officers of my own training to the front. The only thing that reconciles me to the work is that I know it is useful'. Total casualties for the first year of the war are 381,983 killed and wounded. Howell sends Harmer 'best love to you all', and ends, 'I hope you have good news of Russell – God bless him'. Russell is Harmer's eldest son and Howell's nephew. He is a 2nd Lieutenant in the Royal Engineers and has been in France since the spring. He will be 19 in November. In his reply, Harmer tells Howell that they have had 'a very cheerful letter' from Russell 'written just before our advance began. He said he did not expect to be able to write again for some time; and I hope,' his apprehensive father ends, 'no news is good news'.

30 SEPTEMBER 1915 The Museum section of the 31st London Voluntary Aid Detachment of the British Red Cross Society now numbers 11 active members – from attendants to an assistant keeper – and five more who can be called on in an emergency. The Commandant of the 31st Detachment is a local businessman, Stanley Joseph Toms, who enrolled in the Red Cross just seven months previously. He tells the Museum section that they are 'ready and resourceful', but there are things that are 'in need of great improvement'. These include, 'discipline while marching…and there should be no smoking, talking or slackness of any kind'. Perhaps most important – and a little worrying – 'First Aid knowledge must not be forgotten'.

1 OCTOBER 1915 Because of the threat from enemy aircraft, a new order for the reduction of lighting in London comes into force. Bright lights must be shaded, windows concealed with blinds and particular attention paid to skylights which must be covered so no light is visible through them. Under the Defence of the Realm Act 1914, severe penalties can be imposed for any breach of the orders, including life imprisonment or death if the breach is committed to assist the enemy. For some months now, the Museum has been operating lighting restrictions. These are now intensified by new instructions from the Office of Works, together with heating restrictions because of the shortage of coal. The Museum now has to restrict 'to its narrowest limits the consumption of fuel and light'. In case of doubt, a notice is circulated outlining the details. Fires are not to be made up after 3pm, unless it is known that the room will be occupied after 5pm. Fires should only be lit 'when the weather renders it absolutely necessary', and – this is underlined – each light should be extinguished 'the moment it is not required', even if it may be wanted again a few minutes later.

5 OCTOBER 1915 Dr Harmer writes to Lieutenant Thomas Cyril Bruce Joy of the 1st Devonshire Regiment, attached to the 2nd

In order to avoid waste of Coal, it is requested that Fires shall not be made up after 3 p.m. unless it is known that the room will be occupied after 5 p.m., and in no case should a Fire be made up later than two hours before the time of leaving.

Fires should only be lighted when the weather renders it absolutely necessary.

Care should be taken to extinguish all Lights whenever the room is vacated, and to extinguish each Light the moment it is not required, even though it may be wanted again in a few minutes' time.

H.M. OFFICE OF WORKS.

(6438). Wt.30,153—647. 10,000. 10/15. Gp.133. A.&E.W.

The shortage of coal for heat and light was such that the Office of Works issued notices restricting its use 'to avoid waste'.

Battalion, the Dorsetshires, serving in Mesopotamia (now Iraq). He has not previously been associated with the Museum, but Harmer tells him that he has heard from his father, the well-known artist George William Joy, that 'you have very kindly offered to collect specimens for us. We should gladly avail ourselves of your kindness as the district in which you are fighting is one from which we have but little material'. There are many things 'we might like to have', Harmer tells him, 'but I can imagine the difficulties of collecting in camp, and in a hostile country; and it seems to me useless to suggest specimens which require preservation in spirit or by any complicated methods'.

Harmer suggests instead that perhaps he might 'collect some shells for us more easily than anything else', and encloses typewritten instructions. As small mammals and birds would also be very welcome, he sends instructions for the collecting, preserving and packing of these too, but adds, 'they are more trouble, and are useless unless done properly'. He closes with renewed thanks, 'and my most earnest wishes for the success of your operations'.

13 OCTOBER 1915 The National League for Physical Education and Improvement sends a copy of their leaflet, *How to prevent the spread of epidemics by insects in wartime*, for approval by the Museum. It is revised and corrected by the Keeper of Entomology, Dr Gahan, and the Trustees permit the League to mention that the leaflet has met with their approval. Since its formation in 1905, the League has been endeavouring to improve the health of the nation. It draws attention to the 'potent factors for evil', as one of its founders, the physician and pharmacist Sir Thomas Lauder Brunton described them to a meeting of head-teachers: overcrowding, alcoholism, insufficient or imperfect food and poor personal hygiene – including tooth care and understanding how spitting spreads disease. By targeting 'the coming generation' through the schoolroom, the League hopes to transform the health of the nation.

This evening a Zeppelin raid on London kills 32 and injures nearly 100 people.

18 OCTOBER 1915 Dr Harmer informs the Director that an attendant in his department, Isaac James Frederick Kingsbury, has requested permission to join the army for service abroad. He hopes he will be allowed to join the Royal Army Medical Corps, 'for which his previous experience in connection with the Boy Scouts Association would be useful'. Kingsbury, who is 22, works for Georges Boulenger, the head of the department's reptile and fish section. Boulenger tells Harmer that he will be extremely sorry to lose him, but he will not object to his application. However, he considers Kingsbury's health is not very robust, and that the work of the RAMC 'might suit him better than some other kinds of work'.

Across the Museum, the depletion of staff is becoming critical, in administrative as well as human terms. As Harmer tells the Director, 'With every new loss of a member of staff it naturally becomes more difficult to carry on the work of the Department. But Kingsbury (who has recently lost his mother whom he helped to support) considers it his duty to go; and I therefore support his application'.

To Kingsbury himself Harmer writes: 'I am very glad to be able to congratulate you on your decision to come forward, and I hardly need say that I wish you every good fortune while you are fighting for the country'. Kingsbury enlists in February 1916. Two years later he is killed in action.

19 OCTOBER 1915 The politician Lord Derby has been active in recruiting volunteers since the outbreak of war. Two weeks ago Lord Kitchener appointed him Director General of Recruiting. Now Derby has devised a scheme that 'is the last effort on behalf of voluntary service'. Conscription is something the Government still wants to avoid. There are some two million men of military age yet to enlist. Today he spells out the details of his scheme. All men aged between 18 and 41 will be asked either to enlist immediately or to attest their willingness to serve. 'A mere promise', the government's recruiting posters proclaim, 'is of no value'. Their commitment has to be registered and they will be issued with a khaki armband to show they have attested. They will then be called upon only as necessary and in the meantime they will continue with their usual occupations. They will be given a fortnight's notice before being expected to join up. Only after all single men have enlisted will married men be called up.

20 OCTOBER 1915 The Keeper of Zoology, Dr Harmer, recommends to the Director that Guy Coburn Robson, an assistant in his department in charge of molluscs, should be granted permission to go to the Italian front with the 2nd British Ambulance Unit for Italy of the Red Cross and St John's Ambulance. Robson, who is 27, has just been declared unfit for active military service by the Central London Recruiting Depôt. Robson has made 'a special appeal' to be allowed to serve. His knowledge of Italy and Italian, and his recent experience with the Red Cross detraining the wounded makes him, he argues, especially useful in a unit which is short of men with such knowledge. His application is supported by Colonel Valentine Matthews, County Director of the British Red Cross Society. Robson wishes to apply for special leave for six months, with full pay and pension rights. He tells Dr Harmer, 'I need hardly say how anxious I am to avail myself of this opportunity of service and I would be most grateful if by any personal influence you could convince the Trustees of this'.

22 OCTOBER 1915 The Hon Arthur Stanley, MP, Chairman of the Joint War Committee of the British Red Cross Society and the Order of the Hospital of St John of Jerusalem, writes to the Museum asking for Robson's services on the grounds of his 'special qualifications'. It is difficult, Mr Stanley points out, to obtain suitable personnel, as men eligible for the army cannot be accepted by the Red Cross. But neither this request, Col Matthews' support, or Harmer's 'personal influence' prevail. Treasury sanction would be needed for the payment of Robson's salary, and the Trustees, unwilling to ask for it 'under present conditions', refuse his application.

On learning this Robson writes to Dr Harmer with barely disguised bitterness: 'Thank you for letting me know the Trustees' decision. It is rather sickening to have such an uncompromising refusal'.

23 OCTOBER 1915 Every newspaper across the land carries an appeal from King George V to 'men of all classes to come forward voluntarily and take your share in the fight'. The King tells his subjects, 'The end is not in sight. More men and yet more are wanted to keep my Armies in the field, and through them to secure Victory and enduring Peace'. It is a last appeal for a voluntary army.

The Trustees hold one of their regular meetings. Dr Rendle, Keeper of Botany, reports on the department's war work. He has recently been consulted by Major Clive Maitland Waterlow, the Squadron Commander and Experimental Officer at the Royal Naval Airship Station, Farnborough, on the subject of a suitable wood for use in airship construction. He has made suggestions and has indicated sources of supply. Dr Rendle reports that his department has also been consulted on an organism which was damaging fabric used for airships. It proved to be a fungus. They have also examined samples of fodder with a view to the discovery of poisonous seeds in connection with an outbreak of presumed fodder poisoning at a military veterinary hospital. Such enquiries, Dr Rendle tells the Trustees, are part of the usual work of the department. Many are answered directly and in other cases the enquirer is referred to sources of expert information. Any reduction in efficiency of the department, he warns, would seriously reduce its value as a source of help and information to other Government departments and the general public.

A four-page leaflet has been prepared on *The Danger of Disease from Flies and Lice*. There is a great demand for information. Ten thousand copies are printed. The Local Government Board, which oversees local government throughout the country, is asked to co-operate in making the leaflet as widely known as possible to medical officers of health. A guide is also being prepared by the anatomist Dr Walter George Ridewood to the exhibits in the Central Hall of disease-spreading insects. Houseflies, fleas, mosquitoes and bed-bugs are exhibited – every stage of their lives illustrated – and these have recently been joined by specimens and models of tsetse-flies as well as more mosquitoes and ticks. The labels are detailed and graphic in their descriptions of both disease and how easily, particularly with poor hygiene, they are spread.

A further 3,000 copies of *The Louse and its Relation to Disease* are printed. The Director informs the Trustees that the War Office has requested that 2,000 copies be supplied to the Army Medical Department for distribution to Military Medical Officers. The Director of Medical Services, Canadian Contingent, has asked for 500 copies. At the request of the Director-General of the Medical Department of the Navy, a further 100 copies of *The Housefly as a Danger to Health* pamphlet are supplied to the Admiralty for distribution.

27 OCTOBER 1915 Charles Fagan writes to the Chief Medical Officer at the India Office asking if he would be interested in the pamphlets on the housefly and the louse for distribution to Indian medical officers. The India Office asks for 200 copies of both pamphlets. They are to be sent to the Indian Medical Service at the front.

Examples of disease-spreading insects, such as these models of house-flies, were exhibited in the Central Hall.

29 OCTOBER 1915 In response to the Derby scheme and the King's appeal, the Assistant Secretary, Charles Fagan writes to all the keepers, enclosing a list of the 28 members of staff who are of military age (18–41) and are not at present serving in the navy or army. He asks that they be informed of this. He would like the list returned as soon as possible, indicating on it those who are married.

30 OCTOBER 1915 Dr Harmer tells Fagan that there are nine men in his department of military age, of whom five are married. Two attendants have indicated they will enlist, and as Harmer again writes, 'The difficulty of carrying on the work of the Department is becoming more and more serious'. One of the attendants, Herbert W England, is essential to the work of the departmental library, the other, 21 year old Stanley Thomas Wells, to work in the mammal rooms. He is applying to enlist in the Civil Service Rifles. It is Wells's third attempt to enlist – he has twice been rejected on medical grounds. 'The work of the Mammal Rooms would be very seriously interfered with by Wells' departure', Harmer writes, 'This part of the Museum will undoubtedly suffer in efficiency with so diminished a staff. In the ordinary course of things it would be my duty to point out that it would not be possible to spare Wells. In the face of a National emergency, everything else ought to be subordinated to the needs of the country'. And, in this case at least, it is. On this third attempt Wells is successful. He is killed in action within a year.

5 NOVEMBER 1915 The Office of Works has urgent need of the services of 'thoroughly reliable carpenters' to help build anti-aircraft stations for the defence of London. The Permanent Secretary, Sir Lionel Earle, writes to the Museum 'that they would be extremely grateful if, in the present emergency, you could see your way to lend

THE PRIME MINISTER'S
ADVICE TO THE YOUNG UNMARRIED MEN
and
PLEDGE TO MARRIED MEN

" I am told by Lord Derby and others that there is
" some doubt among married men who are now being asked to enlist
" whether, having enlisted, or promised to enlist, they may not be
" called upon to serve, while younger and unmarried men are holding back
" and not doing their duty. Let them at once disabuse themselves of
" that notion. So far as I am concerned, I should certainly say
" the obligation of the married man to serve ought not to be
" enforced or held to be binding upon him unless and until - I
" hope by voluntary effort, but if it be needed in the last resort by
" other means - the unmarried men are dealt with.

" I have far too much confidence in the patriotism and
" the public spirit of my fellow-countrymen to doubt for one moment
" that they are going to respond to that appeal - that the young men,
" the unmarried men with whom the promise of the future lies, are
" not going in this great emergency to shirk and to leave the fortunes
" of their country and the assertion of the greatest cause for which
" we have ever fought, to those who have given greater hostages to
" fortune and are least able to bear the brunt".

HOUSE OF COMMONS, NOVEMBER 2ND 1915.

MARRIED MEN !
ENLIST NOW. YOU HAVE THE PRIME MINISTER'S PLEDGE THAT
YOU WILL NOT BE CALLED UPON TO SERVE UNTIL THE YOUNG
UNMARRIED MEN HAVE BEEN SUMMONED TO THE COLOURS.

SINGLE MEN !
SURELY YOU WILL RECOGNISE THE FORCE OF THE PRIME
MINISTER'S STATEMENT AND ENLIST VOLUNTARILY. YOU CAN
GO INTO YOUR PROPER GROUPS TILL YOU ARE WANTED.

Reluctant to introduce conscription, the Government devised the Derby scheme to encourage more men to enlist. This poster was to reassure married men that single men would be called upon first. Under the Derby scheme, this armband or brassard showed that the wearer had attested that they were willing to serve.

some of these carpenters to this Office for the time being to assist in this important work'. Five carpenters are loaned. They are to work on a gun-battery station in Holland Park, west London.

8 NOVEMBER 1915 The Treasury sends out a circular letter regarding the enrolment of civil servants under Lord Derby's scheme. The letter expresses a desire that every possible encouragement is given to men to respond to the King's appeal. The letter also states that the Treasury will be prepared to consider proposals for the employment of men substitutes who are either not of military age or are 'physically incapacitated' for military service, and draws attention to the possibility of employing women as substitutes for men during the present emergency.

The Keepers report that, with very few exceptions, there are no strong official reasons why the remaining men of military age left in the Museum should not offer themselves for enrolment. The Director, Lazarus Fletcher, tells the Trustees that enquiries have been received from the recruiting authorities regarding certain men who had given the nature of their work as a reason for not enlisting, and asks that the Trustees' views on this should be made known to the staff.

The Trustees resolve that every man who can possibly be spared should be encouraged to enlist. However, they authorise the Director to mention to the recruiting authorities the case of any man attested whose services are considered indispensable either to the safety of the collections or for such work in the Museum as is essential for the public. The Keepers are directed to tell their staff that no man may inform the recruiting authorities that his service cannot be spared, unless he has the Trustees' permission, through the Director, to that effect, and that if he has any doubt on the subject he should refer the recruiting authorities to the Director.

17 NOVEMBER 1915 Dr Harmer tells Dr VJ Woolley of the Military Hospital, Tooting that there is considerable interest from the naval and military authorities in the Gallipoli leech and he has been asked to publish his paper. The species of leech, he notes, is well known to those who have experience of the eastern Mediterranean, and the problem is of long-standing. 'Napoleon's army', Harmer writes, 'suffered greatly from it in the Egyptian campaign; and there is no doubt that it is a real danger'.

22 NOVEMBER 1915 Guy Coburn Robson submits a further application to Dr Harmer for leave to go on foreign service for six months with the British Red Cross Society. This time he says he is prepared to go on half, rather than full pay, while still retaining all service and pension rights. Dr Harmer presents his case to the Trustees, recommending its acceptance. Robson, he tells them, would go to France or Belgium if required, but he would greatly prefer Italy, 'for which his previous experience specially qualifies him, and where work could be found for him without delay'. Robson's application points out that under the Red Cross he has no pension rights, and also has the considerable expenditure of life insurance, uniform and equipment. Dr Harmer even suggests a replacement for Robson – the former assistant keeper of Zoology, Edgar Smith, 'who would be very glad to do all he could' in the event of Robson being allowed to go away. The Trustees, however, are adamant. With Treasury sanction still necessary, they again regret they are unable to see their way to granting Mr Robson's application.

The Assistant Secretary Charles Fagan sends out another call to the Keepers for men to enlist, again enclosing the names of those of military age. 'The appeal of the King is being addressed to all Civil Servants of military age,' he writes. The Trustees wish to know whether the Museum has any strong official reasons why staff of military age should not enlist under Lord Derby's scheme. They also wish to know whether their absence on military service would involve the closing of any part of the Museum. Fagan reiterates to the Keepers that in the case of urgent work, 'the Lords Commissioners of His Majesty's Treasury have intimated that they would be prepared to consider applications for the employment of substitutes' – male (if unfit for military service), or even female.

23 NOVEMBER 1915 Dr Harmer tells Fagan that the absence of some of the men on the list 'would practically stop work in the branches they are in charge of'. He has already mentioned to Fagan the importance of the attendant, Herbert England who is in charge of the departmental library, and now he spells it out. 'So long as any work at all is done in the Museum, the members of staff are dependent on the Library. It is, for instance, impossible in many cases to reply to a question having a practical bearing on the War without having access to books. A substitute would be unable to find the books or give the assistance required, if introduced from outside; and there is no-one, among the Attendants who remain, capable of replacing England satisfactorily.' Furthermore, Harmer continues, 'England is very sensitive to cold and his health far from strong. I feel very doubtful if he could stand the exposure to which he would be subject if accepted.' Harmer thinks it very probable that his health would give way and believes there are sufficient reasons for attempting to obtain exemption for him.

Fagan replies the same day, asking whether any men in his department would wish to be examined by a competent medical officer in order to obtain an official opinion as to their medical fitness for military service. Harmer tells him that there is only one who would – who in any event already has a medical certificate pronouncing him unfit. Six other men have similar certificates, and the remaining two consider they have sufficient evidence that they are physically unfit, though Harmer is unsure whether they have certificates to prove it. In other departments, the answer to Fagan is almost invariably, 'No'.

24 NOVEMBER 1915 The problem of lice is still rife. Dr Charles Gahan, Keeper of Entomology, reports that he has received a letter from Mr Alfred Ferris, the Police Surveyor, New Scotland Yard, asking for advice on the subject of body vermin on human beings being transported in prison vans. Ferris is responsible for keeping the vans clean and writes that several disinfectants cannot be used because of their effect on paint, wood and iron. Information is given to him, together with copies of *The Louse and its Relation to Disease*, written by the Entomology assistant and reluctant louse expert, Bruce Cummings. Ferris is told that lice do not live for more than a few days away from a host, and that he could try some of the remedies suggested in the pamphlet. If these do not work, he could also try fumigation with sulphur, or 'better still', hydrocyanic acid gas. This is a fumigant so toxic that if not applied correctly, it can as easily kill those using it, as insects. A further 2,000 copies of the *Louse* pamphlet are printed.

Dr Gahan also reports that the Commanding Officer of the 3rd London General Hospital, Wandsworth Common, Lieutenant-Colonel HE Bruce Porter, has telephoned him to say that lice have been introduced into some of the wards by wounded men returning from the Dardanelles. Cummings is dispatched to the hospital and is shown the wards, infected clothing and specimens of the insect. The hospital is especially anxious to know whether fumigation of the wards will be necessary. Cummings reassures them that he does not consider the case to be very serious and that sufficient precautions will be to disinfect the clothing from time to time and to give infected patients hot baths with cresol soap lather, a coal-tar based disinfectant.

A few days later, Lt Col Bruce Porter asks whether a party of about 20 wounded soldiers being treated at the hospital might be conducted round the Museum by the Official Guide, John Henry Leonard, on one day a week. His request is granted. Since his appointment in 1912, Leonard's knowledge and enthusiasm have made him enormously popular with the public. A graduate in zoology, botany and geology from University College, London and a former teacher, his communication skills draw young and old to his twice-daily tours of the Museum's treasures. He is also much in demand for private tours, such as this for the wounded soldiers.

30 NOVEMBER 1915 The staffing problems in the Zoology department are mirrored throughout the Museum. This is the fifth anniversary of Entomology assistant Kenneth Gloyne Blair's appointment to the Museum. For the last year he has been on military service. The Keeper, Dr Gahan, reports to the Trustees that Blair had 'but a few months training' as a private in the 4th Seaforth Highlanders, when he was sent out to France with his battalion. During most of his time there, he was 'incapacitated' for active service at the front because of fatigue and illnesses he contracted – first scarlet fever and then pneumonia. He convalesced in England and Scotland and then a few months ago returned to France. He was one of those Gahan recommended to the War Office in June for service in the special section of the Army Sanitary Corps dealing with 'the fly peril', but he was not transferred.

The latest news from him, Dr Gahan writes, 'is that he has been declared medically unfit for the fighting line', and has been placed as storekeeper at the Royal Engineers' Headquarters. In 1922, the *Report of War Office Committee of Enquiry into "Shell Shock"*, published by HMSO, noted that 'thousands of men were passed "fit" into the Army every week without any medical examination worth the name'. The result was 'they were being flooded with men, who, after a few weeks or months of military service, broke down and contributed an ever-growing quota to the sick returns and casualty lists'.

At the Museum, Blair specialized in beetles and was engaged in 'valuable work'. Dr Gahan, whose depleted department is contributing vital work to the Museum's war effort, clearly thinks Blair would be of far more use in the Museum and 'greatly regrets the temporary loss of his services'.

DECEMBER 1915 Earlier in the year, there were 11 members of staff enrolled as members of the 31st London Voluntary Aid Detachment of the British Red Cross Society. From mid-May, they were mobilized under the authority of the War Office, for regular duty as stretcher-bearers in the London Ambulance Column which, since the outset of the war, has handled every wounded man arriving in London. To date, the Museum members of the 31st VAD have attended 148 separate calls to hospital trains and to hospitals. They have taken their regular turn on night-watches (for Zeppelins), and as relief-orderlies at the Kensington Red Cross Hospital. Now the Ambulance Column has had to be reorganized, as only men unfit for military service may be retained. This has reduced the Museum cohort to six men, who, nonetheless, are continuing with their duties as far as is possible.

1 DECEMBER 1915 To what must have been Dr Harmer's considerable relief, Herbert England, the library attendant, is rejected by a recruiting depôt doctor as medically unfit, as are two other members of his staff.

5 DECEMBER 1915 John Stanley Gardiner, Professor of Zoology at Cambridge, writes a letter in haste to Dr Harmer. It is barely decipherable, written in pencil and marked 'confidential'. He tells him that the Royal Society is authorised to select a number of trained microscopists 'who will undertake 1) to come up for training when called upon, 2) to serve anywhere in the diagnosis of a protozoological nature'. Protozoology is the study of micro-organisms, in this case those carried by ticks, mosquitoes and flies that can cause severe and often fatal illnesses in humans. Diseases such as typhus, malaria and dysentery are of great concern in the military, and also in the civilian population. 'Such men', Gardiner writes, 'will be badged [as if they had attested under the Derby scheme], if called on and trained, as they are likely to be sent out as expert civilians directly under the Director General of the Royal Army Medical Corps. The men wanted, Gardiner writes, 'are research workers, lecturers, demonstrators, etc in botany and zoology, professionals'. Others, a 'second class', may be needed for work at home.

Gardiner wants to know within four days if there are any men in the Museum Harmer could recommend for consideration. 'Ability, tact, and other qualities than pure microscopy are advisable'. He asks if Harmer could recommend botanists as well as zoologists. By return, Harmer tells him he may safely assume that the Museum is anxious to co-operate in every way possible 'with well designed attempts to assist the country in its great struggle'. He says it is 'not improbable' that the Museum could release two members of staff. However, he writes, 'you will no doubt be prepared to hear that I cannot speak in the name of the Trustees without express permission', and Harmer has had no opportunity yet to obtain it.

7 DECEMBER 1915 The pressure to encourage staff to enlist continues. Charles Fagan circulates to the Keepers a further Treasury letter on the subject of civil servants and military recruitment. He tells the Keepers that recruits under the Derby scheme are more likely to be assigned to the new army. Men who prefer to join a Territorial unit such as the Civil Service Rifles or a local battalion, 'may be well advised to offer themselves for enlistment without awaiting a summons'. Within a few days, 12 men from the permanent and temporary staff have attested under the scheme.

9 DECEMBER 1915 The Museum's Director, Lazarus Fletcher and Charles Fagan, Assistant Secretary, attend a conference of the great London museums and art galleries. It is held at the Office of Works to consider whether any further steps can be taken to safeguard the national collections against air raids. They discuss measures such as the use of wire-netting to prevent damage from falling glass, and methods for packing and storage. Water is thought to be 'more efficacious' than sand for dealing with fire. The naval and military experts present, however, unanimously agree that no public building can, by any structural device, be protected against attack by bombs, or at least not without incurring considerable expense. While incendiary bombs – at least those in use at present by the enemy – were unlikely to penetrate a concrete roof, it is thought that an explosive bomb would get through. As for the Museum's spirit building, the conclusion, again, is that 'the building must be left to take its chance'. The Museum asks the Office of Works to set out its agreement to this in writing.

11 DECEMBER 1915 At Kut-al-Amara in Mesopotamia the weather is bitterly cold. An Anglo-Indian force consisting, according to War Secretary, Lord Kitchener, of 'a gallant garrison' of fewer than 9,000 men, is besieged by 30,000 Turkish soldiers. The troops include the 2nd Battalion the Dorsetshire Regiment. They have limited food and few medical supplies. Day after day they are shelled, shot, or repel infantry assault. Thomas Joy, now promoted to temporary Captain, is killed in action. His surviving colleagues are forced to surrender to the Turkish army four months later. Most of them die in captivity. The war memorial in Wadham College, Oxford, where Joy was a student, records that he was a 'keen and gallant soldier and a gentle friend'. He was 29 years old. His zoological collecting career on behalf of the Museum lasted barely two months.

14 DECEMBER 1915 Charles Fagan writes to the secretary of the Parliamentary Recruiting Committee. He asks to be sent 150 copies of a pamphlet the Committee has recently published by the barrister Professor John Hartman Morgan. *Germany's Dishonoured Army, additional records of German atrocities in France*, is the report of Morgan's investigation into alleged violations of the laws of war by German troops. During four or five months in France, he interviewed nearly 3,000 officers and men. His report is a searing indictment of the German forces' disregard for the Geneva Convention and what Morgan calls their 'brutal and licentious fury'. Fagan tells the Committee that 'we shall be glad to distribute [copies] to scientific correspondents of the Natural History Museum in Neutral countries'. Within a week, he asks to be sent an additional 150 copies. Fagan sends a dozen of them to each of his contacts in museums abroad. He offers to send more, if required. He asks his Museum colleagues to do the same.

Professor Stanley Gardiner has replied to Dr Harmer regarding the need for protozoologists. He tells him the deadline for names has been moved forward by a week. Harmer, however, needs clarification on a number of points. As Gardiner had marked his letter 'confidential', Harmer asks him if he may explain the general nature of the Royal Society's scheme to the Trustees. No member of staff can offer his services without the Trustees' permission, he tells Gardiner. He also needs to know whether those selected would be sent abroad in a civil or military capacity, and whether the scheme includes bacteriology as well as protozoology.

Unfortunately for the Museum, all this is taking too long for Professor Gardiner and he has looked elsewhere. He tells Harmer, 'The matter had to be done in a hurry and…I'm only sorry I troubled you. Time scarcely permits an august body like the Trustees to deliberate before we conclude names tomorrow'.

The Museum decides to approach the Royal Society independently of Professor Gardiner. Dr Harmer accordingly writes to the Secretary, William Bate Hardy, suggesting they could offer two or three members of staff and asking whether it would be desirable for them to acquire experience at once, by working at the Lister Institute of Preventive Medicine. Hardy's reply could not have been welcome. 'I think the best thing would be to call on you later if there is any urgent need for men,' he tells Harmer. 'It looks as though the names we have would more than satisfy present need'. And there the matter rests – until January.

Chapter 5
January–April 1916

The year 1916 opens with a great row
over Government plans to close all museums
and galleries to the public in the interests of
economy. The policy is ridiculed by the press, and
fought tenaciously by supporters of all museums,
including the Natural History Museum. Lord Derby,
director-general of recruiting, reports that 651,160
single men have still not offered themselves for service.
Voluntary recruitment has failed; conscription is
now introduced. By the spring, 56 men on the staff of
the Natural History Museum are absent on military
service and more will soon follow. As well as the
pressure this places on those remaining just to keep
the Museum functioning, their work is becoming
of increasing importance to the war effort. At
the request of the War Office an exhibit of
pigeons is displayed in the Central Hall, and
the Assistant Secretary is sent a suggestion
for entomological warfare.

THE EVENING NEWS.

SATURDAY, JANUARY 29, 1916.

HOUSE FULL

BOOKING OFFICE

TO-DAY

PRICES
1/-
TO
5/-

ADMISSION FREE

CLOSED

BRITISH MUSEUM

How to Save.

It is estimated that by closing the museums the nation will save £50,000. This would pay for the war for *very nearly a quarter of an hour!*

This cartoon from *The Evening News*, 29 January 1916, was typical of the ridicule newspapers heaped on the Government's plans to close Museums and galleries. The saving was estimated at £50,000. 'This would pay for the war for very nearly a quarter of an hour!' is the mocking comment.

3 JANUARY 1916 Charles Fagan writes a confidential letter to the Keepers. There have been rumours that the Treasury wishes to close the national collections to the public for the duration of the war 'in the interests of economy'. These have now been 'officially intimated'.

The Treasury wishes to save money in terms of staff, cleaning, light and so on and states that closure 'will no doubt make it possible' for additional members of staff to be freed for either service in the Army or to assist other Government departments which are in need of extra staff. Fagan tells the Keepers that the Director would like a report as soon as possible on how their departments would be affected and what measures would be necessary 'for the proper protection and conservation of the collections'.

4 JANUARY 1916 Dr Charles Gahan, Keeper of Entomology, replies to Fagan regarding the proposed closure. He wishes to know whether it is suggested that students should be excluded. Amongst others, there are two Japanese and one Indian student studying the collections. The Imperial Bureau of Entomology is also housed in the Department. 'If students are still to be admitted', Gahan writes, 'and if the work of the Bureau is not to be interrupted, I cannot see how the staff of the Department, already so much depleted, can be expected to work elsewhere'. In any event, not more than one or two men could be spared unless the Department's work and care of the collections 'cease altogether', with consequent damage to specimens. Closing the exhibition galleries makes little difference to the Department and would not enable Gahan to spare 'more than, perhaps, one man'. Lack of heating in the galleries would make little difference either, but it would make work in the Insect Rooms 'most uncomfortable'. As for removing specimens as a precaution against air raids, he adds, his main concerns are the 'expensive models' of various insect species in the Central Hall. He thinks it desirable for them to be moved to a position of greater safety.

5 JANUARY 1916 The Military Services Bill which will, for the first time, make military service compulsory, is introduced in Parliament. Yesterday Lord Derby reported that in spite of intensive

Dr Harmer's views on the Government's proposed closure of the
Museum were politely scathing. He detailed the heavy expenditure
and impracticability of moving specimens, and in this paragraph
on the proposal itself, he comments: 'the wisdom of closing it
seems questionable'.

publicity for his voluntary recruiting scheme, just 350,000 men have
volunteered. In the Museum, under his scheme, two members of the
higher staff, five attendants and five weekly staff have attested – a
total of 12. Thirteen men have been rejected as medically unfit –
six from the higher staff and seven attendants. Across the country,
651,160 single men have not offered themselves for service in the
military. The choice will no longer be theirs.

Dr Harmer, Keeper of Zoology, replies to Charles Fagan's letter
regarding the proposed closure of the exhibition galleries. His tone –
towards the Treasury's scheme – is politely scathing. Like Dr Gahan,
he writes that closure of the galleries would not automatically
release his staff for service elsewhere as none have duties primarily
connected with them. It would be 'neither practicable nor expedient'
to remove zoological specimens from the exhibition cases as they
'must be protected from dust and insect-enemies'. Temporary
cases for them would incur 'heavy expenditure' and there would
be nowhere to put them. Mounted specimens, moreover are 'very
sensitive to alterations in temperature and humidity' and 'serious
deterioration is likely to result' in specimens moved to the basement.

If the galleries were not properly heated, not only the specimens, but also 'the expensive cases' would suffer.

As to the proposal itself, Harmer adds, 'If the last man and the last shilling are really required in order to bring the War to a satisfactory conclusion everything else ought to be sacrificed'. But if it is at all possible to keep the Museum open on current lines, then 'the wisdom of closing it seems questionable'. Any further reduction of staff will interfere with help requested by government departments or other public bodies. Zoology, Harmer writes, 'is so much specialised', that no member of staff 'can be expected to be competent' to assume the responsibilities and special knowledge of an absent colleague. As for attendants and boy attendants, the Department has already lost 10, leaving just eight – and one of those has been lent to Entomology.

It also seems to Harmer that 'some consideration' is due to the general public. 'The proportion of visitors in uniform – often wounded – is an appreciable one.' Many of them, he notes, take a special interest in the economic exhibits in the Central Hall, and he hopes they acquire 'information of a practical value'. He concludes that if closing the galleries results in a comparatively small saving, 'it seems more than doubtful whether it is in the public interest to take this step'.

The Botany Keeper, Dr Rendle, also sends his thoughts. The biggest saving, he writes, is in cleaning the public gallery, which would probably need to be cleaned once a week instead of daily. Two of his assistants have already said they wish to undertake war work, which will leave him in any event with two assistants instead of five, as one is already serving. He too thinks that the collections would probably suffer more damage from moving and storage than from an air raid. He does not anticipate damage in the galleries if the present temperature was not maintained, but he is concerned that damp could affect the Herbaria if the temperature was reduced too much.

6 JANUARY 1916 George Thurland Prior, Keeper of Mineralogy, writes today that his department will be little affected by the closure, provided that his staff could still access and work on the collection. He has no more staff remaining who could be spared for service elsewhere. As for the temperature, he too is concerned that damp might affect certain specimens.

In his response to the proposals, the Keeper of Geology, Dr Arthur Smith Woodward, writes that his 'most experienced' staff would still be needed to 'watch and deal with the numerous cases of natural decay among the fossils'. Accidental discoveries of fossils are continually being made, and they have to be obtained and preserved, he writes. It is just a few months since two members of his staff were occupied excavating the Chatham elephant. However, closure of the exhibition galleries, Smith Woodward thinks, might enable one attendant and two boy attendants to be spared for service elsewhere. What he does not want is to remove specimens from the exhibition cases and store them elsewhere. This would be 'most harmful' and 'many would be destroyed' by decay. Labels might disintegrate and cement in fractures would tend to perish. Packing away the specimens would take a considerable time, even if the Treasury agreed to defray 'the great expense' of the necessary packing materials. As for heating, what Smith Woodward is most concerned about, like his colleagues, is keeping fossils and furniture 'perfectly dry'. Dampness will accelerate the decay of certain specimens, he writes, and destroy the glue-based products by which the fossil bones are preserved.

8 JANUARY 1916 Today the Trustees consider the Treasury's proposal to close the Museum to the public. They have before them the Director's detailed arguments against closure, which include many of the points raised by the Keepers. The Director, Sir Lazarus Fletcher (who has just received his knighthood in the

New Year's Honours), concludes that closure would result in a comparatively small saving – £2,500. 'The wisdom of closing the doors of the Museum to our soldiers, many of them wounded, and of depriving the public and students of the opportunity of seeking relaxation, edification and instruction in this time of stress seems very questionable', Fletcher writes, and 'under these circumstances it appears very doubtful whether it is in the public interest to take the proposed step'. The Museum's cause will be taken up over the next few weeks by the national newspapers and journals from the *Daily Mirror* to *Nature*.

10 JANUARY 1916 Dr Harmer sends a memo to Charles Fagan regarding his correspondence in December with William Hardy of the Royal Society. The Museum is anxious to keep the zoologist and leech expert Harry Baylis in the Museum and hopes that work as a protozoologist [or bacteriologist] – might give him a claim for exemption from ordinary military service on the grounds of his specialist knowledge. However, as Hardy has told Harmer that they have more names than they need at present, it looks, Dr Harmer thinks, that Baylis 'offering himself might have no chance of being accepted'. He suggests to Fagan that he might recommend that Baylis should start a special course of training in protozoology on the chance of it being wanted later. 'Considering our interest in blood-sucking Arthropods [insects, spiders, crustacea and so on] that carry Protozoal diseases, it would not be a bad thing for some members of our staff to have some knowledge of the Protozoa concerned'. He tells Fagan that if Baylis is allowed to go on a course, he will inform Hardy and send him Baylis's name.

12 JANUARY 1916 Harry Baylis's future is almost immediately secured. Charles Fagan tells Dr Harmer that Baylis and Guy Robson (who the Trustees would not permit to go to Italy with the Red

Cross) are to attend a course at the Protozoology Laboratory, Wellcome Bureau of Scientific Research. This is just what Harmer has hoped for – it is part of the Royal Society's scheme. They will be taught by Clifford Dobell, a brilliant young scientist at the Imperial College of Science and Technology, seconded to the Wellcome. Dobell has been released from Imperial for service with the War Office, 'to conduct protozoological investigations of dysentery cases and carriers among the troops'. He also trains biologists to diagnose protozoal infections.

17 JANUARY 1916 Charles Fagan writes to the Military Representative of the Chelsea Recruiting Office in an attempt to prevent the call-up of another essential member of staff, Louis

Fleas as a Menace to Man and Domestic Animals, the latest popular pamphlet to be published as part of the Museum's war effort to improve public health. Two thousand copies were printed. The author, James Waterston, was an assistant with the Imperial Bureau of Entomology based in the Museum.

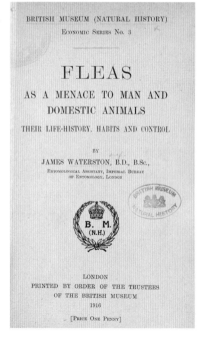

BRITISH MUSEUM (NATURAL HISTORY)
ECONOMIC SERIES No. 3

FLEAS
AS A MENACE TO MAN AND DOMESTIC ANIMALS
THEIR LIFE-HISTORY, HABITS AND CONTROL

BY

JAMES WATERSTON, B.D., B.Sc.,
ENTOMOLOGICAL ASSISTANT, IMPERIAL BUREAU
OF ENTOMOLOGY, LONDON

B. M.
(N.H.)

LONDON
PRINTED BY ORDER OF THE TRUSTEES
OF THE BRITISH MUSEUM
1916

[PRICE ONE PENNY]

Parsons, preparator in the Geology department. 'He is at present engaged in a difficult piece of work requiring considerable technical skill', Fagan writes, 'necessary for the preservation of a very important specimen of a fossil elephant discovered at Chatham'. Parsons worked on the excavation in the summer of 1915. The bones are fragile and friable 'and the specimen must be prepared at once and the work completed to prevent deterioration'. His services are essential to the work, which should take about six months to complete.

A few days later, Fagan has to write to the recruiting office in Fulham to argue for the continued Museum service of the entomologist Frederick Laing. He, Fagan writes, 'has frequently to consider enquiries of sanitary or economic importance. His expert knowledge may at any moment prove to be of considerable value to the Naval or Military authorities'.

Dr Gahan, Keeper of Entomology, reports to the Trustees that James Waterston, an entomology assistant with the Imperial Bureau of Entomology based in the Museum, has prepared a pamphlet on another disease-spreading insect, *Fleas as a Menace to Man and Domestic Animals*. Two thousand copies are to be printed.

Just how important the Museum is to the public and military is witnessed every day by the Official Guide, John Leonard. He writes to Charles Fagan on the subject of the proposed closure, emphasizing the frequent visits by men from the Royal Army Medical Corps and the Army Veterinary Corps who are lectured by their own officers. He writes that the Museum 'is a common resort of soldiers "on leave" with their friends or with their children – the exhibits here affording them the material for mental recuperation, entertainment and instruction'. Many tell him that they find their visit 'a real comfort'. Wounded men from different hospitals attend regularly. And from his own knowledge of museums and 'general observation of our visitors I can add that, to the majority of folks, no other Museum in London can give a tonic to the war-weary like the Natural History Museum'.

22 JANUARY 1916 The Government announces that all museums and art galleries are to be closed. The date of closure will be announced later.

26 JANUARY 1916 The outcry is such that today *The Times* reports that a few exceptions have already been made: the National Gallery, Victoria and Albert Museum and the Reading Room of the British Museum (but not the galleries) are to remain open.

William Pycraft, who is a journalist as well as a senior assistant in Zoology, writes a six page letter to Dr Harmer on the subject of the closure. 'Since the fatuous policy of closing this Museum seems to have been formed with a supreme disregard to the consequences which may follow,' he begins, and proceeds to outline to Harmer 'a few facts' which should be known about the part played 'only by my small section of the Museum, in the prosecution of the War'.

He reminds Harmer of how in 1914 he helped the Royal Army Medical Corps deal with the critical levels of frostbite that were incapacitating the army in France by advising on the use of whale oil and supplying tins immediately. He has advised a captain in the Army's veterinary department who was lecturing to classes from the cavalry and Field Artillery on the care of horses. Just now he is helping Captain Cope of the RAMC who is studying human crania in the Museum's Osteological Room. The captain wishes to understand how to deal with the problem of bullet wounds in the skull and how bullets might be extracted. 'It is imperative I should be with him', Pycraft tells Harmer, 'since I am able to render him very material assistance'. The captain needs a number of skulls bisected, 'by no means an easy task', and one that Pycraft cannot entrust to another.

He tells Harmer of a conversation with a postman he had this morning. The man remarked, Pycraft writes, 'that if things had got so bad as implied by this proposal, then we had better "throw up the sponge". That is a dangerous spirit to encourage'. Pycraft is also most concerned about the thousands of troops in London, recovering from wounds at the front, who will find 'all doors' shut in their faces for the sake of saving money 'to carry on the War at its present rate of expenditure for about 36 minutes!' That is estimated at £50,000, approximately the amount that would be saved if all museums and galleries are closed as the Treasury proposes. Pycraft scarcely has to tell Harmer that 'I feel very strongly on this subject' and that he fears the result 'may be disastrous'.

27 JANUARY 1916 Closure of museums is debated in the House of Lords. The Archbishop of Canterbury, a Trustee of both the British Museum and the Natural History Museum, expresses his 'greatest regret' and that of his fellow Trustees that they have felt the need to acquiesce in the Government's decision, especially given the importance of the Museum to wounded officers and men recuperating in convalescent homes near to the Museum.

Although no firm decisions regarding the implementation of closure have yet been made, the Command Pay Office of the Army's Eastern Command have requested taking over the Museum's refreshment room to accommodate their clerks. As the very popular refreshment room seats 80 people and the Museum is still open, Basil Harrington Soulsby, a clerk in the Director's Office, informs the Pay Office that an official letter will have to be written to the Museum Secretary and that will be laid before the Trustees for their decision.

The Military Service Act today becomes law. All unmarried men between 18 and under 41 on 2 March 1916 are deemed to be enlisted from that date for the period of the war. Between now and the end of the war, 2.5 million men are conscripted into the armed forces.

There are a number of categories for possible exemption, however, including those who are ill, disabled, or more useful to the country in their present employment. Conscientious objectors may also be exempt, provided they engage in work of national importance.

28 JANUARY 1916 Miss Winifred Thomson writes to Charles Fagan. Several times a week she brings parties of wounded soldiers to the Museum from King George's Military Hospital near Waterloo Station. With 1,650 beds it is said to be the largest military hospital in Britain. The Museum 'is such a resource' for them, she tells Fagan, 'and it has the great advantage of having so much that is interesting on the ground floor – steps and stairs being impossible for the lame men. The bird gallery and the Central Hall alone are so fascinating that the soldiers have always left unwillingly at closing time'. As the Victoria and Albert Museum is exempt from closure,

Sir Edwin Ray Lankester (1847–1929), zoologist and former Director of the Museum, was one of the many scientists who wrote to *The Times* protesting against the closure proposals. He condemned the 'disastrous ignorance' of politicians.

she writes, 'Could you not persuade the powers that be to keep this open?' It would be rather sad, she adds, 'to be reduced to picture palaces as their only place of amusement'.

29 JANUARY 1916 *The Times* reports the 'public indignation' at the Government's policy to close museums and galleries, and says it has received an 'unusual' number of letters of protest. One of these is from the Museum's former Director, Sir Edwin Ray Lankester. He fulminates against the paltry sum closure will save, the contempt towards science shown by politicians, and condemns their 'disastrous ignorance'. The highly regarded geologist and palaeontologist, Professor Sir William Boyd Dawkins, speaks for many when he writes to *The Times* of the importance of museums to the 'general education' of the public. He refers to a visit to the Natural History Museum just three days previously of 45 soldiers and their instructor to study flies so 'that they might be prepared to deal with that deadly pest in the field'.

Dr Harmer reports to the Trustees that he has been asked to take part in the work of the Light Observation Detachment, organised as part of the Anti-Aircraft Corps by the Admiralty. To do this, Harmer has to enrol as a special constable. His hours of duty are 7pm to 11pm, every fourth night. Lighting restrictions are a key part of London's defences and it is crucial they are obeyed. In the event of a daytime air-raid, Harmer is also liable to be called for duty.

31 JANUARY 1916 Zeppelins attack the east coast of England and the east Midlands – there are six or seven of them. Nearly 70 people are killed and more than 100 injured.

1 FEBRUARY 1916 The famous surgeon, Sir Frederick Treves, adds his voice to the outcry over closure, citing in a letter in *The Times*, 'the thousands of sick and maimed men' for whom museums, and

The Hon Mrs Graham Murray (1871–1947) was an influential and well-connected ally of the Museum in the fight against closure. Among those she contacted on its behalf was Sir Alfred Keogh, Director General of Army Medical Services.

'especially the Natural History Museum… are a great delight and a most desirable resort', particularly in 'inclement weather'. In 1915, 433,581 people visited the Natural History Museum. Treves' letter is followed by others over the next few days, highlighting the essential war work of the Museum.

2 FEBRUARY 1916 Another influential and well-connected ally in the fight against closure is the Honourable Mrs Graham Murray. She is co-founder and superintendent of the King George and Queen Mary's Club for the Overseas Forces, which opened in 1915 and can accommodate 400 men. She tells Charles Fagan that she has had 'quite a satisfactory interview' about the Museum with Sir Alfred Keogh, Director General of Army Medical Services, '& others', which she underlines but does not specify. She wants answers to a number of questions including, 'roughly speaking', how many soldiers visit the Museum daily, how many are wounded or convalescing, and how many are from the colonies. 'Without mentioning names', she writes, 'we want to make our case as strong as possible so please err on the generous side when mentioning numbers! I shall anxiously await your message or letter'.

Fagan's four-page reply is by return. 'I do not think there is a Hospital for wounded soldiers in or near London which does not send parties of convalescents to the Museum', he writes. Just four hospitals send around 100 soldiers a week, with at least another 50 each day who come with different groups or friends. It is hard to judge, he writes, as they 'do not sit down idly, but walk or hobble about, evidently taking great interest in the exhibits'. There are well over 50 soldiers daily who are on leave, and at least that number who are from the colonies. Sometimes there are hundreds at a time – troops route-marching through London come to the Museum when they can. The numbers he gives Mrs Graham Murray amount to many hundreds of soldiers each week.

7 FEBRUARY 1916 Chares Fagan writes to the Superintendent at his local police station asking that he be communicated with 'at once' at home in the event of an air raid. He would like his name added to 'your Official List of Persons to be warned on receipt of news of the approach of a Zeppelin'. He gives his home address and telephone number. After 10.30pm he asks that a constable 'or other messenger' should be sent to his house to warn him.

8 FEBRUARY 1916 Dr Harmer receives a letter from the entomologist Frank Milburn Howlett who is giving a series of lectures at Imperial College on measures 'likely to be useful against flies and vermin in the different war areas'.

Howlett writes that he doesn't know 'if you want evidence of the utility of the Museum, but you might like to know that I send between 50 and 80 men there every week'. These are officers and men who will be engaged in sanitary work at the front. The exhibits in the Museum, he tells Harmer, 'form a most useful adjunct' to the lectures.

10 FEBRUARY 1916 A strong protest against the closure of museums and galleries is made to the Prime Minister, Herbert Asquith, at Downing Street by a deputation including the Museums Association and the National Art Collections Fund. One of their many criticisms, as *The Times* reports, is that the savings represent only 'a fleabite' compared with the costs of the war. Mr Asquith replies briskly that all savings made in Government departments are 'flea bites', but it is necessary for government and individuals to save every pound they possibly can.

However, for the Natural History Museum, there is a reprieve – for some of its galleries at least. The Prime Minister announces that he now concludes it would be 'desirable and expedient' for its more 'popular' galleries – those showing 'exhibits of animals, birds etc' – to remain open, and also facilities for students to pursue their studies there.

11 FEBRUARY 1916 The Museum is still receiving so many letters asking when or if it will be closed, that the clerk Basil Soulsby replies with uncharacteristic exasperation: 'The Museum is not closed, never has been, nor is it going to be'.

12 FEBRUARY 1916 The importance of the Natural History Museum in disease control is reported in *The Times*. It describes how men of the Royal Army Medical Corps and the Royal Army Veterinary Corps attend for instruction in groups of 20 or 30, accompanied by an officer. Their interest is particularly in exhibits in the Central Hall of pests – both specimens and models – such as the malarial mosquito, tsetse fly, the plague flea, clothes louse and the common housefly. 'The character, habits and dangers', *The Times* reports, 'of these insects are cleverly illustrated, and it is much easier for the men to acquire the necessary knowledge of these minute but disease-spreading creatures by explanations

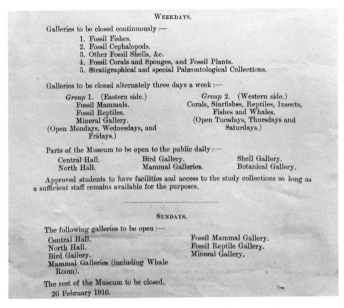

WEEKDAYS.

Galleries to be closed continuously :—
1. Fossil Fishes.
2. Fossil Cephalopods.
3. Other Fossil Shells, &c.
4. Fossil Corals and Sponges, and Fossil Plants.
5. Stratigraphical and special Palæontological Collections.

Galleries to be closed alternately three days a week :—

Group 1. (Eastern side.)
Fossil Mammals.
Fossil Reptiles.
Mineral Gallery.
(Open Mondays, Wednesdays, and Fridays.)

Group 2. (Western side.)
Corals, Starfishes, Reptiles, Insects, Fishes and Whales.
(Open Tuesdays, Thursdays and Saturdays.)

Parts of the Museum to be open to the public daily :—

Central Hall.
North Hall.

Bird Gallery.
Mammal Galleries.

Shell Gallery.
Botanical Gallery.

Approved students to have facilities and access to the study collections so long as a sufficient staff remains available for the purposes.

SUNDAYS.

The following galleries to be open :—

Central Hall.
North Hall.
Bird Gallery.
Mammal Galleries (including Whale Room).

Fossil Mammal Gallery.
Fossil Reptile Gallery.
Mineral Gallery.

The rest of the Museum to be closed.
26 February 1916.

Following strong protests against the Museum's closure, there was a reprieve for some of its galleries. Regulations were published stating how the partial closure would take effect.

given in front of the cases than by lectures illustrated only by drawings'.

The Museum's Director, Sir Lazarus Fletcher, submits a scheme to the Trustees for partial gallery closure to take effect on or after 1 March 1916. Some galleries, such as Fossil Fishes, are to be continuously closed; others, including Fossil Mammals and Whales, are to be closed on alternate days of the week. Those which will remain open daily include the Central and North Halls, and the Birds, Mammals and Botanical galleries. This will save four commissionaire and three police constable posts. On Sunday afternoons, when policemen on duty act as warders in the galleries, eight constables only will be wanted, instead of the usual 15.

16 FEBRUARY 1916 Louis Parson's status is still uncertain. This is partly because his temporary exemption from military service was asked for before the Military Services Act came into force. Charles Fagan tells the Geology Keeper, Dr Arthur Smith Woodward, that he does not think the Museum can take any further steps to postpone his call-up for six months. The only thing now, he writes, 'is for Parsons himself to find out what his position is under the Act and to obey the Law'.

19 FEBRUARY 1916 Ernest Edward Austen, an assistant in Entomology and author of the pamphlet on *The House-fly as a Danger to Health*, is currently serving in Egypt. He is a captain with the Sanitary Branch of the Royal Army Medical Corps who are battling against a range of parasitic and insect-carried diseases amongst the troops. Dr Harmer reports to the Trustees that Austen is investigating the disease bilharzia, caused by *Schistosoma*, a species of parasitic worm, which is 'one of the most dreaded parasites known to man'. If it gets into blood vessels, 'very often those of the bladder, it gives rise to many kinds of trouble according to the organs affected'. Austen suspects that certain molluscs are its intermediate hosts and as it is a matter of urgency, Dr Harmer has dispatched to him 10 duplicate specimens of molluscs not required for the collections.

22 FEBRUARY 1916 The Office of Works writes to Charles Fagan requesting once again the loan of carpenters. This time it is to assist in building a gun emplacement in Lambeth Palace Park. Four carpenters are lent.

26 FEBRUARY 1916 At their meeting, the Trustees agree to the closure of certain galleries in the Museum, 'in compliance with the request of His Majesty's Government', for the duration of the war.

This pigeon exhibit was placed in the Central Hall in 1916 to illustrate differences between species used by the army for essential war service and other species.

The study collections are to remain accessible to approved students, provided sufficient staff are available.

The Keeper of Zoology, Dr Harmer, reports to the Trustees that a new exhibit of pigeons has been placed in the Central Hall. Homing pigeons are now in use solely for military work, and under the Defence of the Realm Act 1914, it is an offence to shoot them. The messages they carry are vital communications – whether of strategic plans or saving lives. There are thousands of birds at the front with the army and also carried by ships and planes. Pigeon fanciers have willingly loaned their birds for war service. Pigeon breeding, racing and shooting has long been a popular pastime. Just a few days previously, a 16 year-old boy was fined 10 shillings (50p) – a very large amount for a youth – for wounding one. Captain Alfred Henry Osman, head of the War Office Pigeon Service, said the bird was on war service when it was shot. There are many similar offences reported, with severe financial penalties or even prison sentences being imposed on the perpetrators. The War Office has issued a public notice prohibiting their shooting, but a number of offenders plead ignorance as they cannot read and did not know of the ban. Often homing pigeons are mistaken for wood pigeons and shot.

The pigeon exhibit has been arranged at the suggestion of Captain Osman. He is a leading pigeon racer and breeder and editor of the *Racing Pigeon* weekly magazine. In 1914 he was consulted on the possibility of using pigeons for war service and in 1915 he was commissioned as army captain and set up the Pigeon Service, overseeing recruitment of men and pigeons. The Museum's exhibit illustrates the differences and likenesses 'between the type of Racing or Homing pigeons, as used by the Army for war service, and other pigeons'. Dr Harmer tells the Trustees that Captain Osman has 'sent for the purpose three very fine specimens' of racing pigeons from his own loft. The public are told that any pigeon flying alone, steadily and in a straight line, must not be shot, and if one is found injured, it should be taken at once to the nearest police station or military depot.

2 MARCH 1916 Zoology assistant and parasitic worm expert Harry Baylis has completed his training at the Wellcome Laboratory. Now he has been nominated by the Royal Society to be transferred to the Admiralty for temporary service as a protozoologist for the duration of the war. He is to work at the Royal Naval Hospital, Haslar in Gosport, Hampshire. Because of this, Baylis is now exempt from military service at the front. Dr Harmer tells Charles Fagan that the course at the Wellcome under Mr Dobell 'has been very successful', and mostly devoted 'to the study of amoeboid dysentery'. Guy Robson has also been on the course, and Harmer suggests that it 'would be desirable to extend the permission to study this subject for another six weeks'. Robson, he thinks, would probably spend part of the time studying bacteriology at either St Mary's or University College Hospitals.

Basil Soulsby in the Director's Office writes in reply to an application for employment at the Museum. Since the outbreak of war, there has been a marked increase in the number of women applying for jobs, and almost invariably, the reply is 'there is at present no vacancy. Should an occasion arise, a further communication will be sent to you'. Soulsby's reply to this applicant is no different, but she is. Her name is Evelyn Cheesman, and she will become a renowned explorer and entomologist, and subsequently a volunteer at the Museum. She becomes a significant donor, presenting the Entomology department with more than 50,000 insects she collects in Papua and the New Hebrides.

8 MARCH 1916 Dr Harmer reports to the Trustees on the results of the examination of a tinned food sold as 'Finest Pacific Lobster'. Harmer had been told the previous summer by the Board of Agriculture and Fisheries and the London Chamber of Commerce that there was some concern about the actual contents of the tins – it was suggested it might be Japanese spider crab – but there had been a delay in sending samples. In February he and his department's crustacea expert, Dr William Calman opened a tin and 'it was at once evident' that the contents were from a large crustacean, but not from 'any lobster-like animal'. Dr Calman made a comparative study of tendons from the tin and concluded there was a 'complete resemblance between it and the corresponding tendon of *Paralithodes camtschatica*, a Pacific species of *Paralithodes* or 'Stone-crab'. It was neither lobster nor Japanese spider crab. Harmer reports that this morning a second tin was opened and the contents proved to be 'precisely similar'. He suggests that the tinned food might therefore be described as Japanese or Pacific crab, or Japanese stone crab, a 'genus remarkable for appearing to possess only three pairs of walking legs'.

Harmer takes this opportunity of pointing out to the Trustees the importance of having large collections which have been assembled without reference to any practical utility of the species, but which enable such economic questions to be answered. Furthermore, the incident is also an argument, he writes, 'for leaving the Museum as far as possible in possession of its Scientific Staff, who are able to give assistance to public bodies, from time to time, in matters of considerable practical importance'.

9 MARCH 1916 Entomology assistant Harry Baylis commences work at the Royal Naval Hospital, Haslar. His task is to examine material from dysenteric patients for the amoeba of dysentery and other intestinal protozoa. Over the next two years he will examine roughly 1,000 cases. He has to identify which men are 'merely "carriers" of the amoeba, having been invalided home for other causes such as Typhoid or bacillary dysentery' and which are suffering from acute amoebic dysentery. He follows up these cases with repeated examinations during and after treatment, to ensure that a cure has been effected.

23 MARCH 1916 The Museum receives a letter from the Controller of HM Stationery Office, drawing attention to the 'imperative need of the strictest economy' in the use of paper of all descriptions, caused by the restrictions on the importation of wood pulp. He requests that, as far as possible, government departments reduce their demands to two-thirds of the amount used during a normal year. He makes various suggestions as to how reductions might be obtained – for example, by using both sides of a sheet of paper and not using large sheets when smaller will do. The Trustees order that these suggestions are carried out 'as far as may be'. Twelve copies of the letter are made for the various departments within the Museum.

25 MARCH 1916 The Director reports to the Trustees that, as a measure of precaution against bombs from hostile aircraft, instructions have been given to allow the Museum firemen prompt access to dangerous points on the upper floors of the Museum, that the doors of the Upper Mammals gallery and Botanical gallery should be left open during the night, and the fire-hose so placed as to be ready for instant use.

Two more members of staff enlist: Thomas Douglas, a labourer, joins the 11th Battalion County of London Regiment (Finsbury Rifles). Isaac James Frederick Kingsbury, a 22 year-old attendant in Zoology, joins the 15th Battalion, London Regiment (Prince of Wales' Own Civil Service Rifles). His request last autumn to join the Royal Army Medical Corps has been refused. He has been working for the Zoology assistant and reptile specialist Georges Albert Boulenger since his appointment in 1914. Boulenger finds him 'intelligent and well-trained' and very punctual in his work. He will clearly be missed as Boulenger notes 'he is of great assistance to me'.

28 MARCH 1916 The economies that the Museum now has to impose are impacting the work of the Official Guide, John Leonard. Charles Fagan has to inform the Education officer of London County Council that Leonard's services conducting teachers – and all special parties – round the Museum can no longer be without charge. 'However,' Mr Fagan writes, there is 'no objection to your making any arrangement you may desire with Mr Leonard for continuing the classes in his own time, and on terms to be agreed between you'. In 1915, Leonard conducted a total of 11,005 visitors round the Museum.

3 APRIL 1916 The Eastern Pay Command that had wished to take over the Museum's refreshment room for its clerks has instead been accommodated in temporary buildings in the grounds. All is not going well, however, as the clerk, Basil Soulsby tells the Office of Works which maintains the Museum buildings. 'I am desired by Mr Fagan', Soulsby writes, 'to state that necessary steps should be taken to prevent the lady clerks...obtaining access to the Museum grounds through the windows of the lavatories lately erected by the Office of Works with the sanction of the Trustees, and it is also desired that the lady clerks should not throw orange peel & other rubbish on to the Museum grounds'.

6 APRIL 1916 Georges Boulenger is one of the scientific staff whose 'expert knowledge' Charles Fagan suggested in 1914 might be of use to the government – an offer not taken up. Boulenger was born in Belgium but is a naturalised British subject. Now Fagan tells the War Office that his 'thorough' knowledge of French and German 'may be useful in the present emergency in some capacity at the War Office, in the Department of Military Intelligence or elsewhere, and if so the Trustees of the British Museum will be glad to place his services at the disposal of the Army Council'. Fagan also informs the Ministry of Munitions that the mineralogist, Dr George Herbert Smith, 'is available for war service in an administrative or technical capacity...if you have suitable employment for him'. Herbert Smith, who at 43 is too old to be called-up, is an expert in the study of crystals and has designed instruments in connection with this. He is also 'acquainted with the theory and construction of many forms of optical instruments' and he has recently 'designed and patented a Range Finder'.

7 APRIL 1916 The matron of the Prince of Wales' Hospital in Staines, Middlesex has requested permission for members of the hospital staff to study the Museum's osteological collections. Permission is granted for the following week.

9 APRIL 1916 For months now, the newspapers have been reporting stories revealing the appalling conditions of the Wittenberg prisoner-of-war camp in Germany. Today the Government publishes *The Horrors of Wittenberg, Official Report to the British Government*. It reveals a camp grotesquely overcrowded, with systematic brutality, freezing conditions, lack of clothing, food or any washing facilities for either the prisoners or their clothes. Lice spread unchecked and resulted in a typhus epidemic which raged from December 1914 to early summer, 1915. Of the 700–800 British prisoners, nearly half caught the disease. Sixty of them died. As the German medical staff refused to deal with the epidemic, six doctors from the Royal Army Medical Corps were eventually allowed into the camp. Three of them died.

A few days after the report is published, Charles Fagan writes to the Foreign Office. He tells them that the Museum proposes to distribute the *Wittenberg Report* to correspondents in neutral

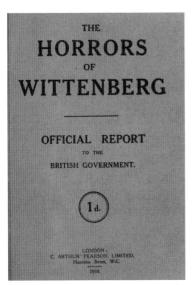

This report to the British Government on the Wittenberg prisoner-of-war camp in Germany detailed the horrific treatment and living conditions of the inmates, where typhus raged unchecked for months. Charles Fagan asked the Foreign Office for 500 copies to send to the Museum's contacts in neutral countries. In June he sent hundreds more.

countries. He requires about 500 copies. He also asks whether it is proposed to translate it into foreign languages as the Museum has 'correspondents (Professors and others) in all the neutral countries'. The Foreign Office supplies the Museum with 100 copies in Spanish and in French, and 25 copies in Dutch and in Portuguese.

10 APRIL 1916 RH Carr of the Ministry of Munitions writes to the Director, Sir Lazarus Fletcher. 'We are finding great difficulty now in obtaining a sufficient number of clerks to perform ordinary routine duties', he begins. Acknowledging that the Museum has probably already lent any available men to other Government departments, Carr writes that it would be of great help 'if by any chance 'they could still spare some men 'for work of this kind'. The Museum agrees to transfer temporarily one departmental clerk and three attendants to the Ministry immediately.

11 APRIL 1916 The Treasury sends a circular to all government departments asking for a return on the number of men who have joined the 'Naval or Military Forces' since the outbreak of the war. In the Museum, there were 84 men of military age in August 1914. By 1 April 1916, 56 have enlisted. Of the remaining 28, two have left the Museum, 11 have attested, 14 have been rejected on medical grounds, and one is a conscientious objector. With four men temporarily transferred to the Ministry of Munitions, the shortage of attendants now in the Museum is acute. Part of their role is correspondence and clerical work, and the situation is now so serious that the Trustees authorise an application to the Treasury to sanction the employment of two 'female shorthand-writer-typists' as 'substitutes'.

13 APRIL 1916 Four months after the Museum asked the Office of Works to confirm in writing that the Spirit Building must 'take its chance' in the event of an air-raid, it at last receives a reply. It confirms that it is 'questionable' as to whether any effective safeguards could be provided, and that in any case, the cost would be prohibitive. What it suggests instead is that any measures should be directed towards preventing fire. The Museum informs the Office of Works that special facilities for extinguishing fires are in place in the Spirit Building, and general fire arrangements are as efficient as practicable 'in existing circumstances'.

18 APRIL 1916 Charles Fagan writes to William Eagle Clarke, Keeper of Natural History at the Royal Scottish Museum in Edinburgh who has asked him what measures the Museum has taken to protect its exhibited collections against bombs. An air raid on Edinburgh a couple of weeks earlier, with bombs falling 'pretty near to us', prompted Eagle Clarke to write. Fagan outlines for him the measures they have taken, but tells him that they found the cost of doing anything 'really effective' was prohibitive. 'I am of the opinion', Fagan writes, 'that short of moving all the collections to some remote place in the country, very little can be done to protect them from destruction if an explosive or incendiary bomb fell on the Museum'.

The same day, Fagan replies to queries from RH Carr of the Ministry of Munitions, regarding the medical fitness and marital status of three of the attendants of military age who have been loaned for clerical work. He tells him: 'You may be interested to know that with no exception the whole of the staff of the Museum of military age have either joined the colours or attested, or been rejected for military service as medically unfit'.

19 APRIL 1916 John Hartley Durrant, the entomologist whose work on the Army Biscuit Enquiry and many other economic matters is highly regarded, has an idea which he conveys to Charles Fagan. 'As

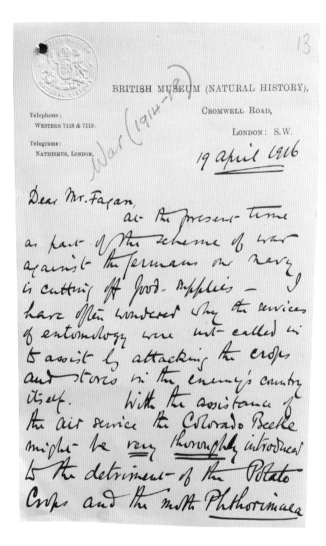

Beetle bombs. Entomology assistant John Hartley Durrant, who worked on the Army Biscuit Enquiry, suggested to Charles Fagan that German crops might be destroyed by dropping particular species of beetles and moths from aircraft.

Operculella would continue to
work on the stored tubers.

If this suggestion were accepted
there should be no difficulty in
obtaining supplies of them itself,
and others attacking other
crops could be added to the
list — but the question should
receive immediate attention so
that no species should be lost
through application too late in
the season.

Perhaps you might like to
bring this suggestion to the
notice of those whom it might
interest

Jn. V. [signature]
Jno. Hartley Durrant

C. S. Fagan Esq
British Museum (Nat. Hist.)
P.W.

part of the scheme of war against the Germans our navy is cutting off food supplies', he writes, 'I have often wondered why the services of entomology were not called in to assist by attacking the crops and stores in the enemy's country itself. With the assistance of the air service the Colorado Beetle might be <u>very thoroughly</u>' – and this is underlined twice –'introduced to the detriment of the Potato Crops'. Durrant also suggests introducing *Phthorimaea operculella*, the potato tuber moth, to continue the work on stored potatoes. He thinks that if his suggestion were accepted, there would be no difficulty obtaining supplies of the insects, and also others to attack a wider range of crops. The matter is urgent. 'The question should receive immediate attention so no species should be lost through application too late in the season', and he suggests that Fagan brings this to the notice 'of those whom it might interest'.

27 APRIL 1916 As last year, the officers stationed at Cromwell Garden Barracks are granted permission to use the grounds at the back of the Museum for cricket net practice. Charles Fagan adds that if any of the men make use of this permit, 'it is understood that they will be accompanied by Officers who will be responsible for seeing them off the Museum premises at the close of play'.

29 APRIL 1916 The Museum receives a supportive letter from an American, Charles M Clement from Idaho, expressing sympathy with Britain and her allies 'in this terrible war, in which they are upholding the cause of freedom and enlightenment against militarism and the ascendency of brute force'. Charles Fagan replies, expressing his grateful thanks. 'You may be sure,' he writes, 'that had the United States been involved in a war with Germany you would have had the sympathy and practical help of this country.' He sends Clement 'some official war literature' that gives 'plentiful evidence of the methods of German barbarism'.

Chapter 6
May–August 1916

In May, the clocks are changed under the
Summertime Act for the first time. In July, a huge
offensive is launched against the Germans at the
Somme. The battles rage for nearly four months, with
horrendous casualties on both sides. The enormity
of it hangs over the Natural History Museum, as it
does over the whole of Great Britain. The Museum is
active in spreading propaganda to its international
correspondents. It is also contributing to the fight
against grain-infesting insects, wood-boring marine
molluscs, rats in the trenches of the Western Front
and in the development of camouflage. The first
female clerical staff are employed by the Museum as
so many men are now at war, and assistance is offered
to the founder of the Women's Institute in Britain.
One more member of staff is killed on active
duty. Another is seriously wounded.

10 MAY 1916 Charles Fagan writes to the Foreign Office requesting further copies of *The Horrors of Wittenberg, Official Report to the British Government*. He asks for translations in Swedish, Danish, Romanian, German and Italian, 'say 50 in each language'.

12 MAY 1916 He sends six copies of the Wittenberg report to every senior member of staff, including senior assistants. He tells them that the Foreign Secretary, Sir Edward Grey, 'will be glad if it can be distributed among your correspondents in neutral countries... whom you know to be in sympathy with Great Britain and her Allies', and that they should be asked to distribute them among their countrymen. The Foreign Secretary, Charles Fagan writes, 'will be happy to supply as many copies as may be required in any of these languages for wide distribution'. In addition to the languages Fagan has asked for, he learns that it is also being translated into Greek.

15 MAY 1916 Pressure on men of military age to enlist is unrelenting. Today Charles Fagan writes to the Keepers, telling them that he needs to know which of their remaining staff are of military age. The information is required for a list 'which is to be compiled and posted up in the Museum for inspection'.

16 MAY 1916 Charles Fagan sends the Civil Service Commission, 'in accordance with Treasury instructions', a list of members of staff who can be temporarily transferred to other government departments 'as occasion may arise...in connection with the war'. He gives their qualifications and how they might be of use. Dr Francis Bather, Assistant Geology Keeper, speaks Swedish, German and French. Fagan suggests he could be useful for administrative or editorial work – possibly a post in the Censor's Office. The qualifications of others range from chemistry, which 'might be of value in the Ministry of Munitions', a taxidermist experienced in electrical battery work and mechanics, who also has a knowledge of mechanical plumbing, and a bacteriologist who could 'fill a post under medical or sanitary authority'. Dr Knud Andersen, a temporary technical assistant in Zoology, is a Dane with 'a considerable' knowledge of languages. These include fluent Danish, Norwegian, Swedish, German and French, a 'less thorough' knowledge of Russian (learned in Bulgaria), Dutch and Spanish. Fagan suggests he could be useful in the Foreign Office.

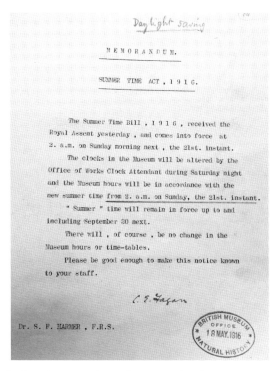

Charles Fagan's memo advising the Keepers that the new Summertime Act would come into force on Sunday, 21 May 1916 at 2am. He told them that the Office of Works Clock Attendant would alter the Museum clocks during Saturday night.

21 MAY 1916 The Summertime Act 1916 comes into force at 2am. The Government has introduced it in the interests of economy and efficiency as part of the war effort. It has also just been introduced in many European countries, including Germany. As this is the first time it has happened, Charles Fagan tells the senior staff that 'There will, of course, be no change in the Museum hours or time-tables'. He informs the messengers and police that arrangements have been made for the Office of Works' Clock Attendant to adjust the clocks between the hours of 4am and 11am on that date.

22 MAY 1916 Dr Sidney Harmer, Keeper of Zoology, reports that he has received a request for certain specimens of ticks (Ixodidae) and flies (Diptera) from Dr E Pawlowsky of the Laboratoire Zoologique, Académie Impériale de la Médecine Militaire, Petrograd, Russia. He requires them for teaching purposes. Dr Harmer writes that there is plenty of duplicate material, so it would be easy to send about 11 specimens of ticks and 8–10 of the Diptera. 'Any help which can be given at the present moment to an Academy of Military Medicine belonging to one of the Allied Powers', Dr Harmer reports, 'would be well bestowed'. It is no sacrifice to the Museum, he thinks to send the specimens as there is 'the probability – though not the certainty – of receiving a useful return hereafter'.

23 MAY 1916 Botany assistant Dr Herbert Fuller Wernham writes to the Keeper Dr Rendle. He tells him he is 'partly sorry, partly glad', that he has just relinquished his commission as a lieutenant in the 28th Battalion, London Regiment (Artists' Rifles) because of poor health. Wernham volunteered in August 1915 when he was 35, but his 'supersensitive digestive apparatus' as he calls it, caused him endless trouble, which was compounded by blood-poisoning and other ailments. Medical treatment and leave did not help and eventually 'a medical Board offered me the chance of relinquishing my Commission'. He refused at first, but then 'felt bound to accept...The fact is, I was too old – considering my sedentary lifestyle of study for twenty odd years – to enter upon a military career. But I am glad that I tried'. He tells Rendle he wants to resume work at the Museum 'as soon as possible', after he has taken some leave.

Dr Rendle scrawls a hasty note to Charles Fagan asking if this would be in order, adding, with a degree of cynicism in the light of the constant pressure on all men to enlist, 'I presume he will not be called up as a private!'

24 MAY 1916 Dr Gahan, Entomology Keeper, reports to the Trustees that John Hartley Durrant – whose invaluable work on the Army Biscuit Enquiry is well-known – has been asked to serve on a Committee appointed by the President and Council of the Royal Society to enquire into the bionomics and economics of grain-infesting pests. The investigation will cover the relative 'economic importance of the species and varieties of insects infesting grain, and to suggest measures for combating them, and to enquire into the extent of the actual loss from these pests'. The Royal Society, Dr Gahan writes, 'believe [Mr Durrant's] experience would prove of great value'. The Trustees approve.

27 MAY 1916 Dr Harmer, Zoology Keeper, reports to the Trustees at their meeting today that the Eastern Telegraph Company has recently submitted 'a portion of the core of a submarine cable injured by marine organisms'. The company has also sent specimens of the organisms for identification. Dr Harmer reports that 'injuries' to submarine cables caused by 'the depredations' of marine animals are not infrequent. The conducting wires are embedded in gutta percha (a type of latex widely used in electrical insulation), and if this is punctured, Harmer writes, 'the insulation

These small wood-borers, *Chelura terebrans* (left) and *Limnoria lignorum* (right) were identified by the Museum as being the cause of damage to submarine cables belonging to the Eastern Telegraph Company.

is destroyed and the cable is put out of action. Injuries of this kind done to deep-sea cables may involve the Companies in heavy expenditure'. He tells the Trustees that he has reported on several earlier incidents of damage to cables where punctures have been caused by deep-sea fish or the powerful jaws of particular species of worms.

In this instance, the damage has been caused by two small crustacea, 'well-known wood-borers: the amphipod, *Chelura terebrans* and the isopod, *Limnoria lignorum*, which are often destructive to submerged piles. He notes that in the earlier enquiries, he drew attention to the probability that these 'wood-borers' would also be found capable of injuring cables. There is nothing to show in this latest example how these crustacea obtained access to the core, which should be protected by 'outer investments of wire and jute'. On a previous occasion, Harmer had found that the gutta percha core had been exposed owing to some 'twisting action', by which 'the spirally wound wires forming one of the protective sheaths had been separated from one another'.

Dr Harmer reports to the Trustees that he has suggested that the gutta percha 'might be made distasteful to predaceous animals by some appropriate treatment'. How practical this might be, however, 'remains to be seen'. He suggests to the company that the construction of the protective layers might be improved. In the meantime, 'anything like a twist or a kink of the cable should be avoided as far as possible'.

The Eastern Telegraph Company subsequently informs Dr Harmer that since about 1880, the gutta percha has been protected 'against injury from boring animals in shallower water by means of brass tape laid spirally over the core'. This has proved most effective. The damaged core sent to the Museum had not been so protected as it was manufactured prior to 1880.

29 MAY 1916 Dr Harmer sends Charles Fagan details of a system for exterminating rabbits and other animals. He suggests it might be worthwhile informing the War Office 'in connection with the plague of Rats in our trenches at the front'. It is a method devised in Australia by William Rodier, who, so he told Dr Harmer in correspondence in 1910, 'had great success' in destroying rabbits which were devastating Australian agriculture. 'Briefly stated', Harmer tells Fagan, 'his system is to catch the animals alive, to kill the females and to liberate all the males. In this way the natural proportions of the sexes are interfered with, the males becoming the more numerous. They worry the females to such an extent when the disproportion is sufficiently great, that breeding is affected and fertility declines'. Harmer, who is Zoology Keeper, suggests Rodier's claims are worth examining, though when he first heard of the system, he thought, 'it was hardly our business to conduct an experiment in the extermination of animals'. However in 1911 he tried to interest the Zoological Society and the Board of Agriculture, but 'my efforts had no practical results, so far as I know'.

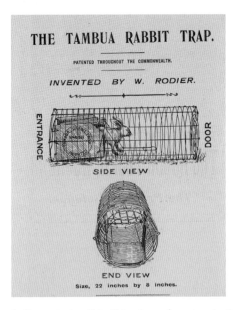

THE TAMBUA RABBIT TRAP.

PATENTED THROUGHOUT THE COMMONWEALTH.

INVENTED BY W. RODIER.

ENTRANCE

DOOR

SIDE VIEW

END VIEW

Size, 22 inches by 8 inches.

William Rodier sent a booklet of his scheme for exterminating rabbits, to Zoology Keeper Dr Harmer, who thought it could be applied to 'the plague of Rats in our trenches at the front'.

Fagan writes immediately to the Army Council at the War Office, briefly outlining the system. 'The Museum does not, of course,' he concludes, 'in any way guarantee the success of the method, but it seems to have possibilities of success'. Fagan also writes to the Australian High Commission, asking if they have any information as to the success of Rodier's system.

31 MAY 1916 Just two weeks after Charles Fagan suggests to the Civil Service Commission that Dr Bather's qualifications might be of use to another Government Department, the Military Intelligence Division of the War Office requests the temporary loan of his services. Much of his work will be assisting with propaganda for Sweden.

JUNE 1916 A trench at Maricourt on the Somme, on the eve of the great battle. A soldier named AA Tullett captures a butterfly,

Iphiclides podalirius, a swallowtail – scarce in England though common in France. Somehow it has fluttered into a trench, Tullett has secured it and, almost miraculously, brought it remarkably undamaged, back to England. There it is acquired by a passionate collector, James Joicey. His collection is acquired by the Museum in 1934 and Tullett's butterfly from the Somme has been preserved in the Entomology department ever since.

3 JUNE 1916 The demand for the Wittenberg report is such that Charles Fagan has to ask the Foreign Office for 50 more copies each in Swedish, Danish, Dutch and Portuguese. To send out any printed publications, the Museum needs a permit, issued by the Censor of Printed Matter at the General Post Office. When it sends the packages for posting, the Museum has to compile a list of everything it is sending, detailing country of destination, addressee, address and title of the publication and this, together with the package, is then sent to the Censor.

TAKEN IN FRONT LINE
TRENCH,
MARICOURT, SOMME
VALLEY. FRANCE.
A.A. TULLETT,
JUNE. 1916.

This scarce swallowtail butterfly, *Iphiclides podalirius*, was captured in June 1916 in a trench at Maricourt on the Somme by a soldier named AA Tullett. In 1934 it was part of a collection acquired by the Museum, where it has been preserved ever since.

5 JUNE 1916 Lord Kitchener, Secretary of State for War and the driving force behind the new army which saw nearly two and a half million men voluntarily enlist between August 1914 and December 1915, is killed. He and his staff die while on their way to Russia. The headlines in *The Globe* the following day are typical of all: 'Lord Kitchener drowned. Our greatest soldier goes down in British cruiser. Sunk off the Orkneys. HMS Hampshire torpedoed or mined: all on board feared lost.' There are just 12 survivors, washed ashore on a raft. Flags on the War Office and Admiralty are flown at half-mast. 'Britain and her allies', *The Globe* reports, 'are plunged into mourning'.

Charles Fagan tells the keepers that the list of names they provided in May of staff who are of military age is to be posted up in 'some conspicuous part' of the Museum for inspection 'by or on behalf of the Naval or Military authorities'.

9 JUNE 1916 Charles Fagan receives a reply from the Australian High Commission about the Rodier system for exterminating rabbits and it is not good news. In 1905 an official investigation on Rodier's land in New South Wales concluded his system was 'mere theory, no good in practice', and that much better results would have been obtained if all the rabbits trapped had then been killed. An official experiment carried out the following year appeared 'to entirely disprove Mr Rodier's theory'. Both were reported in the *Agricultural Gazette of New South Wales* in 1905 and 1906.

20 JUNE 1916 Dr Harmer reports on a letter received from Captain William Garforth, Royal Engineers, who is at the French front. It is about the possibilities of applying the principles of protective coloration of animals to practical purposes in warfare – in other words, camouflage. Garforth's concern is how to conceal gun-positions from aircraft observation, and he writes that, 'The main difficulty lies in getting rid of the shadows caused by the mound

The Museum offered advice to the military on methods of concealment – camouflage – based on the protective coloration of animals. Netting to cover weapons and men was found to be highly effective. Here hessian strips are being attached to netting at a British camouflage factory.

of earth which has to be thrown up, round and over the gun pits – they are really little "houses", strongly built, covered with earth and other materials'. What he is looking for are some rules to help concealment. 'What are less conspicuous at a distance,' he asks, 'a series of coloured (?black and white) <u>squares</u>, or a series of parallel lines, or splodges of paint? Excuse me troubling you', he concludes, 'and excuse this hurried scrawl in pencil'.

In suggesting possible solutions, Dr Harmer writes that 'it was natural to think of the views' of the American painter and amateur naturalist, Abbott Handerson Thayer, expressed in his son Gerald Thayer's book, *Concealing Coloration in the Animal Kingdom*. Thayer's theory of what he calls countershading is exhibited by means of model birds in the Central Hall. His principle is that with many animals, the upper surface of their bodies are of a dark shade, while the under surface is almost invariably white, or nearly so. William Pycraft described this at the beginning of the war in an article in *The Illustrated London News*. As long as the animal is at rest, the light undersurface is in shadow and the upper is illuminated, giving an obliterating effect so 'the body merges into the background and is invisible against it'. Dr Harmer points out that the chief difficulty in applying Mr Thayer's principle to the gun emplacements 'is probably that the shadows change with each advance of the sun', and that 'this difficulty might prove so great as to deprive the artificial shading of most of its value'.

He suggests to Garforth in a detailed report that 'the use of a broken surface – which you indicate towards the end of your letter – may perhaps help you here'. While he would be only too pleased to assist him, 'theory and practice are not always in accord, and you may very well get more information from your own observations than you could from any amount of advice given by persons who have no practical experience of your own particular problem'. Dr Harmer informs the Trustees that he has suggested to Captain Garforth that it might be useful if he experimented 'to test the value

Painting of a male ruffed grouse in a forest, from Thayer's book on concealing coloration. 'The bird is in plain sight, but invisible – such is the wonderful power of full obliterative coloration', Thayer wrote.

of the ideas in practice'. He adds that it might perhaps be worthwhile alerting the military authorities to the possibilities of protective coloration.

Charles Fagan sends a memorandum to Sir Frederic Kenyon, Director and Principal Librarian of the British Museum on behalf of the Museum's Director, Sir Lazarus Fletcher, who is technically subordinate to Kenyon. He states that 'Treasury sanction is requested' for the temporary employment of two female shorthand-writer typists. They are required for clerical duties, he writes, 'as substitutes for Attendants who have been enrolled for military service during the present emergency'. There is considerable correspondence between the Museum and other government departments, much of it being 'directly connected with questions of an economic or sanitary nature arising out of the war', and there is now a backlog. It has meant 'the costly expedient of some of the higher officers of the Museum having to devote a considerable amount of their time to clerical work of a more or less routine nature'. Payment for the typists is to be made from savings for the current financial year.

22 JUNE 1916 Dr Charles Gahan, Keeper of Entomology, reports to the Trustees that his department has recently received visits from Fleet Surgeon Munday of the Medical Department of the Admiralty, and from Lieutenant Colonel HJ Barnes of the Royal Army Medical Corps, an Inspector of Detention Camps. Fleet Surgeon Munday's problem is with rice. Polished rice, he explains to Dr Gahan, 'is believed to be responsible in many cases for the disease known as beri-beri', and he had proposed to 'do away with it altogether' in 'ships of His Majesty's Fleet' and replace it with unpolished rice. However, as it has also been suggested that unpolished rice is 'much more subject' to attack by the rice-weevil, 'an objection had been raised to his proposal'.

This is a problem on which Dr Gahan is unable to give any information based upon actual experience, as he reports to the Trustees, nor can he find any reference to it in any entomological publication. However, from what is known of the history of the weevil 'and of its mode of attack', he sees no reason to think that polished rice would be any less liable to attack than the unpolished. He does consider that this is something that should be put 'to an experimental test'. He suggests to Fleet Surgeon Munday that as the weevil can be destroyed by heating rice for a short time at a temperature 'not exceeding' 140 degrees Fahrenheit, 'it ought not to be difficult to make sure that the supply of rice would be entirely free of attack by the weevil'. Fleet Surgeon Munday tells Dr Gahan that he believes that this can 'easily be acted upon'.

Lt Col Barnes's problem is with drinking water at Eastcote Camp in Northamptonshire, where Germans are detained. In two of the compounds, many of the detainees are suffering from stomach complaints which they say is caused by the drinking water. Lt Col Barnes has brought in some larvae found in the water. Dr Gahan reports that the larvae are 'blood worms', as the reddish-brown larvae of the genus of flies *Chironomus* are known. Dr Gahan tells Lt Col Barnes that these are not known to cause stomach complaints, 'nor was there any reason' to suppose that they might. However, as Dr Gahan reports, their presence in the water is an indication that there is a certain amount of vegetable organic matter present – and that serves as food for the larvae. The larvae are liable to be present in any open tank or cistern where there is a slight sediment of organic matter at the bottom, and they are not the cause of the problem. The water has been analysed chemically and bacteriologically, Lt Col Barnes tells Dr Gahan, and 'found all right'. He says they are 'pretty certain' that the water has nothing to do with the stomach complaints of the detainees, as only one or two compounds are affected and the water supply is common to the whole camp.

24 JUNE 1916 The Danish zoologist Dr Knud Andersen – a temporary member of staff – whom Charles Fagan recommended to the Civil Service Commission because of his language skills, has been temporarily lent to the Military Intelligence Division of the War Office for part-time duty. He is to report to Lieutenant Colonel Wake of Section M.I.7(b), at Winchester House, St James's Square. Charles Fagan has arranged with Col Wake for Dr Andersen to attend four days a week at Winchester House, and two days at the Museum. As Dr Andersen is paid by the hour, he is to continue to submit his monthly bill to the Museum. His duties are reading the foreign press and compiling a daily review.

The Director reports to the Trustees that a further six men have enlisted. Two members of staff have been exempted from military service because of the importance of their work to the Museum. Frank Barlow, mason in the Geology department, is exempt on grounds that his technical services are 'indispensable' and needed for 'the proper preservation of fossil specimens'. John Ramsbottom, an assistant in the Botany Department and expert on fungi, is exempt because of his work 'of a sanitary character' which is of use to the War departments. And there is some good news for the depleted staff. The Botany department has regained Dr Herbert Fuller Wernham who relinquished his commission on the grounds of ill-health and has now returned to the Museum.

26 JUNE 1916 Charles Fagan writes to the Military Representative, Local Military Tribunal, Stanmore, Middlesex. He informs him that Entomologist Frederick Edwards, who is eligible for military service, has applied for exemption on the grounds of conscientious objection. However, Fagan writes, 'the Museum authorities have no intention of asking for an exemption from military service for Mr Edwards on the grounds of being indispensable here'. Edwards' application is refused and he appeals to the Middlesex Appeal Court, Westminster.

27 JUNE 1916 The Treasury sanctions the employment of the two temporary 'female shorthand-writer-typists' to take on the clerical work of attendants absent on military service.

1 JULY 1916 This is the first day of the battle of the Somme. It will not end until November. Its aim is a clear victory over the Germans – or at least to wear them down. The British attack along a 20-mile front. Casualties on this first day are 57,000 British and allied troops killed or wounded. In one battalion alone, there are more than 500 casualties out of a complement of 800 men. They are fighting in the mud of farmland, on soil enriched with manure and so contaminated with bacteria. There is danger of fatal infection to every soldier wounded along the Western Front in every battle of the war.

8 JULY 1916 Educating the public on health and sanitary matters and the dangers of infection is crucial at home. Miss Winifred Thomson, who regularly brings parties of wounded soldiers to the Museum from King George's Military Hospital near Waterloo, has suggested to Charles Fagan that the Local Government Board should be involved in disseminating the Museum's pamphlets on the dangers of insects. She suggests the LGB might be induced to persuade every Post Office to put up a notice informing people about them. Fagan himself writes to the Secretary of the General Post Office, sending notices of the different pamphlets available. He tells him that several societies and 'prominent people' have suggested 'the desirability of making [the pamphlets] known as widely as possible'.

Fagan also writes to Mrs Alfred Watt of the Agricultural Organisation Society about the pamphlets. She is giving a series of lectures on 'the prevention of epidemics, the extermination of flies etc'. Fagan suggests to her that the Museum's pamphlets might be of assistance and sends her some copies. 'I shall be glad to do anything

Mrs Alfred Watt (1868–1948) of the Agricultural Organisation Society, gave lectures on health and the danger of flies. Charles Fagan sent her copies of the Museum's leaflets saying 'I shall be glad to do anything in my power to help you in your work'. Mrs Watt is better known today as Madge Watt, the founder of the Women's Institute – the WI – in Britain.

in my power to help you in your work', he tells her, 'and trust the literature sent will be useful to you'.

Mrs Watt, a Canadian, is perhaps better known as Madge Watt, the founder of the Women's Institute in Britain. She brought the idea with her from Canada, where the WI was founded in farming communities in 1897. She arrived in England in 1913 after the death of her husband, and, under the auspices of the Agricultural Organisation Society, formed the first WI here in 1915. Its aim is to help increase the supply of home-grown food by encouraging countrywomen to grow and preserve it. Over the years, Mrs Watt founded more than 300 branches.

10 JULY 1916 The Treasury sends a letter to all government departments stating that the question of women's employment after the war is being considered by the Reconstruction Committee, and that the Royal Commission on the Civil Service has recommended that the Treasury should institute an inquiry into which posts in each government department 'might with advantage to the public service' be filled by qualified women.

Each department is asked to send details of numbers of women employed and their duties, together with suggestions as to further grades they might occupy.

In the Natural History Museum, there is just one woman on the Museum's establishment in 1916 – the Ladies' Attendant. Not counting the two new shorthand typists, the Museum employs another eight women, 'some constantly, some at intervals, as artists and preparators. 'Women', the Director informs the Trustees, 'have been employed by the Museum from time to time on a definite piece of work on groups of which they were known to have made a special study...It may be said', he continues, 'that sex has not been a bar to the temporary employment of women on scientific work where opportunity has arisen of making use of their special knowledge on a particular group'. The Trustees postpone consideration on the question of the appointment of women until after the war.

14 JULY 1916 Dr Harmer reports that he has received through the Colonial Office a report from the Falkland Islands on the 'South Shetland Whaling Season'. It complements a report he has earlier received on whaling near South Georgia which showed so great an increase in the number of blue whales caught as to 'give cause for serious anxiety'. The total number of blue and fin whales caught in the South Shetland area of the South Atlantic in 1915–1916 is 4,431, which produces 212,336 barrels of oil. Just 219 humpback whales have been caught, indicating there are now comparatively few of these left in this whaling area. Dr Harmer lays stress on the 'grave danger' which threatens the whale through 'wholesale and indiscriminate slaughter', and he stresses the importance 'of losing no opportunity' to suggest the need for caution. A letter is to be written to the Colonial Office outlining Dr Harmer's report. His concerns are those of preservation and sustainability – and of course the study of these magnificent animals. The letter is to include 'strong representation, and especially refer to the possibility of total extinction of Humpback and desirability of preventing killing for some years'. Dr Harmer warns that 'the responsibility of the Falkland Islands is great, as by their authority over the Whaling in South Georgia and South Shetlands they control by far the larger part of the whaling operations of the far south'.

Whales however, are vital to the war effort. Among many uses, their oil is used in the production of glycerin, used to make the high explosive nitroglycerin, vital to British artillery shells and ammunition. It is also used to make lubricants in rifles and many military instruments and machines, and, as William Pycraft has highlighted, to protect soldiers' feet from frostbite and trench foot.

19 JULY 1916 So many members of the Entomology staff are now absent on military service, that, as Dr Gahan reports to the Trustees, it is difficult for those remaining to give the necessary attention to students and visitors. Since there are one or two still liable to be called upon for service in other government departments, Dr Gahan writes that it is possible that by September, the department will be left without a single attendant. The situation is so critical that Dr Gahan thinks the question of closing the Insect Room to students may arise. He asks that the Director might be given authority to act in the matter, or in any other way the Trustees may consider most suitable.

Dr Gahan is not alone. Dr Harmer too reports to the Trustees that the depleted condition of Zoology staff means it is difficult to provide attendance for visitors to the Bird Room. The egg collection cannot be studied unless there is proper supervision, and this, Dr Harmer writes, 'is hardly possible, except at the expense of more important parts of the work of the Bird Room'. He thinks it would be desirable to close the egg collection to visitors 'for the present' and asks the Trustees for their approval.

20 JULY 1916 Despite the shortage of staff, Dr Gahan's department has produced three new economic pamphlets. Public health is a matter of great concern. Newspaper articles warn of the dangers of vermin and insects. The magazine *Dawn of the Day* advocates 'the waging of war against flies' as a patriotic duty. 'Our soldiers and sailors are fighting against the Germans, let those who stay at home fight against insects', it urges.

Entomology assistant Bruce Cummings has completed *The Bedbug and its Relation to Disease*. Frederick Wallace Edwards, the conscientious objector, has prepared *Mosquitoes and their Relation to Disease*. James Waterston of the Imperial Bureau of Entomology based in the Entomology department has finished *Fleas as a Menace to Man and Animals*. He notes that about 500 kinds of fleas have been described, of which 46 species are found in Britain. Eleven species, 'up to the present', he writes, are known to be 'capable of transmitting plague'. Five of these are common British species. 'Even in the absence of the actual disease', he warns, 'it is well to remember that the menace of plague will remain so long as rat and flea control is neglected'. Bubonic plague, 'may quickly become a potential source of Pneumonic plague, which, being contagious and air borne, is all the more to be feared in crowded centres'. The chief source of fleas in houses, he says, is 'want of cleanliness' and also proximity to animals. He details the necessary remedies.

In Zoology, Arthur Stanley Hirst has prepared *Species of Arachnida and Myriopoda (scorpions, spiders, mites, ticks and centipedes) Injurious to Man*. Dr Harmer reports to the Trustees that in many parts of the world, the Arachnida 'are no less formidable enemies of man and domestic animals than are the insects, by reason of their agency in carrying disease-producing Protozoa'. In fact, Harmer writes, 'Tick-carried diseases of Cattle and other domestic animals are responsible for losses which can only be measured in millions of pounds, while other diseases similarly carried affect Man'. Hirst's guide book deals with these practical questions.

22 JULY 1916 The Trustees consider Dr Gahan's proposal regarding the possible closure of the Entomology department to students and do not approve it. The Director is to apply for the return of 'necessary attendants' who have been loaned to other Government departments. 'Serious students' engaged on research work are still to be admitted.

29 JULY 1916 John Gabriel is an attendant in the Entomology department at the Natural History Museum, joining in 1905 when he was 16. On the outbreak of war in 1914 he enlists in the 15th Battalion, London Regiment (Prince of Wales' Own Civil Service Rifles), and is sent to France. For nearly two years, Private Gabriel survives uninjured. In July his battalion is sent to front-line trenches at Neuville-St Vaast in northern France. Today he is on guard duty. He is struck by an aerial torpedo and killed instantly. He is 27 years old. He is buried in the British Cemetery at Maroeuil, Pas

Private John Gabriel, Entomology attendant, is killed at Neuville-St Vaast, France on 29 July 1916.

de Calais. In the official Museum papers regarding his death it is noted: 'Gabriel discharged his duties with diligence and fidelity to the satisfaction of the Trustees'.

31 JULY 1916 Earlier this month, 18-year-old George Pagnoni, a boy attendant in the Geology department and a private in the 13th (Princess Louise's Kensington, County of London) Battalion, was severely wounded at Albert in France. Today Charles Fagan writes to his aunt who brought him up. 'I was very sorry to hear that your nephew has been wounded,' he writes, '...and shall be much obliged if you will let me know how he is getting on'.

14 AUGUST 1916 Private Kenneth Gloyne Blair, an assistant in Entomology, was declared 'medically unfit for service abroad' by the military authorities in November 1915 and has been working as a storekeeper for the Royal Engineers since then. He is currently stationed at Ripon in Yorkshire. The Entomology Keeper, Dr Gahan would dearly like to have him back. Today Charles Fagan writes to the War Office, making the case that as he is unfit, and as his department 'is very much depleted owing to the absence on military service of so many of its members...it is hoped that he may be released' to resume his civil duties in the Museum. His work, Fagan writes, is research 'of an economic character of national importance'.

22 AUGUST 1916 Charles Fagan writes to the Secretary of the War Office on the subject of countershading, enclosing a copy of Dr Harmer's detailed report. Since Dr Harmer reported on this in June, Fagan tells the War Office that the Trustees have heard that the well-known portrait painter, Solomon Joseph Solomon, has been appointed by the Army Council as chairman of a committee to advance the uses of camouflage, including the disguising of gun stations. Solomon came to the notice of the War Office when he wrote to *The Times* on 27 January 1915 describing the applications of 'the protection afforded animate creatures by Nature's gift of colour assimilation to their environment'. In his letter Solomon describes how it can be applied to uniforms, to heavy artillery and to warships. 'Artists, I feel certain,' he writes, 'would be only too pleased to place their knowledge and experience at the disposal of the authorities. They discuss these matters among themselves, but so far there is no useful connecting link between the makers of the arts of peace and the designers of the munitions of war'.

The War Office responds quickly to the letter and Solomon, with the rank of lieutenant colonel in the Royal Engineers, is sent to Flanders, first to work with the French military 'camoufleurs' unit, and then to set up a British camouflage section. The section is known as Special Works Park, Wimereux. He experiments with strips of muslin and bamboo, paints canvas in shades of brown, green and grey, and applies leaves and moss to it. The pattern is denser in the centre but more transparent towards the edges. The elimination of shadow, Solomon believes, is 'the essence of invisibility'.

The Museum too is 'only too pleased' to help, and Charles Fagan now invites the military authorities 'in the first instance' to inspect the models illustrating the principles of protective coloration of animals in the Museum's Central Hall.

24 AUGUST 1916 Ten days after Charles Fagan's letter about him to the War Office, Kenneth Blair returns to work in Entomology. He has been placed in the Territorial Force Reserve, but he is free to resume his civil duties. He remains liable however, to be called up for military service should the need arise. Also returning to work in the Museum is the labourer, James Eden, who served as a rifleman in 12th London Regiment (Rangers) from September 1914. He has now been discharged from the Army 'as no longer physically fit for war service'. He was wounded fighting in France and has lost a finger.

26 AUGUST 1916 Dr Harmer sends a memo to Sir Lazarus Fletcher, the Director. 'I have heard it suggested', he writes, 'that some of the bombs at present used by German aircraft are timed to explode after they have penetrated two or three floors, instead of immediately on striking the building'. If that is the case, he wonders whether specimens in the upper galleries really need to be moved, and suggests that the Fire Brigade might be consulted.

Chapter 7
September–December 1916

In the last months of 1916, the dreadful
battles of the Somme and Verdun finally
end, leaving more than one million dead or
injured – including men from the Museum. One
is killed in action, one dies from war wounds
and a third is reported missing. At sea, German
submarines are terrorising shipping lanes with a
devastating loss both of life and urgently needed
supplies. The situation is so critical that some of
the best scientific minds in the land are engaged on
anti-submarine warfare. In the Museum scientists
deal with enquiries including the nature of
luminous wood found in suspicious circumstances,
mites attacking war stores of oats, and worm-
eaten police truncheons. Senior military officers
discuss Dr Harmer's report on the application of
the protective coloration of animals to practical
purposes in warfare. The Museum becomes
even more active in disseminating propaganda
and young lady guides are to be trained
to take parties of wounded soldiers
round the galleries.

SEPTEMBER 1916 The Office of Works sends a letter to the Director of the Museum, Sir Lazarus Fletcher, marked <u>VERY IMPORTANT</u>. It is to bring to his 'attention the very pressing need which exists for economy in the consumption of coal'. Maintaining coal exports is of the highest importance, and 'in view of the restricted supply of labour available for mining', this can only be done by reducing consumption. It is of grave national importance. Fires should be allowed to die down naturally overnight. In rooms where there are both radiators and open fires, 'the use of the open fire should be abandoned'. The Director tells the Keepers to bring this to the attention of all their staff.

8 SEPTEMBER 1916 On the instructions of the Trustees, Charles Fagan writes to the 'Propaganda Department, Press Bureau, Royal United Services Institute': 'With a view to the distribution of propaganda in neutral countries, I am directed to suggest that this Museum could render useful aid in the circulation of printed matter.' He writes of the work the Museum has already done with the Foreign Office in sending out various publications 'on the German methods of conducting warfare'. As 'German Professors' are active in sending out propaganda to 'scientific quarters in neutral countries', he writes, the Museum would be glad to do the same, 'to place matter forcibly presenting the British and Allied cause'. Without waiting for a reply, Fagan writes to the Foreign Office requesting a further 150 copies of the French *Yellow Book* which details the behaviour of the German forces in occupied districts in France.

11 SEPTEMBER 1916 Frederick Wallace Edwards, the 27 year-old Entomology assistant and conscientious objector is no longer to receive pay from the Museum, as of today. The Middlesex Appeal Tribunal has granted him exemption from military service provided he obtains work of national importance, which they must approve.

Entomology assistant and conscientious objector Frederick Wallace Edwards (1888–1940) spent the war working as an agricultural labourer. A brilliant entomologist, he was promoted to deputy keeper of Entomology in 1937 and was elected a fellow of the Royal Society in 1939.

He has had to answer a long questionnaire detailing his objections to military service. 'I believe that the elimination of war is an urgent necessity', he writes, 'and that one of the best ways, if not the only way, in which this can be brought about, is by the refusal of the people to take part in it'. It is his 'firm belief' that in 'obeying at all costs the dictates of my conscience I am serving not only my God but also my country in the highest possible way'. His precise and passionate answers extend over five closely written pages.

He is given 21 days by the Tribunal to find acceptable employment. He is referred to the Committee on Work of National Importance, which helps conscientious objectors with this. They suggest he applies to the School of Tropical Medicine in London. There he is quickly offered 'special research work' on houseflies in relation to disease – on which he is an expert – but the Tribunal rejects this as 'not work of national importance which they are prepared to approve'. This is in spite of Lt Col Alfred William Alcock, renowned medical entomologist, fellow of the Royal Society and lecturer on General Medical Zoology at the School, describing the work as of 'National, I might say of Imperial importance which Mr Edwards is particularly well qualified to perform'. Edwards instead is offered work as a labourer on a fruit farm at Letchworth in Hertfordshire. This the Tribunal approves as acceptable work of national importance. For the rest of the war, Edwards works as an agricultural labourer on farms round Hertfordshire, even though, according to one of his employers, 'he was willing but not strong'. Far from abandoning his passion for insects, he collects all the time, sending them to the Museum, where many are still. He returns to the Museum after the war, becoming Deputy Keeper of Entomology in 1937 and a fellow of the Royal Society in 1939. In 1940, at the age of 52, Edwards, described by colleagues as 'an inspiration' and a 'brilliant entomologist', is diagnosed with cancer and is dead within a fortnight.

12 SEPTEMBER 1916 Colonel Wilfred S Swabey, Deputy Director Supplies and Transport, Third Army, France, writes to the Museum. He would like information regarding the habits of what he calls 'AGRUS FARINAE which I am told is the name of certain microscopic insects found in large quantities in the oat stores out here'. There is no damage at present, 'as far as can be ascertained', but he wishes to know what damage may in time occur and whether the horses may be affected in any way. It has been suggested to him that a 'five percent Formaline spray' might be used to destroy the insects, but he thinks this could only be partially effective as there are a large number of sacks stacked 40 feet high. The Keeper of Zoology, Dr Harmer, refers the matter to Arthur Stanley Hirst, his department's expert on mites and ticks.

13 SEPTEMBER 1916 The Museum receives a 'confidential' enquiry from the new Munitions Inventions Department of the Ministry of Munitions. The department has recently been established by the Ministry to assess and possibly develop some of the thousands of war-related proposed inventions submitted by servicemen and the public.

There are at least half a dozen distinct government organisations involved with invention and research. The enquiry relates to some wood which appears to possess luminous qualities. It was found by the roadside in East Anglia, 'under suspicious circumstances'.

A specimen of it is sent to the Botany department for Dr Rendle 'or some gentleman in his Department', to determine whether it has been treated in some way to make it luminous. It is examined by Dr Rendle, who recognises it as 'a perfectly normal example' of infection by a fungus which permeates the tissues and renders the specimen luminous in the dark. The fungus loses its luminosity if dried up, he reports, 'but might acquire it again on damping. The luminosity might be visible for a distance of twenty yards'. Because of the urgency of the matter, the Munitions Inventions Department is informed immediately by telephone.

16 SEPTEMBER 1916 *The Times* reports a 'Great British advance' on the Somme on a six-mile front, with 'New heavy armoured cars used for the first time'. A number of Museum men are fighting there. The development of these vehicles has been top secret, their existence protected by a codename meant to imply new water-carriers. 'The Mysterious "Tanks", our latest military weapon', is The Times headline. A number of code-names were considered, including 'reservoir' and 'cistern', before 'tank' was favoured. The soldiers who handled them, *The Times* reports, 'named them humorously "Willies"'.

17 SEPTEMBER 1916 Private George Pagnoni of the 13th (Princess Louise's Kensington, County of London) Battalion, dies of war wounds at the Fulham Military Hospital in London. He was severely injured in July, fighting near Albert in France. He joined the Geology department as a boy attendant aged 15 in 1913. A member of the Civil Service Cadet Corps, he enlisted in 1915, a

Private George Pagnoni, boy attendant in the Geology department, was severely wounded in fighting near Albert, northern France. He died in hospital in London, 17 September 1916. He was 18 years old.

month before his 17th birthday, and was sent to France. He was, the Museum records, 'keen and efficient in his work, and was liked by his fellows'. He is buried in Kensal Green Cemetery in London. He died four months after his 18th birthday.

19 SEPTEMBER 1916 Stanley Thomas Wells, a private in the Civil Service Rifles, and an attendant in Zoology, is reported missing in action in a battle on the Somme.

24 SEPTEMBER 1916 Zoology assistant Arthur Hirst reports on Colonel Swabey's enquiry of 12 September regarding mites possibly attacking stored oats in France. He also includes a note on the best method 'of killing the pests'. Although no specimens were sent, Zoology Keeper Dr Harmer reports to the Trustees that the mites are *Aleurobius farinae* de Geer, a species well known to damage stored cereals. They are of the same family as the similarly microscopic cheese mite, which, Dr Harmer writes, 'are consumed in large quantities (in Stilton cheese etc) without, so far as is known, producing any injurious effects'. There appears no reason to suppose, he continues, that the mite species 'attacking Oats would be more injurious to horses than those infesting Cheese are to man'. Arthur Hirst, Dr Harmer reports, 'insists on the necessity of keeping the stores scrupulously clean' and emphasises the importance of excluding flies by which the nymphs of these mites are carried from one place to another.

Dr Harmer also consults the Entomology assistant, John Hartley Durrant, who received considerable acclaim through his work on the Army Biscuit Enquiry. He too emphasises the importance of cleanliness, while recognising this is perhaps difficult with an Expeditionary Force. He recommends emptying the store and cleaning it thoroughly with boiling water and spraying it with hot water. Great care should be taken to keep the store as clean as possible and to use any infested grain quickly. He recommends that it should be noted whether the sacks are clean when they arrive, and, if the oats have been threshed, they should be well washed in the way that grain is in wheat-mills. If the fault is in the storage facility itself, he recommends finding a place 'more capable of being kept clean', if possible.

Hirst has suggested fumigation with hydrocyanic acid gas, if necessary, and supplies details of how it should be used, with careful instructions on how to avoid inhalation of the deadly fumes. Durrant reinforces this. He points out that the treatment will not injure the grain if time is allowed for it to be thoroughly ventilated after treatment. However, the gas is so poisonous that treatment must 'in no case commence' while any person is in the room to be disinfected, and 'the most complete ventilation' is necessary afterwards before anyone is allowed back in. All are agreed that the suggestion of formalin treatment to eliminate the mites 'would probably be quite effective'.

1 OCTOBER 1916 Between 9pm and midnight, ten Zeppelin airships cross the east coast, heading towards London. *The Globe*

The remains of the Zeppelin shot down near Potter's Bar, just north of London, on 1 October 1916. The Air Department of the Admiralty brought one of its propellers to the Museum for the material used in its construction to be identified.

describes how one approaches London from the north, 'but is driven off by gunfire and pursued by aeroplanes'. It returns, dropping 39 bombs – with little damage – over an area of about a mile, and is caught in 'the full glare of a very insistent searchlight'. It is again attacked, a 'white arc of flame' enveloping it. The framework is illuminated in the glare, according to the reporter, 'like the giant ribs of a mastodon ripped bare by a tusk of an invisible yet mighty enemy'. This time it crashes in flames, near Potter's Bar in Hertfordshire, just north of London. All crew are killed. Five weeks later, Dr Rendle, Keeper of Botany, is visited by representatives of the Air Department of the Admiralty. They bring with them one of the Zeppelin's propellers for Dr Rendle to identify the 'materials' used in its construction. He gives them an immediate, verbal opinion, but does not reveal what he told them.

2 OCTOBER 1916 Dr Harmer informs the Trustees of the progress of his report on the application of protective coloration of animals to practical purposes in warfare. It was sent to the War Office in August, where it aroused sufficient interest for the War Office to send it to the Admiralty, which in turn sent it to its Board of Invention and Research, established in 1915. The BIR informs the Museum that the report 'will be studied with much interest', and suggests that a copy is also sent to the Comptroller of Munitions Inventions, 'whose Department will deal with the possible military application of the proposals'. In fact the BIR forwards its copy to Munitions Inventions, who immediately ask Charles Fagan for 'a conference on this matter with Dr Harmer, preferably at the Museum'.

The Supervising Examiner for the Comptroller of Munitions Inventions, Captain WHD Clark, informs Fagan that two officials will attend: Colonel Kent of the War Office and Mr Taylor, an Examiner for the Comptroller of Munitions. In the Central Hall Harmer shows them the Thayer models illustrating countershading, and he suggests further reading matter on protective coloration – including a paper published just a few weeks previously. Today Harmer reports to the Trustees that the War Office 'appears to have taken much more interest in the subject of Protective Coloration than might have been expected; and many practical devices are already in use in the field'. He reports that Col Kent and Mr Taylor were aware of Mr Thayer's work, and that when Thayer [an American] was in London recently, he visited a Government department connected with war work.

6 OCTOBER 1916 A letter arrives from Colonel Swabey, thanking the Museum for Dr Harmer's report on mites infesting oats. However, he has decided to issue the infested oats for consumption and replace with fresh ones, ensuring there is no 'infestation from the old to the new oats'. As for the suggestion that the store or sacks might possibly be dirty, 'As a matter of fact', Swabey writes briskly, 'the building is part of a jute factory and its cleanliness (brick floor etc. very carefully laid) cannot be well improved on; moreover all the sacks on which the mites were appearing are clean and new'.

7 OCTOBER 1916 The Director, Sir Lazarus Fletcher, receives a letter from Ernest Arthur Gowers, Chief Executive officer of the Propaganda Department of the Foreign Office. The letter Charles Fagan sent to the Propaganda Department at the Royal United Services Institute on 8 September offering the Museum's assistance in distributing propaganda to neutral countries has been forwarded to Gowers. His department is so secret it is said that most MPs do not know of its existence. It shares a building, Wellington House, with the National Insurance Commission. It is under the Commission's name that the Museum discreetly registers the letters it receives from the Department. The Museum's offer, Gowers writes, is one that the head of the Propaganda Department, the former Liberal MP Charles Masterman, warmly welcomes. The Museum becomes even more active, contacting correspondents abroad, and through them building a network of sympathetic scientists and academics to whom propaganda material is sent for them in turn to disseminate. To one correspondent in America Charles Fagan writes: 'I am very much impressed with the super-importance of doing all we can in this country to make known in the United States the cause of the Allies and the brutal methods and crimes with which Germany is carrying on the war. Personally I shall leave no stone unturned to try to secure the sympathy of Americans, which we value so greatly'.

9 OCTOBER 1916 Charles Fagan sends a letter to all senior staff regarding 'an appeal which is being made on behalf of the Prisoners of War and Wounded Men etc, belonging to the Civil Service Regiment'. The Civil Service Rifles Regimental Aid Fund aims to provide food 'and other necessaries' for prisoners of war, temporary help for widows and dependents of men who are killed, and assistance for men who, through wounds or sickness contracted abroad, are permanently disabled. It also aims to provide 'Comfort, where needed, for men at the Front'. Fagan asks the Keepers to inform their staff. The response, typically, is for Keepers to donate £1 – approximately £60 in today's values – while their staff contribute one shilling (5p or approximately £3 in today's values).

13 OCTOBER 1916 The Man-Power Distribution Board informs the Museum that it is considering a proposal that all men between 18 and 25 inclusive, now working in Government departments, should be freed for military service within a period of perhaps one month. The Board enquires whether the Museum has any objections to the proposal, or whether it will be necessary to ask for exceptions. 'A very early reply is requested'. Ten days before, the Board had asked for the number of men of military age now employed in the Museum, and how many have been rejected for military service.

14 OCTOBER 1916 For more than a year, a Belgian ornithologist, Emile J Lance, has been a temporary worker in the Bird Room. Today he writes to Dr Harmer to inform him that he has been called to join the Belgian army, and 'am thus compelled to give up the work in the Museum for which you have been so good as to engage me'. Dr Harmer tells the Trustees: 'This loss will be much felt by the Bird Room, the work of which will be carried on under increasing difficulties'.

Dr Harmer receives a telephone call from Sir Richard Paget, lawyer, scientist and an assistant secretary to the Board of Invention and Research, One of the Board's primary aims is to develop methods of combatting the threat posed by submarines. Sir Richard follows up their conversation with a letter detailing the information he requires. It is, he writes, 'in connection with investigations which

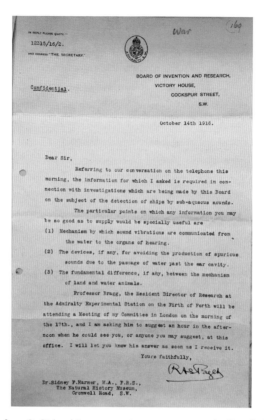

Letter from Sir Richard Paget, an assistant secretary to the Board of Invention and Research, to Dr Harmer detailing the information he required with regard to 'the detection of ships by sub-aqueous sounds'.

are being made by this Board on the subject of the detection of ships by sub-aqueous sounds'. The points that would be particularly useful to know are: '1. Mechanism by which sound vibrations are communicated from the water to the organs of hearing. 2. The devices, if any, for avoiding the production of spurious sounds due to the passage of water past the ear cavity. 3. The fundamental difference, if any, between the mechanism of land and water animals'. Sir Richard arranges a meeting for 17 October.

17 OCTOBER 1916 Dr Harmer arrives at the headquarters of the Board of Invention and Research at Victory House, Cockspur Street. He is there to meet a number of representatives of the Board. As well as Sir Richard Paget, there is the Nobel prize-winning physicist and X-ray crystallographer, Professor William Bragg and Professor Sir Ernest Rutherford, the nuclear physicist who won the Noble prize for chemistry. Their top-secret research is into submarine detection and underwater combat, and they are developing underwater acoustic listening devices. Their work is of the utmost importance given the enormous losses of merchant ships. In September and October this year nearly 100 merchant ships are lost – all sunk by German submarines. They are joined by a staff member of the Board, Commander Middleton.

What they want from Dr Harmer is his expertise on animal auditory organs and whether they could possibly be adapted for military purposes. The following day, Harmer sends a long, detailed report to Paget, expanding on their conversation. He compares the auditory organs of amphibians, reptiles, birds, mammals and fish, discussing which are the most efficient and why, and which might be used as a model. 'From your practical point of view', he writes, 'the sound-receiver has to be insulated as far as possible from extraneous sounds. I presume that these are partly the noise of the waves beating against the side of the ship, and that of the engines and other sound-producing agencies transmitted through the substance of the hull. Does the [auditory] mechanism of Vertebrates perhaps give a hint as to the way in which the sounds you want to hear could be kept distinct?' He then devises 'for your consideration' a series of experiments in considerable detail, 'imitating the conditions found in Mammalian ears as closely as possible'.

He encloses a sketch giving the possible construction of an instrument they might use. 'My ideas may be entirely crude and worthless', he writes, 'in which case you can dispose of them by means of the wastepaper basket. I cannot claim to be either a physicist or a physiologist'. By return, Sir Richard Paget thanks him for 'your very interesting letter and suggestions', and tells him that not dissimilar experiments have 'actually been tried, but it may well be that further experiment could usefully be tried' and he is forwarding Harmer's letter to Professor Bragg.

Dr Harmer's report to the Trustees on this meeting is of necessity guarded, but he does reveal that 'he gave such information on the subject as he was in a position to give, demonstrating some of the facts by means of actual specimens'. He also reports that there has been subsequent correspondence since the interview, although 'it is not possible to say at present' whether the meeting will have any practical outcome. However, Harmer does state that the men he met seemed to be 'really interested' in receiving information with regard to 'certain details of comparative anatomy', and they may possibly institute experiments based on this information.

19 OCTOBER 1916 Dr Harmer reports to the Trustees that a temporary exhibition on the biology of water reservoirs is being prepared. As the matter is of practical importance, he proposes to issue a short guide. It is to be written by Zoology assistant Randolph Kirkpatrick who is also preparing the exhibit. It will show through a series of specimens and diagrams how the animal and plant-life in a water-supply system affects the quality of the water and its delivery to the consumer. Kirkpatrick visits the 'extensive' Hampton works and filter-beds of the Metropolitan Water Board. There, officials explain to him the construction and mechanism of the plant, the type of filters used and the type of 'minute organisms' found in the London water supply. When the exhibit opens, it is of considerable interest to water engineers and medical officers of health, as well as the general public. Enquiries come from the Royal Army Medical Corps concerning water supplies in camp. Within a

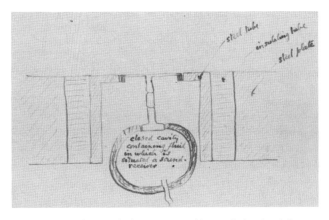

Dr Harmer sent the Board of Invention and Research this sketch for an acoustic listening device as part of his report on auditory organs of animals and whether they could be adapted for military purposes.

few months of publication, a second edition of Kirkpatrick's guide is issued.

At 53, Kirkpatrick is too old to fight, but in October 1914, he joined the Volunteer Training Corps, the London Rifles. He is a qualified machine gunner, stretcher-bearer and has reached the required standard of efficiency in rifle shooting.

20 OCTOBER 1916 Dr Gahan, Keeper of Entomology, receives an enquiry from New Scotland Yard, regarding a consignment of truncheons, some of which are worm-eaten. They wish to know whether there is any risk that apparently sound truncheons in the same consignment might also be infected. Dr Gahan examines the damaged truncheon sent to him and concludes that the wood was already worm-eaten before it was made into a truncheon. He is able to reassure the police that it is 'extremely unlikely' that apparently sound truncheons had been infected. If they had, he writes, 'there should be some external evidence of it in the presence of "shot-holes" or superficial tunnels as in the case of the sample sent'. As the truncheons are dyed and polished all over, it is 'extremely unlikely' that they would be attacked from the outside. The police also consult him on how best to prevent damage to some ambulance stretchers which are being attacked by termites.

28 OCTOBER 1916 At their regular meeting, the Trustees are given the latest information on the military service of staff, some of which has been compiled in response to the Man-Power Distribution Board's request. They are told that two men have been killed – Private John Gabriel in July and Private George Pagnoni in September. Five men serving in the military have been promoted. Six men have been wounded, including a boy attendant who was gassed and is suffering from shell shock, and another man who has been injured twice. Two have been discharged from the army – one who lost a finger fighting in France and has returned to work as a labourer in the Museum, and another whose injuries received in the Dardanelles are such that not only has he been discharged from the Army 'as unfit for further service', but also from the Museum, as he is now 'physically unequal' for his job as a labourer.

Of those still in the Museum, six men have been certified as 'indispensable' for their duties and are exempt from military service. These are Arthur Stanley Hirst, the mites and ticks specialist in Zoology who is engaged in 'economic research of national importance'; Frank Barlow, mason in Geology whose work is essential to the 'preservation of the very valuable fossil collection'; William Ernest Barnett, indispensable as the only attendant left in the Spirit Building, is also a member of the London Ambulance Column. Herbert England is the attendant essential for the running of the Zoology library and is also a member of the London Ambulance Column. Frank Reeley, is now the only attendant left in Entomology, while Geology attendant Harold

Seeley has been granted conditional exemption as long as the department remains in its present depleted state and that he joins the Volunteer Training Corps, which he does. Of these six, he is the only one passed fit for general military service. Six more have been rejected on medical grounds, and two who were at first rejected have now been passed as Class C (iii), which means they are fit only for 'sedentary work as clerks, storemen, batmen, cooks, orderlies, and on sanitary duties'.

Regarding the Man-Power Distribution Board's proposal that all men between 18 and 25 should be called up with one month's notice, there are now just three men left in that age group in the Museum – not one fully fit. Two have been rejected on medical grounds, and the third has been placed in Class C (iii) and is available for limited military service when called upon. The Man-Power Board notes this 'with satisfaction'.

4 NOVEMBER 1916 Dr Harmer writes to Sir Richard Paget of the Board of Invention and Research on another matter connected with the war. He has seen rumours, he tells Sir Richard – he thinks in print – that airship construction is being hampered by the difficulty of getting hold of a key component – 'gold-beaters' skin'. 'This letter has no special point,' Harmer writes, 'if the report is groundless'.

Gold-beaters' skin is animal membrane used by goldsmiths to separate sheets of gold leaf, but it is also of great importance in the construction of airship gasbags. Often made from cows' intestines, it is said that it takes 250,000 cows to make the gasbag for one Zeppelin airship. British airships also use it. Harmer tells Paget that while consulting various works on cetacea, 'with the above rumour somewhere in the back of my mind', he came across references to the uses that the abdominal membranes of the Greenland and also the White whale are put by 'the natives of those parts'. These include

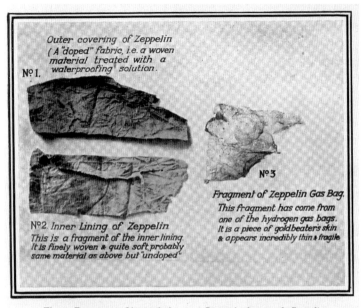

Illustration of the construction of a Zeppelin balloon, including
fragments of the gasbag made from gold-beaters' skin. This was
published in *The Sphere* newspaper 29 July 1916.

clothing, a substitute for glass in windows, and curtains. One report
noted that the membrane of the intestines 'is so nicely prepared that
it nearly resembles "gold-beaters' skin"'.

Harmer writes that he cannot say on this evidence that the
cetacean membranes have any special advantage 'over those which
an ordinary butcher could supply'. However, because of the oily
nature of the cetacea, their intestinal membranes 'might have some

corresponding advantage'. He concludes by telling Paget that as the Museum has an arrangement with the Board of Trade whereby stranded whales are reported by telegram to them, that might provide a suitable opportunity of looking into the question, 'if it is one in which you are interested. There would', he ends, 'be other ways of obtaining the material in large quantities'.

In his reply, Paget tells Harmer that he has 'handed your letter on to the section which deals with aeronautical matters'.

9 NOVEMBER 1916 The Museum receives a letter from the Board of Education that the Foreign Office desires closer contact between British and Russian men of science. The letter states that the Board would welcome any suggestions from the Museum. The keepers are asked for their views, and the response from all is that 'the principal difficulty is undoubtedly the language'. Dr Harmer writes that there are a number of Russian zoologists who 'publish habitually' in German and French, and their work is as well known in this country as if it had been published in Germany or France. 'It must be remembered', he adds, 'that the minimum equipment of a working zoologist, in the way of languages, is a working knowledge of German, French, Italian and Latin, while some smattering of Greek is very useful, if not indispensable'. In addition, 'Danish (Norwegian) and Swedish are very important, while some knowledge of Dutch and even Spanish or Portuguese is useful. It can hardly be expected that many Zoologists will accomplish all this with the addition of Russian'. He suggests, as do the other keepers, that closer communication appears to rest principally with the Russians, and they should be urged 'with great advantage' to themselves to publish their results in some other language, 'which would possibly be French'.

Dr Harmer also suggests that after the war, the exchange of specimens with Russian museums might be encouraged.

Gunner Robert James Swift of the Museum's cleaning staff. He was killed in action on the Somme 10 November 1916.

10 NOVEMBER 1916 Gunner Robert James Swift, 1st Battery, 45th Brigade Royal Field Artillery, a contractor's labourer at the Museum, is killed in action on the Somme. He first joined the army in 1900, serving as a gunner in the Royal Field Artillery in the South African War which ended in 1902. In 1910 he was appointed to the contractors' staff at the Museum. As a reservist, he was called up on the outbreak of war in 1914 and was sent to France with the first expeditionary force. According to the Museum's *War Memorial Record*, 'he saw continuous service, absolutely without a scratch'. He was 35 when he died, and 'he lies near by where he fell'. He was married and had a three-year-old son. Gunner Swift's name is commemorated on the Thiepval Memorial. He is one of the 72,000 soldiers reported missing on the Somme who are commemorated there. A week after his death, major operations on the Somme end in rapidly deteriorating weather conditions. Since 1 July, when the battle commenced, more than a million men on both sides have been killed or wounded.

14 NOVEMBER 1916 The *London Gazette* records that Captain Arthur Knyvett Totton, Duke of Cornwall's Light Infantry and an assistant in the Zoology Department, has been awarded the Military Cross for 'conspicuous gallantry in action'. He was wounded early on the morning of 3 September at Guillemont, but nonetheless led his men to their first objective, enemy dug-outs which they bombed. He was again 'hit by a bomb' – but he still led his men on to their second objective, and was wounded for a third time on the way. The Museum Trustees are told that he is now in hospital in London and 'progressing favourably'. The Trustees 'desire' the Director to convey their congratulations to him.

The Board of Invention and Research replies to Dr Harmer's gold-beaters' skin suggestions of 4 November. The letter tells him that the rumour he heard is correct. 'There is a considerable shortage of gold-beaters' skin for airship work, and that any additional sources of supply would be welcomed'. He is also told that there are 'many problems arising from time to time in connexion with the manufacture and use of gold-beaters' skin, and you could probably be of assistance in dealing with them'. He is asked to communicate with Squadron Commander Cave-Brown-Cave, Royal Naval Airship Station, 'Kingsnorth', Hoo, Rochester. 'He will supply you with particulars of the problems requiring investigation'.

17 NOVEMBER 1916 Dr Harmer writes at once to the Squadron Commander. 'I have no knowledge of the details of the manufacture of gold-beaters' skin', he tells him, 'but I have taken a special interest in whales. These animals are being killed in very large numbers; and if their product could be utilized it ought to be obtainable in very large quantities'. He tells him that the Museum is notified immediately on any whale stranding. 'If there is any way in which I can give assistance that would be of practical value it would give me much pleasure to do so', he concludes. 'I have a good deal of information with regard to capture of whales, the majority of which are caught from December to March'.

22 NOVEMBER 1916 Dr Harmer informs the Trustees of this correspondence – although he does not reveal the exact subject matter – simply that he has had an idea relating to whales. He tells them that it is at a preliminary stage and may not be worth pursuing, but the response he has had so far indicates it may prove to be important. In that event, Harmer asks whether he may give part of his official time to work arising out of his suggestion, should his assistance be of value to the Admiralty or the War Office.

24 NOVEMBER 1916 Dr Rendle, Botany Keeper, reports that he has recently been consulted by the Air Department of the Admiralty on the identification of samples of so-called 'Silver Spruce' from North America. He has been able to give 'helpful information and advice'. 'Silver spruce', better known as Sitka spruce, is lightweight, strong and was recognized as ideal for aircraft construction for which it becomes a key material.

25 NOVEMBER 1916 The Trustees are informed that Private Stanley Thomas Wells, 15th Battalion, London Regiment (Prince of Wales' Civil Service Rifles) and an attendant in the Zoology department, has been reported missing in action since September and that 'hope has been given up of obtaining any information of his fate'. Wells joined the Museum as a boy attendant in 1908 when he was 14. On the outbreak of war he attempted to enlist, but could not because of health issues. He was promoted to attendant three weeks later. Early in 1915 he made another attempt and was again rejected. His annual report for that year relates that he was 'turning into an excellent Attendant'. He was 'keen, tidy, intelligent and methodical'. A key part of the attendant's job is writing – registering specimens as well as correspondence, and Wells was 'a remarkably good writer, his keeping of the registers and other books is admirable'. On his third attempt to join up, he was accepted by the London Irish Rifles,

Private Stanley Thomas Wells, Zoology attendant, missing in action on the Somme since September 1916. By November 'hope has been given up' for him.

transferring in November 1915 to the 1st Civil Service Rifles. In September 1916 his battalion suffered heavy casualties in 'severe battles' on the Somme. On 19 September he was reported missing in action and 'nothing has been heard of him since'. In the Museum's *War Memorial Record*, the Curator of Mammals, Michael Oldfield Thomas under whom Wells worked, wrote: 'Owing to his unusually beautiful handwriting and his care and interest in the work, the registers were kept in a way which has never been equalled, and still remain as a model as to how such things should be done'. Stanley Wells was 22 years old.

They are also told that twelve members of staff, including Zoology Keeper Dr Harmer, an assistant, attendants and carpenters, have enrolled in the Volunteer Training Corps, 1st Battalion Central London Regiment (United Arts Rifles). The Museum Secretary, Charles Fagan, writes to the Keepers to tell them that the Trustees desire that 'as far as maybe', all facilities should be given to the Volunteers to train. 'The drills, I believe', he wrote, 'can normally be done in the men's own time. The question of a few hours' leave may be left to the discretion of the Keepers, since circumstances vary in each Department. In the case of absence for a more extended period, reference should be made to the Director'.

The Trustees also see the Museum's budget estimates for 1917–1918. Included are sums of £100 for Zoology and £50 for Entomology to provide for expert assistance 'as occasion may arise, in view of the dearth of Assistants in these two departments'. There is an urgent need for the employment of 'properly qualified persons', if only for a few hours a week, to maintain the collections 'in their proper scientific order and arrangement'.

2 DECEMBER 1916 For some time there has been increasing concern about how to entertain the thousands of soldiers in London. The Museum is already hugely popular with them but there is just one official guide, whose services are already oversubscribed. An acquaintance of Charles Fagan, Lady Glover, suggests that young ladies might be asked to act as guides to visiting soldiers. Charles Fagan writes to her, telling her that if she organises the 'young ladies', he will arrange for the official guide to make two or three special tours of the galleries for them alone. He suggests they also join the public tours, as the more they accompany the guide, 'the more they will learn'.

14 DECEMBER 1916 Charles Fagan sends a memo to the Keepers regarding the use of electric light. 'Owing to the scarcity of carbon', he writes, 'and to the uncertainty of future supplies, HM Office of Works is compelled to exercise a strict control over the supply of electricity. The service of electric light in the Museum will be maintained as far as possible, but any complaints or applications for more light should be sent to the Director's office'.

Chapter 8
January–April 1917

The winter of 1917 is harsh. The manpower shortage is acute and shipping losses mount. Germany announces 'unrestricted naval warfare', and that it will blockade sea traffic in wide zones around France, Italy and Great Britain. There are already food shortages and this will gravely aggravate the situation. Increasing home-grown food production is now essential. Allotments are created wherever possible, in public parks, golf courses and government land, including the grounds of the Natural History Museum. Public health and hygiene is of great concern, both at home and at the front. The Entomology department plans leaflets to warn the public and the troops on the dangers posed by houseflies and mosquitoes – and how to deal with them. The Museum's expertise in the protective coloration of animals, or camouflage, is again called upon. Annie Lorrain Smith, an eminent botanist and – in the male-oriented Museum – a rare female scientist, volunteers for work the Botany Keeper calls 'of supreme national importance'. The Museum is so depleted of its staff that, without volunteers, it would have grave difficulty in functioning. At the front, the expertise of Museum scientists is invaluable. In April, the United States at long last enters the war.

1 JANUARY 1917 The *London Gazette* records that Captain Walter Campbell Smith, 28th London Regiment (Artists' Rifles), is awarded the Military Cross. The medal is awarded to captains or officers of lower rank for acts of exemplary gallantry during active operations against the enemy on land. At the Museum Campbell Smith is a Mineralogy assistant. An authority on Antarctic minerals, he curated the rock collection from Captain Scott's Terra Nova expedition. Now, because of his scientific expertise, he is attached to what the Museum Trustees are told is the 'Gas Company' of the Royal Engineers – one of their special units to counteract aspects of the German offensive, particularly the use of poison gas. When the Americans join the war, it is Campbell Smith who instructs the American First Battalion, First Gas Regiment in offensive gas training. He leads them in a five-week course consisting of fieldwork and lectures. In 1937, Campbell Smith will be appointed Keeper of Mineralogy.

4 JANUARY 1917 Captain Frederick Courtney Selous, 25th Royal Fusiliers (Legion of Frontiersmen) is killed in action in East Africa. He is 65 years old. He had attempted to enlist at the outbreak of war, but was repeatedly rejected for nearly a year because of his

The London Gazette recorded on 1 January 1917 that Mineralogy assistant Walter Campbell Smith (1887–1988), a Captain in the 28th London Regiment (Artists' Rifles) but attached to the Royal Engineers, was awarded the Military Cross. In 1937 he was appointed Mineralogy Keeper.

Captain Frederick Courtney Selous, the renowned big-game hunter and donor to the Museum, was killed in action in East Africa on 1 January 1917. His bronze memorial was unveiled in the Museum's Central Hall in June 1920.

age. A renowned big-game hunter, his association with the Museum began in 1881 when he donated a series of mammals from South Africa. Since then he has been a significant donor, presenting many magnificent mounted specimens, including antelope, moose and caribou. A committee is formed to promote a national memorial to him as explorer, naturalist and sportsman. It is unveiled on the staircase of the Museum's Central Hall in June 1920 – a bronze sculpture of Selous, in uniform, carrying his rifle.

9 JANUARY 1917 Botany assistant John Ramsbottom has been attempting for nearly a year to obtain a commission in the 1st London (City of London) Sanitary Company, Royal Army Medical Corps, Territorial Force. Today he writes to the Assistant Secretary, Charles Fagan, telling him that although the Company is keen to have him, he has repeatedly failed a medical examination because of his eyesight, even though he was passed as fit for general service under the Derby Scheme. The Officer Commanding the Company has even noted on the medical officer's report, 'I am of the opinion that this gentleman's vision is satisfactory for duty in this unit', but to no avail. Ramsbottom now asks if the Museum could bring his case to the notice of the Director General of the Army Medical Service, Sir Alfred Keogh, 'or some other authority'.

12 JANUARY 1917 Charles Fagan writes to the War Office about Ramsbottom. He tells them that he is 'a very capable' member of staff, who should 'be well fitted' to the position he seeks and that 'his services should prove especially welcome to the Sanitary Corps'. Fagan attaches a note of Ramsbottom's qualifications – which are particularly relevant to the Sanitary Corps, not least because of the courses he has recently taken at the Lister Institute studying bacteria pathogenic to man and at the Wellcome Institute on amoebic dysenteries.

Dr Harmer receives a telephone call from the Board of Invention and Research, asking why he has not been in touch with Squadron Commander Cave-Brown-Cave who has been expecting to hear from him. Dr Harmer writes to the Commander at once, enclosing a copy of the letter he sent in November, which has evidently gone astray. 'I venture to suggest', Harmer writes, 'that this is a serious matter which ought to be looked into it'. He tells Commander Cave that the Museum would be 'only too glad' to do anything of practical value and that he had not sent a second letter as he had thought his suggestion regarding the possible use of whales for gold-beaters' skin was not of interest. 'I greatly regret the delay', he concludes, 'especially as the most favourable season [for capturing whales] is rapidly passing'.

15 JANUARY 1917 Harmer's letter to Commander Cave is answered by Neil Kensington Adam, a 25-year-old chemist whose research at Cambridge into the biochemistry of muscle protein was interrupted by the war. He was appointed chemist to the Royal Naval Airship Service in September 1914. Adam's work is principally on the fabric of airships, the quality of which has to be capable of retaining hydrogen. He tells Harmer how gold-beaters' skin is used. 'A perfect gold-beaters' skin', Adams writes, 'measures some 10 inches by 30 inches', though not all is of that quality. 'Roughly 900,000 skins are

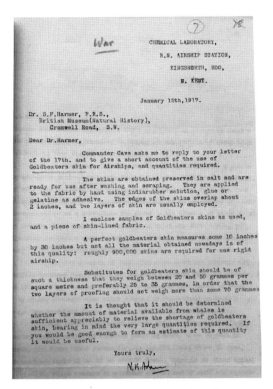

Letter 15 January 1917 from Neil Kensington Adam, chemist to the Royal Naval Airship Service, to Dr Harmer outlining how gold-beaters' skin was used in airships and the quantities and size required.

required for one rigid airship'. He tells Harmer that the skins are obtained preserved in salt, and are ready for use 'after washing and scraping. They are applied to the fabric by hand using indiarubber solution, glue or gelatine as adhesive. The edges of the skins overlap about 2 inches, and two layers of skin are usually employed'. He sends Harmer samples of the skin and a piece of skin-lined fabric. Substitutes, he writes, should preferably weigh between 25 to 35 grammes per square metre, 'in order that two layers of proofing should not weigh more than some 70 grammes'. He asks Harmer to estimate whether the amount of material available from whales would be sufficient 'appreciably to relieve the shortage of gold-beaters' skin, bearing in mind the very large quantities required'.

16 JANUARY 1917 Dr Harmer replies immediately, sending a four-page, closely typed and very positive letter. He describes the different species of whales and their respective sizes. 'There is no other animal in existence', he writes, 'which reaches so colossal a size; and if only the Whales' product is suitable there can be no question that it can be obtained in larger quantities from them than from anything else'. He gives various ideas as to which are the best whaling grounds and why and tells Adam that in South Georgia waters alone, 4,000–5,000 whales are caught annually. He also suggests that if immediate results as to the suitability of the whale material are required, then it might be advisable to contact the principal fish-markets, asking them to send a porpoise or small whale to the Museum as soon as possible. The Museum would do the basic dissection, preserve the parts and have them sent to 'someone skilled' in the manufacture of gold-beaters' skin.

Adam forwards a copy of Harmer's letter to the Air Department (part of the Admiralty), and draws attention to his idea of procuring samples from fish-markets 'in order that as little time as possible may be lost'. He tells Harmer that the shortage of skins 'is serious', and that he expects the Air Department will contact Harmer 'with little delay'.

18 JANUARY 1917 *The Times* reports the loss at sea of the Canadian Pacific Railway's steamer *SS Mount Temple*. She is one of ten vessels sunk in the Atlantic by the Germans in late December. Included in her cargo is the 'second half of a collection of Canadian Cretaceous Dinosaurs', destined to be a gift to the Museum. The first half of the collection is currently being worked on in the Geology Department. Dr Arthur Smith Woodward, Keeper of Geology, informs the Trustees that the 22 cases were 'fully insured against war risks'. He hopes to persuade the donors 'to renew their generous intentions… when circumstances are favourable'.

19 JANUARY 1917 John Guy Dollman (known as Guy), a 2nd class zoology assistant, will shortly have completed 10 years' service in the Museum and is therefore eligible to be considered for promotion to 1st class assistant. Since May 1915 he has been on military service, holding the temporary rank of captain. He is a bombing instructor, engaged in work which Dr Harmer describes as exposing him 'to considerable danger'. He has been wounded more than once, the last time almost losing his life. He has just returned to duty after a month in hospital. Dr Harmer reports to the Trustees that he 'has done much useful work' in the Mammal Room, and is 'an excellent artist' with 'plenty of ability and industry'. Dr Harmer recommends his promotion.

Dr Harmer also reports to the Trustees on the critical shortage of spirit needed to conserve the collection. The Government is taking 80 per cent of all spirit produced. 'If some National disaster could be averted only by the disuse of alcohol as a preservative', Harmer writes, 'the Trustees would probably be prepared to acquiesce in the deterioration of the collections if this were necessary to save the country'. However, if it is possible to obtain the spirit that is 'really necessary without endangering the successful prosecution of the war', Dr Harmer thinks this should be done. Re-spiriting the collection cannot be deferred safely, he argues, and 'irreparable injury, including the loss of type-specimens' will occur if spirit lost by evaporation cannot be replaced. At least 500 gallons are needed and Dr Harmer recommends that application should be made to the Treasury to purchase what is necessary.

20 JANUARY 1917 Harry Baylis, the Zoology assistant working temporarily at the Royal Naval Hospital, Haslar, sends several specimens of ascidians – minute marine animals – which are apparently blocking seawater pipes at Portsmouth Dockyard. Dr Harmer reports to the Trustees that they feed off microscopic particles, and suggests to Baylis that filtering the water might resolve the pipe blockage.

23 JANUARY 1917 Ramsbottom's case suddenly becomes critical. He is called up for general service and is expected to join the army in four days' time. Fagan writes in haste to the War Office to request a certificate of exemption from military service for him, as he 'is engaged on research work of direct national importance. Sir Alfred Keogh', the head of the Army Medical Service, 'is acquainted with the facts of the case'. Fagan again attaches a note giving the range of Ramsbottom's work and recent courses he has undertaken.

24 JANUARY 1917 Dr Charles Gahan, Keeper of Entomology and an expert on beetles, now spends a considerable amount of his time answering practical and urgent queries from the government and military. He reports to the Trustees that he has just been dealing with a problem for the Admiralty Medical Department concerning bedbugs that had infested a ship in harbour at Gibraltar. Fleet Surgeon Richard Cleveland Munday had written to him in November that a trial had been made of fumigating the ship using hydrocyanic acid gas – the highly toxic chemical. They had followed instructions given in the American publication, *Public Health Reports*. At Gibraltar, however, it was 'a complete failure as far as its effect on bed-bugs was concerned, but was more or less successful in killing off the cockroaches'.

Munday asks Gahan if he can explain the failure, but Gahan tells him he cannot until he receives the report from the officer under whose direction the fumigation had been carried out. Gahan also researches statements from American entomologists who have successfully fumigated with hydrocyanic acid gas. He sends Munday their conclusions, which include details of the quantity and proportions of gas they have used. In his reply, he writes that the commercial product is sold in different grades of strength, and suggests that the failure of the fumigation was probably because the gas used was either of 'much too low a grade of strength', or, if it had been of the highest grade, then the amount used 'was not quite sufficient'.

25 JANUARY 1917 Dr Gahan replies to a letter from the Surgeon General and Commandant of the Royal Army Medical College, Sir David Bruce, who wishes to know about the distribution in Britain of the *Anopheles* mosquito – the species which can spread malaria. Bruce is an eminent bacteriologist and parasitologist and fellow of the Royal Society. As Gahan tells him, 'unfortunately' his two assistants who are specialists in Diptera (the order of insects which includes *Anopheles*) are serving in the military, but he sends detailed references from a paper by one of them. He also offers to send Bruce a list of all the British localities from which the Museum has *Anopheles* specimens in the collections. He tells him that by researching 'the various scattered records' and by writing to the dozen or so collectors of British Diptera, it would be possible to obtain sufficient information to map the distribution 'with some approach to accuracy and completeness'. As the matter 'seems to be one of importance', and he has no-one available in the department to undertake the work, he suggests that Bruce 'tries to secure the services of Mr James E Collin, a very competent specialist on the Diptera'.

James Edward Collin, a renowned amateur entomologist, is serving as a motor transport driver with the Army Service Corps at

Catford near London. Gahan suggests that if Collin 'could be put to work here' at the Museum to look up the records and communicate with other specialists and collectors, he would be able to get Bruce 'all the information possible'. With such a depleted staff, Gahan can do no more except assure the Surgeon General that 'I shall be glad to supply you with any information I can with the means at my disposal'.

So many of Gahan's staff are now in the armed forces or occupied with dealing with enquiries from government and military, he has difficulty in simply maintaining the normal running of the department. In 1914, 12 assistants and attendants left to join the armed forces. Those left are either too old for military service or are unfit. A volunteer in Entomology, Rowland Edwards Turner, a specialist in wasps and bees, offers to work full-time for the duration of the war, and to undertake, unpaid, any of the duties normally carried out by scientific assistants. At 53 he is too old for military service. Dr Gahan's recommendation to the Trustees that Turner should be recognised – temporarily – as an unpaid member of staff is accepted.

Zoology is similarly depleted through war and illness. William Lutley Sclater, a 54 year-old naturalist and ornithologist, has for many years been a temporary worker in the department. Dr Harmer informs the Trustees that 'it would be very advantageous' to secure the voluntary assistance 'of so well-known an ornithologist'. Sclater is editor of *The Ibis*, the journal of the British Ornithological Union. He is asked to act temporarily as a volunteer assistant and take charge of the Bird Room, under Dr Harmer's supervision. Sclater is most willing to do so.

27 JANUARY 1917 How important volunteers like Turner and Sclater are to the Museum becomes all too clear when the Trustees are informed of an instruction to all Government departments that no new men are to be engaged without the consent of the Department of the Director General of National Service. The War Office has already announced that 30,000 men currently engaged as agricultural labourers are to be called up.

To help avert a food crisis, allotments are being set up throughout the country. Cultivation of all available land is crucial – parks, golf courses, unused building land and government land – and that includes the grounds of the Natural History Museum. In the last few days, Germany has threatened what it terms 'unrestricted naval warfare' to prevent any sea traffic in wide zones round Britain, France, Italy and the Eastern Mediterranean. That includes hospital ships, which the Germans threaten to sink – and do. Imports will clearly be affected. Fuel and food are already in short supply; there are now far fewer men available to work the land and there is a world shortage of corn. The situation is so serious that the Controller of Food, Lord Devonport, has already asked for voluntary restriction of food consumption to avoid compulsory rationing. The Government has announced that the quantity of beer permitted to be brewed is to be reduced to 50 percent of the immediate pre-war output in 1913–1914, as barley, sugar and other ingredients are essential for food. Lord Devonport tells *The Times* 'it is really a question of "bread versus beer"'.

Dr Harmer writes to Dr Peter Chalmers Mitchell, Secretary of the Zoological Society of London. 'Dear Mitchell', Harmer begins his confidential letter, 'There seems to be a serious shortage of white mice, which are required for various purposes connected with the war'. Harmer has discovered this after receiving a telephone query from a Government department (which he does not identify) as to where supplies might be available. They are urgently wanted, and in large numbers. He has tried the department stores Hamlyn and Gamages, which have none. The Lister Institute recommends a zoologist who cannot help, but who suggests the Pasteur Institute

Dr Harmer was asked by a Government department (unnamed) where they might obtain a supply of white mice. As this photograph from *The Sphere* illustrates, white mice were essential for detecting fumes on board submarines.

in Paris, but they have none. Harmer tries four more people, one of whom can only suggest advertising and 'arranging for breeding in hospitals'. He tells Dr Mitchell, 'I can safely say that the available supplies are to a large extent depleted'. White mice have an essential role in all British submarines, where their squeaks alert the crew to noxious fumes. While Harmer has 'no official authority' to ask him, he suggests to Dr Mitchell that 'perhaps if you know that the matter is urgent you may feel disposed to consider whether you could take any practical steps'.

Dr Mitchell replies at once, telling Harmer that the Zoo has recently received a similar enquiry and they have already 'on a small scale' begun breeding the mice. After receiving Harmer's letter, he has 'sent out today' to get in all that they can, though 'they are not likely to breed for some weeks yet'.

29 JANUARY 1917 The interventions on behalf of John Ramsbottom have succeeded. He is no longer to be called up for ordinary military service. He receives a certificate of exemption which is marked 'absolute'.

30 JANUARY 1917 Dr Harmer notices an article in *The Times*, reporting on the vast resources available within the Empire, particularly fish and whale oil. 'I am not sure,' he writes to the Director, Sir Lazarus Fletcher, 'that the authorities are sufficiently informed with regard to the resources of the Empire'. He suggests this might be an opportunity of calling attention to the value of whale-meat 'which is perfectly good to eat'. He wonders if something might be done by reviving the British whaling stations – 'unless the submarine menace is too serious'. 'Rudolphi's Rorqual', he thinks is 'specially appreciated by connoisseurs'.

1 FEBRUARY 1917 Dr Harmer has not heard from the Air Department in spite of the apparent urgency of the gold-beaters' skin shortage, and writes to Neil K Adam: 'I hope the matter will not be allowed to drop without further enquiry'. He asks Adam to put him in touch with a manufacturer of the skin so he can see for himself the entire manufacturing process, 'from start to finish'. In the meantime, Harmer researches the subject as far as he can.

2 FEBRUARY 1917 The Assistant Secretary, Charles Fagan, writes to the Keepers informing them that it is proposed to provide allotments in the back grounds of the Museum 'for the cultivation of potatoes & other vegetables'. The plots will be assigned to members of staff 'who may apply for them in so far as the area of land will allow'. Fagan asks the Keepers to bring this to the notice of every member of their staff, 'irrespective of grade'. Those interested should send their applications to him. Priority, he writes, 'will of

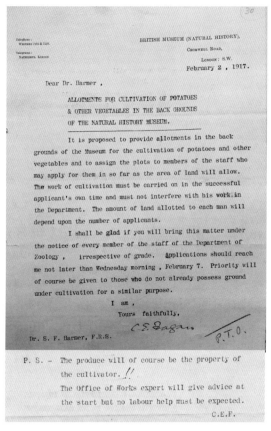

Charles Fagan's letter of 2 February 1917 to Dr Harmer and
the other Keepers advising them that it is proposed to provide
allotments for the staff in the Museum grounds.

course be given to those who do not already possess ground under
cultivation for a similar purpose'. The successful applicants, Fagan
writes, may only work on the allotments in their own time and it
must not interfere with their work. The produce, he adds, 'will of
course be the property of the cultivator'.

5 FEBRUARY 1917 For days the temperature in London has been well below freezing. There is skating in Regent's Park, ice is seen on the Thames, but in the Museum the intense cold brings discomfort and complaints. All Charles Fagan can do is repeat what everyone already knows: there is a 'great shortage of coal' for all government departments, a low temperature in the building 'cannot be avoided', and it is likely to continue during the cold weather.

6 FEBRUARY 1917 Dr Harmer has been asked by the Director to draw up a list of exhibits that might serve to illustrate a lecture on protective coloration as applied to war – in other words, camouflage. He points out to Sir Lazarus Fletcher that, in several cases, the suitability of particular subjects must be decided by experiment. 'It is possible', he writes, 'that the concealment may prove so complete that a photograph cannot bring out what it is intended to illustrate'. He lists 21 specimens exhibited in the Museum which he thinks suitable, from caterpillars to fish to mammals and birds and including Thayer's models. He also lists a number of illustrations from Thayer's book *Concealing Coloration in the Animal Kingdom*.

For some time now, parties of soldiers of all ranks – from officer to private – have been regularly attending the Museum to receive instruction and demonstrations on the exhibits that illustrate protective coloration. Many of the soldiers are based at the huge military training camp at Aldershot. It is Major Frederick Maurice Crum, Instructor in Sniping at Aldershot, who has requested the set of lanternslides of these exhibits, which he says will be most useful and of special interest to the men. Crum has also said he would be very glad to have a model of the 'disappearing bird', part of the Thayer exhibit, illustrating countershading.

The Trustees authorise two sets of coloured lanternslides of the objects to be prepared, with explanatory text, for loan to the War Office.

These photographs from Thayer's *Concealing Coloration in the Animal Kingdom* were among those selected by Dr Harmer to illustrate a lecture on camouflage. These are images of cardboard zebras against imitation reeds and straw.

7 FEBRUARY 1917 The War Office sends a circular letter to all government departments. New certificates of exemption should now only be issued with the consent of the Army Council. 'In view of the grave need for men', the letter states, the cases of those under 35 and classed fit for general service 'should be closely scrutinised again, and every endeavour made to release for Army Service as many of them as possible'. The Museum informs the War Office there are no fully fit men under 35 now employed there, and sends a list of those who may be 'called to the colours' under the various classes for less fit men.

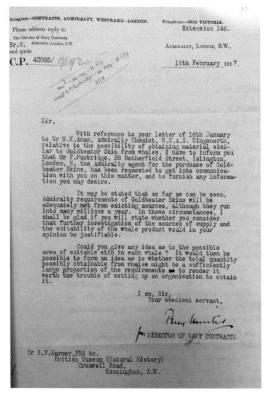

This letter of 10 February 1917 from the Director of Navy Contracts to Dr Harmer regarding gold-beaters' skin, was quite at odds with all other communications Dr Harmer received on the subject.

10 FEBRUARY 1917 Dr Harmer at last receives a response to his suggestions for possibly increasing the supply of gold-beaters' skin. It is a letter from the Director of Navy Contracts. He tells Harmer that the Admiralty agent for the purchase of gold-beaters' skins has been requested to communicate with him. He continues – presumably much to Harmer's surprise – 'It may be stated that so far as can be seen, Admiralty requirements of Gold-beater Skins will be adequately met from existing sources, although they run into many millions a year'. This is quite at odds with all Harmer's previous communications. His probable irritation is also not helped by his being asked by the Director of Navy Contracts for information on the possible area of suitable skin that may be available from the whale – which no-one can answer until the basic research Harmer suggested more than three weeks ago is carried out.

Harmer's reply is brisk, restating the basic points he has already made in his letters to Adam. He adds a further suggestion, however. 'If, as is possible, the supply of "skin" proves to be large, the trouble of setting up a new organisation might be partly repaid by putting other products to use. The oil is largely used, I believe, in the manufacture of explosives. The meat is of good quality and might become an important constituent of the meat-supply of the country'. He also writes to the Admiralty agent for the purchase of gold-beaters' skins, restating his wish to visit a manufacturer so he can see the process.

14 FEBRUARY 1917 Sir Alfred Keogh, Director General of the Army Medical Service who was helpful in securing Botany assistant John Ramsbottom's exemption from military service, now wishes to employ him. It was Keogh who recognised the vital importance of sanitation and hygiene in war, and created a new army sanitary service and School of Army Sanitation. He applied science to sanitation. Without this, as the journal *Nature* records in

1918, 'there would be a terrible and unnecessary loss of life'. Today Surgeon General Sir William Babtie of the Army Medical Service writes to the Museum on Keogh's behalf. 'I am directed to inform you', he writes, 'that it is desired to offer employment to Professor J Ramsbottom [an unexpected elevation for the 31-year old, 2nd class Botany assistant] as Protozoologist in Salonika. ' Babtie wishes to know if there would be any objection 'to the utilization of his services', for which there is great need. Many of the sick and wounded in Salonika were previously evacuated to Malta for treatment. Now, because of German submarine attacks on hospital ships in the Mediterranean, they are to be treated in Salonika with a consequent need for scientists with Ramsbottom's expertise. Hospitals with more than 1,000 beds are created. Conditions in the region are harsh, with malaria and gastrointestinal disease rife. In 1917 to 1918, more than 12,000 men are wounded in battle in Macedonia, while more than 330,000 are admitted to hospital with sickness.

24 FEBRUARY 1917 At their meeting at midday, the Trustees approve the suggestion for allotments. There are 31 plots available and Fagan has received 35 applications. Just a few hours later however, a representative of the War Office arrives at the Museum and informs the Trustees that the military authorities want soldiers to cultivate the land and grow vegetables for the men of the Royal Defence Corps which is based nearby in Cromwell Gardens.

26 FEBRUARY 1917 Fagan informs the keepers and other officials that the offer of allotments has been withdrawn from Museum staff in favour of the military. However, he writes, all those who have been cultivating plots in the grounds in previous years 'will be allowed to retain them on the understanding that such plots must be used exclusively for the growing of vegetables'. To help with

Soldiers of the Royal Defence Corps tending allotments in the Museum's grounds.

this, he circulates an Office of Works leaflet, *Royal Parks – Model Allotment Gardens for Vegetable Culture*, and includes a typed leaflet on manure. It recommends using guano (from seabirds) when farmyard manure is not obtainable. Fagan offers to send as many leaflets as may be necessary. He also sends the leaflets to Major Manners Howe of the Royal Defence Corps, and tells him he should get in touch with the Superintendent of Hyde Park, Mr JA Gardiner, who 'will be very glad to help' by marking out the ground available for cultivation and giving advice on the best plants to grow.

Fagan also has a very different subject to deal with today. The shortage of white mice is evidently widespread, and the Russian Embassy in London has written to ask where some may be obtained. Fagan tells them: 'We have made inquiry from every available source', but with no success. In fact, 'there is a very great difficulty in getting white mice in this country just now'. He suggests to the

Russians that they try the Pasteur Institute in Paris, and tells them that one Government department alone has need of 1,000.

MARCH 1917 Revolution convulses Russia. Food rioters and strikers occupy the streets. Tsar Nicholas II abdicates. Parliament – the Duma – elects a provisional government and many from the previous government are arrested. Newspapers report that all indications are that Russia will continue to fight the war. It is hoped, they write, that constitutional government there will have a future, but little is yet clear.

13 MARCH 1917 John Ramsbottom is instructed to report to Sir William Babtie of the Army Medical Service for service as a protozoologist in Salonika.

14 MARCH 1917 Dr Smith Woodward, Keeper of Geology, reports to the Trustees that the Museum's geological map of Belgium has been loaned to the Geological Survey, which is based in Jermyn Street near Piccadilly. A few weeks previously, a request was received from the Engineer-in-Chief of the Army in France for the loan of a 'spare-copy' of the map. It is believed that 'the Germans have seized the plates, preserved at Brussels, from which the map was printed'. The Museum's copy is in 'constant use' by staff and others, including the Belgian Headquarters' Staff Geologist and the War Office. It is also fragile, incomplete and needs careful handling. There is no spare copy.

It is suggested that the map held by the Geological Survey might be more easily spared, and it is sent to France. This map however, was also much in demand from the military and others in London. It is arranged for the Museum's map to be sent to the Survey, where it will be available for consultation. There are a few sheets missing from the Museum's set and the Geological Survey manages to replace two of these. The Survey is also, at the Director's request, arranging to have the map backed on to linen to strengthen it.

The Geology department's expertise is also called on by the War Office who have queries about the 'geology of the Italian Front', and by an officer of the Belgian Army who has geological questions about the Belgian Front. The department is also consulted on the structure of rocks in Cyprus in connection with the water supply.

16 MARCH 1917 A letter is received from the War Office regarding the Army Biscuit Inquiry, the investigation into 'moth-eaten' biscuits undertaken by Lt Col Wilfred Beveridge and Entomology assistant John Hartley Durrant, first published in 1913. Their report is still in demand and Dr Gahan has requested permission from the War Office to reprint it. There is no objection and Dr Gahan recommends that 250 copies are printed.

17 MARCH 1917 Charles Fagan sends a parcel of about 80 copies of the Museum's various guidebooks to the Chairman of the British Prisoners of War Book Scheme at the Board of Education. He is collecting books for British prisoners at the camp at Ruhleben near Berlin, where there are about 4,000 inmates. Fagan also sends a set of economic pamphlets to the British Mesopotamia Force, which requires them for a series of lectures being given to the men.

20 MARCH 1917 Charles Tate Regan, Zoology assistant and the Museum's fish expert, receives a letter from Rowland Edmund Prothero MP, the new and energetic President of the Board of Agriculture and Fisheries. With the current food shortage, newspapers have been asking why freshwater fish are not being utilised. *The Reading Observer* captures the mood with its headline on 3 March: 'Neglected Food'. In response to the public debate, Prothero is proposing to set up a small expert committee. He tells

Regan, 'It would be a matter of great satisfaction to me if you would do me the favour of serving on the Committee'. Its terms of reference are to consider whether any 'considerable' addition to home food supplies could be provided from the 'rivers, lakes and ponds' of Great Britain. The committee is to consider the practicalities of such a scheme, including labour and transport, the food values of different kinds of fish, and how acceptable they might be to the consumer. Some freshwater fish can, notoriously, be muddy in taste. They will also examine separately possible measures of securing a greater output of eels from UK waters for home consumption.

23 MARCH 1917 The Controller of His Majesty's Stationery Office writes to the Museum and all government departments to urge further economies in the use of paper. The aim is to cut imports of pulp 'to as nearly as possible' half the quantity imported in 1916. The letter warns that there is 'Evidence that larger sheets of paper and larger and thicker envelopes than necessary are still being used by many officials'. It requests that shelves and cupboards should be carefully examined for all obsolete books and papers that can be sold as waste or returned to the Stationery Office for pulping. This would both diminish imports and benefit the Exchequer because of the high prices waste paper now commands. The Museum has in store a considerable number of obsolete guidebooks, and the Director requests permission from the Trustees to send these too.

The letter also reveals the great difficulty the Government has in importing sufficient typewriters to meet the demands of the War Office and the Admiralty. The shortage 'is likely to prove a very serious matter', the letter states, and the Controller of HMSO asks to be informed whether it will be possible to return some of the machines in use at the Museum into stock for re-issue. The Museum, however, barely has sufficient typewriters for its own needs.

31 MARCH 1917 The whaling season in the South Atlantic is ending. Dr Harmer has heard nothing more about gold-beaters' skin.

2 APRIL 1917 President Woodrow Wilson addresses the United States Congress. He asks for a state of war to exist between the United States and Germany. 'Germany,' *The Times* reports him as saying, 'in her submarine ruthlessness is at war with mankind. It is a war against all nations'. America is also outraged by attempts to persuade Mexico to join the war in support of Germany.

3 APRIL 1917 Dr Francis Bather, Assistant Keeper of Geology, is an experienced allotment gardener in Wimbledon where he lives. He tells Dr Arthur Smith Woodward, Geology Keeper, that he has been asked by the chairman of the Wimbledon Home Produce Society, of which he is the Honorary Treasurer, to give further much needed help in organising the work of the Society, which 'has now over 1,000 cultivators and is rapidly growing'. In view of the 'urgent and grave appeal' to those able to help increase the production of food made by the Prime Minister, David Lloyd George, Dr Bather asks to be allowed to devote as much of his official time to this work as may be consistent with the 'bare necessities' of his work in the Geology Department. It is decided to allow him to work there two days a week, and to be prepared to return to the Museum as soon as Dr Smith Woodward requires him to.

6 APRIL 1917 The United States Congress votes by a huge majority on a joint resolution. At 1.13pm, the President signs the resolution. America is now at war with Germany and is mobilising by land and sea. The US War Department calls for one million men to enlist.

12 APRIL 1917 Charles Fagan writes to Dr Frederic Lucas, Director of the American Museum of Natural History in New York. He congratulates him on the entry of the United States into the war.

17 APRIL 1917 Charles Fagan writes to the Nobel Laureate and member of the Board of Invention and Research, Professor William Bragg. He tells him that Alfred Fieldsend, 'who is employed here as a Preparator and seems to have rather a bent for mechanical devices', claims to have 'an invention for meeting submarine attack by means of a torpedo shield'. Fieldsend would like to meet the Professor before sending his sketches to the Board. Fagan makes it clear that his letter is simply a guarantee that Fieldsend is employed at the Museum, nothing more. Two years earlier, Fagan was active – to no avail – in trying to help Fieldsend interest the military with a similar-sounding invention as well as an aircraft bomb-aiming device.

18 APRIL 1917 John Ramsbottom's departure for Salonika has serious consequences for the Botany department – at least as regards fungi. The Keeper, Dr Rendle, reports to the Trustees that during the war his department has dealt with many queries from government departments relating to fodder, fabrics and timber presumed to be infected with or damaged by fungi. With Ramsbottom absent, there is now no-one on the staff with 'highly expert knowledge' of the fungi.

To fill his position as mycologist will take someone of considerable ability. Dr Rendle tells the Trustees that there is one person in the department who is capable of taking on this vital economic work. She is Miss Annie Lorrain Smith who is 62-years-old and has worked as temporary scientific worker in the Department for many years. She is, according to Dr Rendle, 'one of the highest experts in matters dealing with Fungi and lichens', with an international

'Acting Temporary Assistant' Annie Lorrain Smith (1854–1937), an internationally renowned expert in fungi and lichens, worked for many years in the Botany department as an unofficial scientific worker. Her temporary promotion was due to the absence through war of all the male mycologists in the department.

reputation. Dr Rendle tells the Trustees that she has offered 'to carry on this work without additional remuneration, and only asks to be styled '"Temporary Assistant for Fungi"'. The arrangement, he says, will enable the department to continue without a break with work that is 'of supreme national importance' at a time when it is most needed. The increased cultivation of vegetables in gardens and allotments is expected to bring numerous enquiries demanding expert knowledge of fungi – the source of many plant diseases. Dr Rendle strongly recommends that Miss Lorrain Smith's offer be accepted, and it is. Her title is to be 'Acting Temporary Assistant'.

Women are not permitted to become members of the scientific staff until 1928, although by 1917 there are a few women, like Annie Lorrain Smith and the palaeontologist Dorothea Bate, who are unofficial – or temporary – scientific workers, paid piecework rather than a regular salary.

19 APRIL 1917 Dr Sidney Harmer, Keeper of Zoology, reports to the Trustees that he and William Plane Pycraft, an assistant in Zoology who is an expert on birds (and much else), attended a conference at the Home Office, together with civil servants from the Food Controller's office, on the subject of the proposed use of seagulls' eggs as food. The Government has decided that the existing restrictions on the collection of eggs of gulls and other sea-birds might be removed, provided that such collection ceases before the end of the breeding season. The Museum's role, the meeting agrees, is to supply information on the principal protected breeding places in the British Isles of birds whose eggs could be used as food. The Museum suggests 21 June as the end of the breeding season, to allow the birds to rear their later eggs.

The ornithologist William Ogilvie-Grant, who is in charge of the Museum's bird collection (although ill health has caused prolonged absence from work), tells Dr Harmer, 'I cannot see that the taking of eggs of certain species of Gulls for a year or two as food could possibly do any harm. In many places they are a great deal too numerous and do great harm to the young of the rarer and more interesting birds which breed in the vicinity'.

The number of eggs that might be collected under the scheme is estimated by William Pycraft as two million. It could be more, he suggests, but would depend on finding people prepared – or able – to collect eggs from dangerous cliffs. Experienced climbers, Pycraft points out, 'are probably now in the army'. He questions whether 'the cost of collecting will be justified by the results. In pre-war days,' he writes to the Food Controller's office, 'we annually imported 2,580,000,000 eggs of the domestic fowl, valued at £9,000,000'. He suggests that a use for gulls' eggs might be for manufactured egg-powder or custard, which might overcome possible consumer resistance to their unfamiliar taste.

The food crisis is now so grave the Prime Minister has warned that 'our food stocks are low – alarmingly low – lower than they have ever been within recollection'. It is now almost impossible to buy potatoes, and the price of alternatives, such as swedes or turnips, is rising steeply. Newspapers decry 'the crime of waste', and urge economy in the use of food.

20 APRIL 1917 The Museum hoists the Stars and Stripes, side by side with the Union Jack. This is 'America Day', so designated to commemorate the long-awaited entry of the United States into the war. The Stars and Stripes are flown on every public building. The flag has been lent to the Museum by the Office of Works.

24 APRIL 1917 Thomas Henry Withers, an attendant in Geology who has been temporarily lent to the Ministry of Munitions for the last two years, has been passed as fit for general military service abroad. The Ministry has secured a certificate of exemption for him, but they are of the opinion that as he is only on loan to them, the Museum should organise his exemption. Dr Smith Woodward, the Keeper, recommends to the Trustees that he should not be allowed to undertake ordinary military service. He considers it 'absolutely necessary for the safety of the collection', that Withers, with 'his intimate knowledge of the contents of many cabinets', is at the disposal of the Museum in case of emergency. Logic and bureaucracy, however, will not allow this. The Trustees decide that they 'cannot consider him as indispensable seeing that we have already lent him to the M[inistry] of M[unitions]. If he is indispensable to [them] they must say so'.

25 APRIL 1917 Dr Charles Gahan submits a proposal to the Trustees for the publication of two single-sheet leaflets of small poster size, one relating to the danger of disease from flies, especially houseflies, and the other to the danger from mosquitoes. Each leaflet, he suggests, will have one large illustration, and will give, in as few words as possible, 'an account of the breeding places, habits etc.' of the insects, and stating the most approved methods of combatting

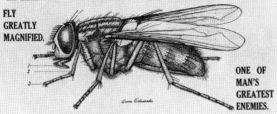

THE FLY DANGER.

FLY GREATLY MAGNIFIED.

ONE OF MAN'S GREATEST ENEMIES.

Grace Edwards

1. The trunk through which the fly sucks up filth, and vomits it back on our food.
2. Leg covered with bristly hairs to which filth and germs cling.
3. Pad on foot, which is capable of carrying thousands of disease germs.

The Fly Carries the Germs of Disease to any Uncovered Food, Liquid or Solid.

COVER ALL FOOD.

BREEDING PLACES.

Refuse, litter, manure heaps, fermenting food stuff, fresh and decaying carcases, rotting vegetation, &c. These should be buried 1½ feet deep in the ground, or burnt, or treated with light wood oil or (failing that) with light paraffin.

N.B.—This treatment does not destroy the value of manure.

Crevices in cookhouses, recreation rooms, pantries, latrines, &c.
Maggots cannot breed in dry refuse.

HOW TO KILL FLIES.

FLAPPERS OR WHISKS. Leather, wire-headed, horsehair, or palm leaves. Fly Killing Competitions are useful and should be encouraged.

FLY PAPERS, TAPES, OR WIRES. BAITED WIRES, prepared with a mixture in the following proportions: Castor Oil, 4 liquid ozs., Crushed Resin, 9½ ozs.; or, Linseed Oil, 4 liquid ozs., Crushed Resin, 7½ ozs.

Heat oil, and then stir in resin. Paint the mixture on wires, about a yard in length : leave a hand-hold at one end unpainted, hook the other, and hang vertically from the hooked top. When covered with flies pass the wire through a flame to clear it of the used mixture and dead flies : heat fresh mixture and paint the wire as before.

SUNLIGHT TRAP. Close all windows and doors, and darken all windows except one, freely dusting the one light window with Keating's Powder.

FLY-TRAPS. (1)—"BALLOON" WIRE GAUZE FLY TRAP.
Baits : Syrup, Jam, Treacle, or Ground Sugar, with a little Rum added.
(2)—IMPROVED FORMALIN TRAP consisting of a narrow necked glass bottle fitted with a cap of blotting paper and two strips of the same material immersed in the liquid (see illustration).
Bait : To half a pint of Lime-water add a table-spoonful of Formalin and a dessert-spoonful of Sugar, make up to a pint by adding Water.
(3)—JAPANESE CLOCKWORK FLY-TRAPS are recommended, but there may be a difficulty in obtaining them in this country.

PREVENTIVE MEASURES.

Food, cooked or uncooked, liquid or solid, should be kept always covered.

FOOD COVERS of muslin or mosquito netting edged with beading. NETS.—Wide mesh netting (tennis or fishing) over doors and windows. REED and SPLIT BAMBOO SCREENS or CHICKS, GAUZE SCREENS, wire and mosquito net, over doors and windows. HEAD VEILS of mosquito netting.

ANTI-FLY PREPARATIONS.

EUCARCIT, a deterrent for Flies, Mosquitoes, and Sandflies. Eucalyptus Oil, 2 ozs.; Liquid Carbolic Acid, 4 drops ; Citronella Oil, 2 ozs.

Mix these together and shake thoroughly before use. The bottle should be fitted with a sprinkler top. A few drops at a time should be used on hands and face and neck.

PREPARATION recommended by PROF. HOWLETT, especially for Mosquitoes and Sandflies. Oil of Cassia, 1 oz.; Brown Oil of Camphor, 2 ozs.; Vaseline, Lanoline, or Salad Oil, 3 ozs.
Mix well and smear on the skin in small quantities.

ISSUED BY THE BRITISH MUSEUM (NATURAL HISTORY), SOUTH KENSINGTON, LONDON, S.W. 7.   PRICE ONE HALFPENNY.

This poster warning of the danger from flies was enormously popular. It advised the military and the general public on the importance of hygiene, remedies and preventative measures.

THE
MOSQUITO DANGER.

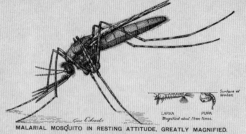

LARVA | PUPA
Magnified about three times.

MALARIAL MOSQUITO IN RESTING ATTITUDE, GREATLY MAGNIFIED.

DANGER: Mosquitoes suck Malarial Fever from a sick man and give it to a sound man when they bite him.

DON'T LET THEM BITE YOU.

BREEDING PLACES.

Water, especially stagnant water, ponds, marshes, pools, puddles, water pockets in hoofmarks and empty tins, bottles, old cans, cut bamboo stumps, &c., cisterns, water butts, slowly running streams.
ONE SMALL BREEDING PLACE WILL INFECT A WHOLE CAMP.

TREATMENT OF BREEDING PLACES.

Drain or fill up all small pools and puddles. Bury empty tins, bottles, cans, &c. Crude mineral oil or Kerosene sprayed on water kills the little wriggling Mosquito Larvae.

HIDING PLACES OF MOSQUITOES.

Shady corners, darkened rooms, or tents, hanging clothes, cupboards, under beds, tables, &c.

PREVENTION.

ROOMS and TENTS. A teaspoonful of Keating's Powder, slowly burnt in a moderate-sized room or tent, will generally drive out Mosquitoes and Sandflies. A teaspoonful of Cresol, heated till it vapourises, has the same effect. A well-lighted window or door should be left for the insects to escape, and shut half an hour later. MOSQUITO CURTAINS or HEAD VEILS. These, or Mosquito ointments, should be used at night by everyone who wishes to escape malaria. The edges of the curtains should be carefully tucked under the mattress so that there is no opening for the insects to enter. All holes should be mended at once. See that no Mosquitoes have got in before going to sleep. WIRE and GAUZE SCREENS. Wherever possible, recreation rooms, mess rooms, cookhouses, pantries, &c., should be fitted with gauze screens to both windows and doors.

ANTI-MOSQUITO and SANDFLY PREPARATIONS.

(1) "EUCARCIT." A deterrent for Flies, Mosquitoes, and Sandflies. Eucalyptus Oil, 2 ozs.; Liquid Carbolic Acid, 4 drops; Citronella Oil, 2 ozs. Mix intimately and put in a bottle with a sprinkler screw top. SHAKE BEFORE USE. A few drops should be used on the hands, face, and neck before going to bed. The ingredients should be stated when ordering.

(2) PREPARATION recommended by PROF. HOWLETT. Oil of Cassia, 1 oz.; Brown Oil of Camphor, 2 ozs.; Vaseline, Lanoline, or Salad Oil, 3 ozs. Mix well and smear on the skin in small quantities before nightfall.

(3) "PARAQUIT" (in tubes),

(4) "AMERIND" (in tubes), and

(5) "PARASITOX" (in sticks), are all good Mosquito ointments, generally obtainable from chemists.

(6) Oil of Peppermint, 1 oz.; Vaseline, Spirit, or Pond's Extract, 2 ozs.; Oil of Cassia, 1 oz.

Scratching the bites of Mosquitoes and Sandflies may lead to sores.
DON'T SCRATCH, BUT PUT ON A GREASE OR LOTION INSTEAD.

ISSUED BY THE BRITISH MUSEUM (NATURAL HISTORY), SOUTH KENSINGTON, LONDON, S.W. 7.   PRICE ONE HALFPENNY.

Another poster, warning of the dangers of mosquitoes.

the danger. Dr Gahan believes the proposed leaflets will be of great service if distributed in the British camps in Mesopotamia, Egypt and other war areas abroad, and will also be of considerable use and have a ready sale at home.

Dr Gahan tells the Trustees that the Dowager Lady Carnarvon, 'is greatly interested in the matter', as is Sir Alfred Keogh, Director-General of the Army Medical Service. In a letter to Lady Carnarvon, made available to Gahan, Keogh writes that 'the widest publicity' should be given to 'the measures which should be adopted for the fly and mosquito danger'. He urges Lady Carnarvon: 'Anything that you can do for the purpose of spreading information on subjects pertaining to the modes in which disease is spread is for the public good'. Lady Carnarvon, Gahan tells the Trustees, 'would be prepared to purchase a considerable number of copies of the leaflets for distribution among the troops in Mesopotamia'. He therefore recommends that 20,000 copies should be printed. The Trustees give their approval.

The health, care and recuperation of the military is of great concern both to the Dowager Lady Carnarvon and to her daughter-in-law, who in 1914, turned her home, Highclere Castle in Berkshire, into a hospital for wounded soldiers. In 1916, she took a lease on a large house in central London and moved the hospital to it. Zoology assistant Captain Arthur Totton is among the wounded who are recuperating there. Sir Alfred Keogh is one of those behind the creation of these auxiliary military hospitals, of which there are hundreds throughout the UK.

The posters, as Dr Gahan has recognised, are also badly needed at home. There is concern throughout the country over hygiene standards and how to improve them. On 2 April, the *Sheffield Daily Telegraph* fears that the 'fly peril' will be 'greater than ever' in the coming summer unless there is 'immediate and continued co-operation between the sanitary authorities and the general public'.

Education, the reporter feels, is the key. He suggests all children in the city should be given illustrated lectures in 'one of the Picture Houses' on the dangers of flies and how to combat them. 'If 80,000 young people', he writes', could be made to realise the danger there is in a fly, the city would be saved many lives and much money. There would be a young soldier in nearly every home with new ideas about dirt and disease'.

The scale of the problem the Museum is trying to help alleviate is national and critical.

28 APRIL 1917 A week earlier, five German destroyers attempt a raid on Dover. There is a fight and at least two are sunk by two British ships. Ten German officers and 108 men are rescued. Some of them are now prisoners at the Cromwell Road Barracks. The Trustees at their meeting today are informed that the General Officer Commanding the London District has asked permission for the Germans to take exercise in the Museum grounds. Provisional permission is granted.

Chapter 9
May–August 1917

The summer of 1917 is marked by more
air raids over London. The Natural History
Museum's basement becomes a public shelter in
the event of attack. Scientific assistants petition
for improved pay and prospects, while attendants
petition for a change of name more fitting to their
role. The open season for edible migratory birds
is extended and 'King Baby' rules. Seagulls are
considered for anti-submarine warfare and Museum
zoologist Charles Tate Regan continues his fight
for exemption from military service. Following the
success of the Museum's best-selling poster on
the house-fly danger, lice and bed-bugs
are next to be targeted.

2 MAY 1917 Charles Fagan writes to Major Crum, Instructor in Sniping at Aldershot, who has said that he is satisfied with the lantern slides illustrating protective coloration and should like to take them to France. Fagan informs him that the Museum had in fact considered preparing one or more sets for that purpose. He suggests having another set made for the Aldershot Sniping School, and that he 'will see what the artist says to your suggestion to take coloured photographs of men disguised in their natural surroundings. The idea seems to me to be a very good one'.

3 MAY 1917 The Propaganda Department in Wellington House (since February part of the new Department of Information under the control of the novelist John Buchan) asks for the Museum's help in connection with a picture representing 'The Freedom of the Seas'. It is one of a series the Department is commissioning, 'The Great

The Government's Propaganda Department asked the Museum's assistance in sourcing an image or specimen to represent a sea monster for the artist Frank Brangwyn's picture, 'The Freedom of the Seas'.

War: Britain's Efforts and Ideals'. It is to be painted by the famous artist Frank Brangwyn, who has produced a stream of striking and powerful propaganda posters since the beginning of the war – many displayed on the London Underground. Today Charles Fagan writes to Brangwyn, suggesting that 'we may be able to place before you something either in the way of pictures or specimens that may answer your purpose'. A few days later an official from Wellington House, Mr T Derrick, meets Fagan and Dr Harmer at the Museum. They arrange a loan for the artist of a picture of an octopus or squid. Brangwyn subsequently creates an allegorical lithograph of a group of desperate-looking men in a small boat, valiantly beating off an attack by a huge, menacing sea monster, reminiscent of the fantastical giant squid or octopus of legend.

4 MAY 1917 The Museum attendants send a petition to the Director, Sir Lazarus Fletcher, asking him to place it before the Trustees. They wish their title changed to 'some other name' more suited 'to their status and the character of the work they now perform'. They believe 'attendant' to be detrimental socially and 'has seriously handicapped' attendants attempting to obtain other employment. They believe the Treasury has 'a wrong impression' of their duties and abilities and are thus prejudiced against their claims for increases in salary. They also think the name 'adversely affects' their children when they apply for situations 'in which official designation and social standing of parents are taken into consideration'. As an example of how the title is misunderstood, the attendants quote the experiences of colleagues who are also working at the War office. 'When it became known that the Museum men were "Attendants", they write, 'they were laughed at and asked whether they had charge of the Lavatories'. They suggest a number of alternative titles, including British Museum Clerks (1st and 2nd class) and British Museum Assistants (3rd and 4th class).

14 MAY 1917 The Treasury sends a circular letter to all government departments marked 'Urgent'. It states that the War Cabinet has decided that a further 2,000 men should be released from the civil service for military service. Newspapers report that 500,000 more men are needed for the army by July. The Trustees are asked to determine 'the quota' to be released by the Museum, and to send the Treasury a list showing the number of men of military age still employed, classified either 'A' – fit for active service overseas – or 'Bi' – able to march five miles, see to shoot wearing glasses, and hear well. There are no men in class A, and just one who is class Bi. He is Frank Oswell Barlow, aged 36, a preparator in Geology who the Museum has been fighting to keep from military service because of the importance of his work. The Treasury also asks for the number of men released for military service since 1 April 1916, and is told 13 men have gone.

15 MAY 1917 Charles Fagan has asked Dr Knud Andersen, the Danish temporary scientific worker who is spending part of his time working in Military Intelligence, for help in identifying Danish scientists to whom it might be beneficial to send propaganda. Andersen is more than happy to do so and agrees to act as the Museum's agent in distributing propaganda literature in Denmark.

19 MAY 1917 The Treasury sends a second 'Urgent' circular letter, directing that any civil servants in London who have not been medically examined since 25 May 1916, should be examined forthwith and providing for their examination by a special medical board. At the Museum, three men are re-examined. Charles Tate Regan is a 39-year-old first class assistant in Zoology whose expertise is fish. He has just been elected a fellow of the Royal Society. In 1927 he will become Museum Director. He is assessed as class A – fit for general military service. Two years earlier a medical examination rejected him as unfit. Botany assistant Herbert Fuller Wernham, also in his late 30s, is classed Ciii – fit only for sedentary work. A year ago he was invalided out of the army through ill health. Lastly there is Frank Barlow, who again is classed Bi.

26 MAY 1917 The Trustees receive a letter from the Local Government Board stating that they think it desirable to direct the attention of sanitary authorities to the fly-danger poster and enquiring whether about 4,000 copies could be placed at their disposal. The National Council of Young Men's Christian Associations asks for 1,000 copies of the posters for use abroad.

Sir Alfred Keogh, Director General of the Army Medical Service, welcomes the efforts the Museum is making. 'The Natural History Museum is no doubt the very best agency the country possesses for disseminating a knowledge of the relation between flies, mosquitoes etc, and disease', he writes.

Within a month of its appearance, the Trustees are told that the fly poster has been widely circulated and is in great demand. More than 20 medical officers of health and sanitary surveyors have requested supplies of the poster. The first edition of 20,000 copies has been exhausted, and a second 20,000 is being printed. Its striking and simple design is dominated by a much magnified fly, drawn by Grace Edwards, a skilled scientific artist employed on an unofficial basis by the Entomology Department to prepare illustrations and models of specimens.

The poster's list of recommended methods of fly killing includes the use of flappers or whisks – of leather, wire, horsehair or palm leaves – and notes that 'Fly Killing Competitions are useful and should be encouraged'. It also suggests using baited wires, and various forms of flytraps – gauze, formalin or Japanese clockwork fly traps, although with these last, the poster text observes, 'there may be difficulty in obtaining them in this country'.

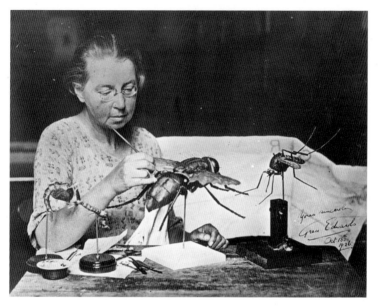

The entomology illustrator and model-maker, Grace Edwards, whose skills during the war were of considerable importance. This photograph is from 1926.

4 JUNE 1917 Charles Fagan writes to the Recruiting Officer, Hounslow, challenging the findings of the medical examination which placed Charles Tate Regan in Class A. He tells him that Regan was rejected in 1915 on medical grounds by the Inns of Court Officers Training Corps, but 'the authorities at Hounslow' did not give him an exemption form. Regan suffered from acute nephritis – a kidney complaint – in 1901 and again in 1906, Fagan writes, when he was on sick leave for six weeks. He has only been able to keep it in check by a careful diet and his own doctor has told him that the nephritis is extremely likely to recur if he is subjected to exposure. Under these circumstances the Museum 'would like him to be medically re-examined'.

13 JUNE 1917 The Keeper of Zoology, Dr Sidney Harmer, also tries to secure Regan's exemption. He reports to the Trustees his own grave doubts as to whether the 39-year-old Regan is physically fit for military service, despite his 'A' classification. He strongly recommends that an application be made to the National Service Department for his exemption on the ground (i) of his constitutional weakness, (ii) the desirability of retaining his services in the Museum, and (iii) that he can do more important national work by carrying out his duties at the Museum and acting as adviser on fishery questions. He has this year been elected a fellow of the Royal Society and is 'an energetic and valuable member' of Harmer's staff. It is decided however that there should be no mention of 'constitutional unfitness' in any action taken.

At midday on 13 June, German aircraft drop explosive and incendiary bombs on London, killing 157 people, including 42 children and injuring more than 400. No air-raid warning is given. Debate rages in the press and in Parliament over whether there should be such warnings, as the occasions when 'air-raids were threatened or impending,' Parliament is told, 'were many times more frequent than when raids actually occurred'. There were concerns that a whole day's work for thousands of people could be lost unnecessarily, potentially affecting the manufacture of munitions and 'therefore our fighting forces'.

15 JUNE 1917 Ernest James Manly, a 26-year-old preparator in Zoology, commences military service in the Royal Flying Corps. In 1915 he enrolled as a seaman in the Royal Naval Division, but was released on health grounds, suffering from 'organic heart disease'. In December 1915 he attested for the Army, but five months later he was medically rejected. However he has now been re-examined and is categorised as class Bii. That means he can walk five miles and see and hear sufficiently well for ordinary purposes. Too unfit for active service, his duties are those of a general clerk.

18 JUNE 1917 The Museum receives a letter from the Office of Works, enclosing a copy of regulations regarding precautions to be taken by government departments in the event of a warning of enemy air raids. It is left to the Director 'to take such precautions as might be desirable and suited to the Museum'.

19 JUNE 1917 Bruce Frederick Cummings, an assistant in Entomology, submits his resignation to the Keeper, Dr Charles Gahan. He has been on sick leave since 6 March and his doctor reports he is unlikely ever to be able to resume his duties in the Museum. He is so ill, the letter has had to be written by his brother. Cummings, an essayist and diarist of extraordinary perception, as well as being a gifted scientist, suffers from 'disseminated sclerosis' – probably multiple sclerosis. Despite this, he has been an invaluable member of staff and his loss will be felt acutely in the much-depleted department. His resignation is accepted 'with great regret' by the Trustees. It is to take effect on 20 July and it is recommended to the Treasury that he should receive a gratuity. With the help of his wife, his diary, *The Journal of a Disappointed Man*, is published in 1919 under the pseudonym WNP Barbellion. It is a searing, exquisitely written portrait of his life and receives high critical acclaim.

A representative of the Museum is sent to the storekeeper of the Office of Works to deliver a letter from the Director's office: 'Please supply the Bearer with one Hand-Bell for use at this Museum in case of Air-raids'. This is in accordance with instructions from Sir Lionel Earle, Permanent Secretary of the Office of Works, received the day before. Earle has also authorised further articles 'in regard to Air raid emergencies'. These include six stretchers with sliding handles and undercarriage, and six sets of appliances for the stretchers, including splints, bandages and tourniquets.

The Director, Sir Lazarus Fletcher, sends a memo to the Treasury, regarding the work of Annie Lorrain Smith, the fungi expert and temporary scientific worker, who is temporarily replacing John Ramsbottom during his absence in Salonika. He writes that the Trustees wish to give her extra remuneration for the additional work she has undertaken, and ask the Treasury to sanction it.

There are now, for the first time, three women working in the Museum who are directly replacing male staff who are in the military. The other two are the shorthand-writer-typists, fulfilling the clerical duties of absent attendants. Their pay is less than that of the men they have replaced, and that extends to Miss Lorrain Smith, even though she is 'one of our highest authorities on fungi', according to the Director. 'It may be noted that the arrangement proposed is a very economical one', he writes to the Treasury, 'as had Miss Smith's services not been available, either the Trustees would not have seen their way to lend Mr Ramsbottom to the War Office, or they would have had to engage some other expert (if indeed this had been possible) at a high salary to deal with a branch of the work of the Museum that could not be neglected without detriment to the public welfare'.

The Museum has asked the Treasury to sanction extra payment of £50 for Miss Lorrain Smith. It will be paid at a rate of £4 a month. In addition, for this year, she will also earn £50 for authorship of the *Monograph of British Lichens* and £100 for preparation of specimens. The total of £200 is roughly what a young 2nd class assistant in his 20s would receive after about three years' service. Annie Lorrain Smith is 62.

20 JUNE 1917 Dr Gahan reports to the Trustees that he has engaged the services of Hugh Scott, the 32-year-old Entomology curator at

Cambridge University. His work will be to collect information in the British Isles on the *Anopheles* mosquito – the species which can transmit malaria – and to map its areas of distribution. Gahan has had to turn to outside help as there is not one assistant left in the department with any 'special knowledge' of the Diptera – the order which includes mosquitoes. Sir David Bruce, the Surgeon General and Commandant of the Royal Army Medical College, had asked for assistance with this work in January, and Gahan had suggested he ask the renowned amateur entomologist James Collin. Collin, however, was unavailable.

Hugh Scott is currently employed in the War Office's Hygiene Department, but he is given permission to work up to six hours a week in the Museum, for which he is to be paid three shillings and sixpence (17.5p) an hour, up to a maximum of £50 a year. Annie Lorrain Smith is paid two shillings and sixpence (12½ p) per hour, up to the same annual maximum.

21 JUNE 1917 In a report to the Trustees, Dr Arthur Smith Woodward, Keeper of Geology, praises Thomas Henry Withers, an attendant in his department who was lent to the Ministry of Munitions earlier in the war but who is to be released for military duty on 1 August. In April Smith Woodward argued fiercely that he should be exempt from military service, but to no avail. Withers joined the Museum as a 15-year-old boy attendant in 1898 and through his ability, enthusiasm and eagerness to learn, Smith Woodward writes, has become 'the chief British authority' on fossil cirripedes – barnacles. His work has also been outstanding at the Ministry of Munitions, and the Minister, Dr Christopher Addison MP, now writes to the Trustees to point out that, because of the high quality of all Mr Withers' work, the Treasury has granted him the acting rank of Departmental Clerk at a commencing salary of £150. By leaving for military service Withers will suffer an appreciable financial loss, as he will, 'in the ordinary course of things', revert to his position as an attendant in the Museum where his salary was just £116. Like Dr Addison, Dr Smith Woodward wants to protect Withers' position. He strongly recommends that application be made to the Treasury to make Withers' promotion permanent and the Trustees agree. The Treasury, however, does not. Their reply, six weeks later, states 'they are unable to agree' to Withers retaining his rank while on military service.

25 JUNE 1917 Miss Winifred Thomson, who regularly brings parties of wounded soldiers to the Museum from King George's Military Hospital near Waterloo, is now active in the national campaign to prevent the spread of epidemics by insects. Charles Fagan sends her copies of the fly and mosquito danger posters. He tells her that he has 'no hesitation in saying that it is of the utmost importance for the welfare of the community to disseminate a knowledge of the relation between flies and disease.'

26 JUNE 1917 At the direction of the Trustees, Charles Fagan writes to the Director General of National Service, Neville Chamberlain, regarding exemption for Charles Tate Regan. The application, he writes, is 'on the ground of the important national work on which he is engaged in the Museum' – both his curatorial work and 'especially as adviser on Fishery questions, many of them of national importance'. He states that Regan is serving on the Freshwater Fish Committee which is enquiring into freshwater fish 'as a possible source of increasing our food supply'. As instructed, he does not mention Regan's 'constitutional unfitness'.

28 JUNE 1917 Regan has received a notice calling him up for military service on 30 June. Charles Fagan today writes to the Recruiting Officer, Hounslow, to inform him that the Museum

Trustees have applied to the Department of National Service for his exemption.

2 JULY 1917 This is the start of National Baby Week. Its aim is to highlight the urgent need to improve the health of mother and baby and attempt to reverse the appalling infant mortality rate – estimated to be about 100,000 babies a year. What is needed, say the organisers, is cleaner and healthier homes with better sanitation, the prevention of disease, proper food, and better care for expectant and nursing mothers. More clinics are needed and more health visitors. According to the Bishop of London, 'while nine soldiers died every hour in 1915, 12 babies died every hour, so it was more dangerous to be a baby than a soldier'.

'King Baby' week, as the newspapers describe it, begins with an exhibition at Central Hall, Westminster, opened by Queen Mary. The centrepiece is a huge model housefly, with a wingspan of 15 feet. The Museum is lending a number of exhibits: the two new fly and mosquito posters, examples of flytraps, an illustration of a fly by the entomology artist Grace Edwards, and a supply of the housefly pamphlets. The Museum has also arranged for the loan of a model of the housefly, larva, pupa and eggs – duplicates of those exhibited in the Central Hall – together with an exhibition case. These models were made by the Board of Trade, which is loaning them on condition they 'are carefully looked after...and are insured during the Exhibition against all risks'. The sum they are to be insured for is the very sizeable amount of £100. A member of the Museum staff is dispatched to Central Hall, Westminster to install the exhibit.

4 JULY 1917 At the request of the Office of Works, the American flag and the Union Jack are again hoisted together at the Museum, to celebrate American Independence Day.

The Director General of National Service's office informs the Museum that they will hear Charles Tate Regan's case for exemption from military service. Charles Fagan writes today that Dr Harmer will appear before them to explain more fully Regan's official position and the work of national importance in which he is engaged.

He also writes to the Dowager Countess of Carnarvon, who has said how pleased she is with the fly danger poster. He tells her that he has just sent Mary, Countess of Wemyss, – the renowned society hostess – 2,000 copies each of the fly and mosquitoes posters. Lady Carnarvon asks for, and is sent, the same number.

7 JULY 1917 Twenty-one German aircraft bomb London on this beautiful summer Saturday morning. Fifty-four people are killed and 190 injured. Private air raid warnings are given, according to *The Times*, but no general warning. One 100lb bomb hits the Central Telegraph Office – part of the Post Office – in St Martin's Le Grand in the City, causing significant damage to the top two floors, though with no fatalities. It takes out the telegraph system for a short time, but the service is restored remarkably quickly.

A German Gotha biplane. On 7 July 1917, 21 of these huge aircraft bombed London on a beautiful summer's morning.

9 JULY 1917 Charles Fagan writes to the Secretary of the General Post Office, inquiring 'whether the Postmaster General is in a position to give the Trustees any information as to the immediate effects consequent on a public building being struck by an incendiary or explosive bomb'. The concern of course is 'to determine the best course of action in the event of this Museum being struck by a bomb from hostile aircraft', and how best to protect its collections. Fagan wonders if there would be any advantage for the Museum's Chief Fireman to make a personal inspection at the Central Telegraph Office of 'the destructive effects of a bomb'. His letter is marked 'Urgent' and receives an immediate reply, inviting the Chief Fireman to inspect the fire damage.

The following day, Fagan also asks the Chief Commissioner of Police at New Scotland Yard and the Chief Officer of the London Fire Brigade for their advice on precautionary measures in the event of an air raid.

10 JULY 1917 At noon Dr Harmer arrives at the Director General of National Service's office to give evidence in support of Charles Regan's application for exemption from military service. He appears before a departmental official, EA Sandford Fawcett, and a representative from the War Office. Neither man, Harmer subsequently reports to the Trustees, think that Regan's work 'has any immediate bearing on the main object, of winning the war', although both acknowledge his scientific distinction and value of work. Later in the afternoon the Museum receives a letter stating that the Director General has considered the statements made at the hearing and he has 'not seen his way' to agree to exempt Mr Regan for a period longer than one month from today. The Director of Recruiting, War Office, concurs.

11 JULY 1917 As a result of Charles Fagan's letter to the London Fire Brigade, a senior officer from the Brigade, Mr SG Gamble, inspects the Spirit Building and recommends a few small structural alterations for the safety of the occupants, including an emergency exit from the basement. In the main building, he advises on the best places for shelter during an air raid and recommends that the Central and North Halls – which have windows and skylights – should be kept clear of people in the event of an attack.

Fagan also informs the Keepers that the following first aid provisions have been made: a stretcher mounted on wheels and a 'Hand Stretcher', two first aid cabinets, and two sets of additional bandages and splints have been placed in the recess by the Museum front doors, near the Director's door; two hand stretchers, two first aid cabinets, and two sets of additional bandages and splints have been placed in the opposite recess, near Geology Keeper Dr Arthur Smith Woodward's door; a stretcher mounted on wheels and a hand stretcher, two first aid cabinets and two sets of additional bandages and splints have been placed by the back doors, near the general foreman's office.

12 JULY 1917 In a sign of the acute tension felt by all following the air raid on Saturday, Charles Fagan issues instructions on how key personnel should be alerted. This includes official telegrams being sent to summon off-duty firemen to the Museum, in case of fire or bomb explosion. The Messenger, Fagan instructs, 'will take care always to have a supply of Official Telegram Forms filled in ready to be despatched immediately'. Within a few days, it is decided to have a further supply of telegrams filled in ready for despatch to the Director and Keepers, in the event the Museum is struck by a bomb at a time when it is not open to the public.

13 JULY 1917 Fagan writes to the War Office to call the attention of the Army Council to the case of Charles Regan. He describes in detail the national importance of Regan's duties and writes that

FIRST AID APPLIANCES.   HOSTILE AIR RAIDS.

A Stretcher mounted on wheels and a Hand Stretcher , two First
Aid Cabinets , and two sets of additional bandages & splints have
been placed in the recess by the Museum Front Doors, near the Director's
door.

Two Hand Stretchers , two First Aid Cabinets , and two sets of
additional bandages & splints , have been placed in the opposite recess
near Dr. Smith Woodward's door.

A Stretcher mounted on wheels and a Hand Stretcher , two First
Aid Cabinets , and two sets of additional bandages & splints have been
placed by the Back Doors , near the General Foreman's Office.

As air raids increased, the Museum had to take preventative measures.
Charles Fagan sent this memo to Dr Harmer and the other Keepers
advising them where first aid appliances had been placed.

'there are very strong reasons for maintaining that Mr Regan is
of greater use to the country as an expert on a subject of which
he is master... than he would be if taken for military service'. The
Trustees, he ends, 'urge' the Council to grant Regan exemption.

14 JULY 1917 The Trustees agree a change of official designation
for the Museum attendants. This is after extensive discussions,
including a meeting of the Director and all the Keepers. Chief
attendants are now to be titled Museum Clerk (first grade).
Attendants are to be 'Attendants (Museum Clerks)'. Their work
remains exactly as it was, but the Trustees recognise that because of
their previous title, attendants 'suffered socially and materially from
a designation which in the public mind denotes a status lower than
that which they actually held'.

16 JULY 1917 There is a meeting of members of staff and
unofficial scientific workers holding first aid certificates. There
are 24 of them – 12 assistants, three attendants, six policemen and

three female employees. They elect three leaders, and organize themselves into teams for the various floors in the Museum. Those who are members of the London Ambulance Column are expected to stay in the Museum unless called out for ambulance duty. In that case, the teams affected will amalgamate to form one central squad. All are urged to renew their knowledge of pressure-points and tourniquet as 'casualties are most likely to be cases of hemorrhage[sic]'.

They are also told that 'Powder scattered from bombs should be washed off with water, if possible rendered alkaline with bicarbonate of soda'. Dr Harmer warns that it is 'most important' to emphasise that 'no one should touch the fragments or contents of any bomb which might fall in the Museum. I have some reason to suppose', he writes to the Director, 'that the yellow powder used by the Germans for filling some of their bombs is dangerously poisonous or injurious'. He does not elaborate. In Parliament, a few days previously, Winston Churchill – just before being appointed Minister of Munitions – tells the House of Commons that he has heard it said that some of the German bombs were filled with shrapnel, which showed that the Germans' main object was the infliction of casualties on civilians.

17 JULY 1917 Still fighting for continued exemption from military service, Charles Tate Regan fills in the Military Service Tribunal application form for exemption. This time he gives his 'constitutional fitness' – his health – as the reason for his appeal: 'I am not fit for general service (the category in which I have been placed), and will produce on the hearing medical evidence in support'. The hearing will take place in August.

19 JULY 1917 The quest continues for an effective air raid warning. The Home Secretary announces that tests will take place in London at 4.30pm of 'sky signals which will combine coloured smoke clouds with a loud report in the air'. The problem, as *The Times* reports, is not to harm public morale by what turn out to be false warnings, while still ensuring there is sufficient time for shelter to be found.

Dr Harmer reports to the Trustees that the unofficial scientific worker, Martin Alister Campbell Hinton, would be available for 'much needed' work in the Osteological Room, if funds could be provided. The sum suggested is an annual maximum of £50 at two shillings and sixpence per hour (the same rate as Annie Lorrain Smith). Harmer wishes him to compile a card catalogue of all the cetacean specimens in the collection. When the Museum receives a telegram from a coastguard reporting the stranding of a whale, it is important to be able 'to ascertain at once', what material of the species the Museum already holds. Hinton has already written a report on the cetacea, and Harmer writes that he could do this and any other osteological work required 'very reliably'. Hinton, who is 34, has been a voluntary worker at the Museum since 1910, although he was a regular visitor for some years before that. He has been rejected on medical grounds from military service. In 1936 he will become Keeper of Zoology.

20 JULY 1917 Still battling to keep Charles Tate Regan from military service, Dr Harmer writes to an old friend at the Royal Society, the marine zoologist Professor William Herdman. Regan was elected a fellow of the Royal Society earlier in the year. Harmer details his qualities and expertise, and mentions the acute nephritis, the kidney complaint that Regan suffered from in the past, and that his health 'is very likely to break down under the strain of life in camp'. Harmer asks Herdman if there is anything the Royal Society can do – although he is aware that there is a rule that any exemption by the Royal Society is 'limited strictly' to chemists.

Herdman's reply is prompt, but he cannot hold out any hope of the Royal Society intervening. However, he tells Harmer that he thinks 'the military authorities refused absolutely those with any trace of nephritis', and suggests that on medical grounds, Regan should be classed as Ciii or rejected. Both men are doing what they can for Regan's exemption from military service. Harmer's son Russell is serving with the Royal Engineers in France. Professor Herdman's 20 year-old son George was killed on 1 July 1916, the first day of the Battle of the Somme.

23 JULY 1917 Still persisting, Dr Harmer now writes to the President of the Royal Society, the physicist Professor Sir Joseph John Thomson, appealing for his assistance for Regan. He also arranges an interview for him with Sir Richard Paget of the Board of Invention and Research. After seeing Regan, Paget tells Dr Harmer there is no work at the Board 'at all comparable in importance with the work that Mr Regan could do in connection with fisheries question', and suggests he should refer to the Board of Agriculture. This Regan does, and tells Harmer that the Board will 'make a noise in the National Service Department'.

The Times reports that the test of the 'sound bombs' is successful and it is announced that fire brigade stations and certain police stations in and around London will henceforth each fire three sound bombs (later reduced to two) at intervals of 15 seconds when an air raid is believed to be imminent in daytime. It is believed that these signals will be heard all over London. Given the 'speed at which aeroplanes now travel', the warning can only be of a few minutes. 'The public should therefore take cover immediately'.

24 JULY 1917 After the great success of the Museum's best-selling posters on the danger of house-flies and mosquitoes, Dr Gahan, Entomology Keeper, proposes the preparation of two large black and white drawings suitable for reproduction, 'one of the Louse and the other of the Bed-bug...with a view to the publication later on of illustrated posters on these pests similar to those on the Fly and the Mosquito'.

25 JULY 1917 Dr Harmer recommends to the Trustees the employment of Frederick William Frohawk on economic work for zoology. He is a well-known naturalist and artist with wide experience of economic zoology. He has worked for the Board of Agriculture and Fisheries. He is needed immediately in the preparation of an exhibition of birds beneficial to agriculture. This is particularly appropriate, Harmer writes, in view of the need to increase the country's food supply. Frohawk is to write and illustrate an accompanying guidebook.

26 JULY 1917 The Museum issues its own regulations for staff in event of 'a probable *impending* air raid'. If there is official notification of an immediate attack, the hand-bell will be rung by the Messenger and the staff should take shelter near their department and be prepared to give any assistance that may be required. The galleries are to be cleared and the public 'recommended' to seek shelter in certain designated places, away from windows. Staff with first aid training should go to preselected points where first aid kit is stored.

Dr Harmer reports to the Trustees that he has been asked for his opinion on rescinding the order which in certain counties prolongs the close season for shooting edible migratory birds. In some cases it has been extended by a month from the statutory end of 31 July to the end of August. It is at the request of the Board of Agriculture and Fisheries acting under the Defence of the Realm Act in an attempt to increase the food supply of the country. A meeting has just taken place at the Museum between Harmer, Charles Fagan, Lord Rothschild – the zoologist and Museum Trustee – and an official from the Home Office. The matter is urgent and the Government wishes to issue the order tomorrow. While normally there would be objections to the plan, this time there are none as it is 'an emergency measure limited to a single year'. The birds affected are on a list drawn up by the Wildfowlers' Association and include the curlew, golden plover, brent goose, woodcock and widgeon, but not the green plover.

A boy attendant in Geology, Frederick John Bean is keen to enlist, but he is still just 17. His 18th birthday is in October. He is learning 'motor mechanics and driving', and is anxious to join the Royal Naval Air Service. Charles Fagan writes today with his details to the Officer Commanding, Royal Naval Air Service at Somerset House in London, and sends Bean to see him. He is 'a very intelligent lad', Fagan concludes, 'and very quick and observant'.

28 JULY 1917 The Museum's scientific assistants petition the Trustees for a review of their salary and promotion prospects. They recall the Treasury promise of an enquiry after the war, and submit 'that few people imagined that the war would have endured for so long as it has, and that at the present time the end is not in sight'. They attach a detailed statement showing 'how unfavourably' their positions and prospects compare with those of corresponding

Golden Plover (*Charadrius pluvialis*), male.

This golden plover is from *Birds Beneficial to Agriculture* by the naturalist and artist Frederick William Frohawk. He was asked to prepare an exhibition on the subject for the Museum, as well as this guidebook.

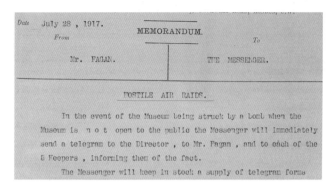

The threat of hostile air raids was so great that Charles Fagan instructed
that telegrams must be sent immediately to the Director and senior
staff if the Museum was struck by a bomb when it was not open.

classes at the Victoria and Albert Museum, and suggest that the
proposed committee of enquiry should be appointed without delay.
That however, will not happen. The Trustees defer consideration of
the petition until it can be taken up in connection with the position
of assistants at the British Museum in Bloomsbury.

The *Labour Gazette* reports official statistics for July showing
that on average there has been an increase of 104 percent in retail
food prices compared with July 1914, the month before the war
began, while taxes and all costs have risen dramatically. The prices
charged by the Museum's printers illustrate the problem. They
have, in some cases, almost doubled through 'the great increase
in costs of all material, rises in wages and War bonuses', they
tell the Assistant Secretary Charles Fagan. 'When War bonuses
cease, or wages drop, we shall be only too happy to revert to lower
charges again'.

31 JULY 1917 At 3.50am the British and French armies launch a
massive attack. This is the start of the Third Battle of Ypres. It is
also known as Passchendaele. In the afternoon it begins to rain and
the battlefield becomes liquid mud. In August it rains nearly every
day. The battle lasts for 103 days and the Allies advance five miles.

There are 320,000 Allied casualties. German losses are estimated at between 250,000 and 400,000.

11 AUGUST 1917 Charles Fagan has received a letter from Dr Frederic Lucas, Director of the American Museum of Natural History in New York, suggesting the possibility of using seagulls to indicate the presence of enemy submarines. Today Fagan replies, telling Lucas that 'I believe something has been done on this side… but I am not sure that any very thorough or systematic inquiry has been made'. He promises to take the matter up and let him know the result as soon as possible.

12 AUGUST 1917 At 6.10pm the Museum receives an air-raid warning. The upper galleries are cleared and the visitors – about 150 of them – take shelter in the basement. 20 enemy aeroplanes attack the east coast of England but they do not reach London.

22 AUGUST 1917 Charles Tate Regan is medically re-examined by the Hounslow Medical Board. He is passed as Bi.

Zoology assistant Charles Tate Regan (1878–1943). In 1921 he became Zoology Keeper and in 1927 he was appointed Museum Director.

23 AUGUST 1917 Charles Fagan writes to the newly appointed Permanent Secretary of the Admiralty, Sir Oswyn Alexander Ruthven Murray, with regard to the possible use of seagulls to indicate the presence of submarines. He encloses a copy of Dr Lucas's letter. He tells Sir Oswyn that the Museum would be very glad to help in any way, and that he has mentioned it to 'one or two of our expert ornithologists', who are inclined to think 'that there is something in the idea from the natural history point of view'.

28 AUGUST 1917 Dr Harmer writes to the Museum Trustee, the geologist Sir Archibald Geikie, who has expressed interest in Regan possibly getting exemption from military service. He asks whether he could give any assistance either by influencing the Director General of National Service personally, or by writing a letter which could be produced at the Tribunal. Harmer has just heard, he tells Geikie, that the case will rest on Regan's general scientific distinction and his work in connection with fisheries and that it will be heard in three days' time.

31 AUGUST 1917 Charles Tate Regan attends the tribunal considering his case. The verdict – at last – is to grant him exemption, 'conditional on continuing to be a member of the Freshwater Fish Committee appointed by the President of the Board of Agriculture and Fisheries' which Regan was asked to join in March. It is also 'in view of the change in his medical category'. Regan warns Dr Harmer that 'the Military may appeal against this decision'. His exemption is granted for three months as of 1 September. So urgent is the need for men for army service, that in 1918, the National Service Department will try to enlist him once again.

Chapter 10
September–December 1917

Autumn and winter of 1917 bring the
threat of compulsory rationing ever closer.
Eels and whale meat may soon be on the menu,
as well as gulls' eggs. The Government hopes that
a little badge will help destroy mutual suspicion
between the classes over food economy. The Museum
is asked to advise on the causes of corrosion of
cement, metal and wood in seawater, and Russia,
in the throes of revolution, is a cause of disquiet
and uncertainty. Enemy aircraft bomb London on
successive nights. The Museum suffers some damage
– from anti-aircraft guns defending the capital.
It faces arguably an even greater threat from the
Government, one that the Museum's indefatigable
Assistant Secretary says could cause its ruin
for many years. One more Museum man is
killed at the front and another is confirmed
missing in action – presumed dead.

1 SEPTEMBER 1917 Sir Archibald Geikie finally receives Dr Harmer's letter regarding Charles Tate Regan's exemption application. He replies at once, enclosing an appeal which he hopes may be of use. 'The pig-headed obstinacy with which some officials insist on putting a round man into a square hole', he tells Harmer, 'sometimes drives one to despair'.

State control on food prices is extended to stop profiteering. Foods for which maximum prices are already in place include bread, meat, jam, oatmeal and some teas. Controlled prices for bacon, ham and other goods are shortly to be introduced. There are queues in the streets outside food shops. To avoid compulsory rationing, the need for food economy remains paramount. Local Food Control Committees are set up to represent the interests of the public. *The Times* reports that German attempts 'to bring us to the verge of starvation' can be foiled either by compulsory rationing or by the voluntary sacrifice of reduced consumption. 'When people read that from 15 to 20 large boats are lost at sea every week they do not always grasp the cumulative effect of the losses. It is essential that they should see the real dimensions of the danger and also realise that there is a world shortage of cereal foods'.

Charles Fagan receives a memo from Dr Harmer regarding the use of whale meat for food. 'I suspect that most if not all the Cetacea are good to eat,' Harmer writes, 'though large Whales and old individuals of other species are probably tough'. A correspondent has told him that the blue whale is usually one of those, 'but that a specimen 65 feet long (and therefore young) was very fat, and its meat was very good, not unlike veal'. Harmer himself has tried Rudolphi's Rorqual. 'It would have been quite good if it had not been cooked without sufficient washing. It had been salted, and tasted like brine'.

4 SEPTEMBER 1917 On a clear moonlit night about 20 enemy aircraft cross the coast and head towards London. Between 11.45pm and 2am, about 40 bombs are dropped. Eleven people are killed and 62 injured.

7 SEPTEMBER 1917 Charles Fagan sends the Keepers a circular from the Treasury regarding possible compensation for civil servants who may be killed or injured while at work as a result of hostile air raids. He asks the Keepers to bring the circular to the notice of all their staff and inform him as soon as they have seen it. The issue has been much discussed in the newspapers, while insurance companies are seizing the opportunity for new business and advertising 'Air raid insurance for employees', urging intending insurers to 'forward proposals immediately, as rates are increasing daily'.

8 SEPTEMBER 1917 Charles Fagan writes to Oscar Ashcroft at the Propaganda department in Wellington House. He asks him

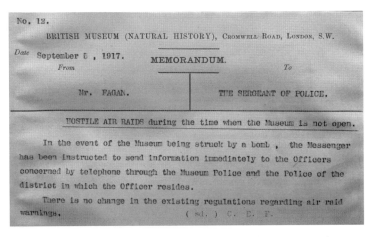

No. 12.

BRITISH MUSEUM (NATURAL HISTORY), Cromwell Road, London, S.W.

Date September 8 , 1917.   MEMORANDUM.

From   *To*

       Mr. FAGAN.   THE SERGEANT OF POLICE.

       HOSTILE AIR RAIDS during the time when the Museum is not open.

In the event of the Museum being struck by a bomb , the Messenger has been instructed to send information immediately to the Officers concerned by telephone through the Museum Police and the Police of the district in which the Officer resides.

There is no change in the existing regulations regarding air raid warnings.   (sd.) C. E. F.

Concern that the Museum might be struck by a bomb was so acute that Fagan instructed the Sergeant of Police to inform the Museum officers by telephone immediately if the Museum was closed at the time.

'whether there is any particular country or part of the world to which you would wish us to give special attention in the matter of the distribution of propaganda literature? I think we could easily arrange through some of our more energetic scientific correspondents to do this in almost any country if you think it necessary or desirable'.

The Museum has already sent out many thousands of copies of propaganda books, reports, posters and pamphlets across the world, including to Argentina, Chile, China, Denmark, France, Greece, the Netherlands, Russia, Spain, Sweden, Switzerland and the United States. Fagan also sends material to British correspondents – particularly public librarians, museum staff and academics, asking them to display the propaganda literature 'as conspicuously as possible'. In addition, he asks for their suggestions for useful recipients in allied or neutral countries who the Museum might contact.

13 SEPTEMBER 1917 Charles Fagan has been pursuing the idea of using seagulls in anti-submarine warfare and he writes to Dr Lucas of the American Museum of Natural History who first suggested the idea to the Museum in July, advising him of the progress he has made. He tells him that it has been brought before the Admiralty, though no 'serious action' has been taken in the way of testing it. He reiterates that he is 'most interested' in the subject and would like to be informed of the results of any experiments that may be made in America. 'Personally it seems to me', he writes, 'that if the birds were fed continuously from submarines, which then submerged and in rising, again fed the gulls, that these birds would in time come to associate the submerged submarine with food, and would follow it in the hope of it rising'. He does not address the rather crucial issue of how the seagulls would know whether the vessel they were following was German or British.

14 SEPTEMBER 1917 Albert Reeley, an attendant in the Geology department, begins military service in the Army Service Corps. He is classed as Ciii, fit only for sedentary duties. He joined the Museum as a boy attendant in 1903 and was still working there in 1953. Reginald Moseley Larking, an unofficial boy attendant in Geology since 1915, resigns his position on reaching 18, military age, and is serving in the 15th Battalion, London Regiment (Prince of Wales' Own Civil Service Rifles). He will return to the Museum after the war.

Arthur William Frederick Hales, a 24-year-old attendant in Botany, is discharged from the Army as 'no longer physically fit for War service'. He had been a private in the 15th London Regiment (Civil Service Rifles), serving in France. He is suffering from shell shock and has been in hospital for several months with what is termed 'neurasthenia'. There are now seven officers and men employed in the Museum who have been discharged from the military as disabled.

14 SEPTEMBER 1917 Charles Fagan writes to Miss G Donnell who wishes to bring parties of blinded soldiers to the Museum. Fagan tells her that the Museum's official guide, John Leonard, has been authorised to arrange the visits with her and to allow the men to handle some of the specimens.

15 SEPTEMBER 1917 Twenty-two-year-old Private Stanley Thomas Wells of the 15th London Regiment (Civil Service Rifles) and an attendant in the Zoology department, was reported missing in action in September 1916. His father, Thomas Wells, who is also employed by the Museum, as Departmental Clerk in the Bird Room, receives a letter from the Army record office stating that no further news has been received regarding his son, and that 'the Army Council has been regretfully constrained to conclude that he is dead'. Wells's name is commemorated on the magnificent Thiepval Memorial which stands overlooking the River Somme.

30 SEPTEMBER 1917 Overnight, the Museum is hit during a bombing raid. In the morning a piece of shrapnel is found at the south end of the Rodent Room, next to the Upper Mammal Gallery. There is a hole of about the same size in a skylight. In another skylight there is a bullet-sized hole. This does not appear to be enemy bomb damage, as Dr Harmer tells the Director: 'I presume that these are incidents of the defensive measures which were adopted by our Forces against air-raids of the last two or three nights'. London has been subjected to air attacks throughout September.

1 OCTOBER 1917 Once again London is attacked and again the Museum is hit. This time the nose cap of a shell falls into the Reptile Gallery. No-one in the Museum is injured, and the damage appears slight. Lieutenant General Sir Francis Lloyd, who is responsible for the defence of London, sends an officer to examine the shell. It is identified as coming from an anti-aircraft weapon, a French .75 gun, a quick-firing field gun used in battle since 1897 and still in use in the 1940s.

The Times warns Londoners of the danger from shells and shrapnel fired from the guns defending London. Their huge bombardment greets the enemy, the newspaper reports. Hundreds of shells burst, releasing thousands of bullets forming what must

The anti-aircraft shell fragment that fell into the Reptile gallery in October 1917. It is now preserved in the Museum's Archives.

seem 'an almost impenetrable curtain' to the oncoming aircraft. As *The Times* points out, 'Shrapnel cases and bullets, if fired into the air, must obviously fall somewhere', and 'it is utter folly' for people to stand in the street. 'A shrapnel shell will not wreck a house', however, but 'it might go through the roof and burst in a top floor room'. Fortunately for the Museum, it is just part of a single shell that penetrates the building.

2 OCTOBER 1917 The Keeper of Zoology, Dr Sidney Harmer, reports that the nose cap of the shell 'hit the projecting terracotta cornice over wall case 7, struck the life-sized photograph of the James Island Tortoise presented by Lord Rothschild, and appears to have fallen on the table-case containing the male North Aldabra Tortoise, glancing off on to the table-case containing a Loggerhead Turtle, on top of which case it was found'. He draws a meticulous diagram of the shell's probable trajectory. Glass was smashed, but no damage was done to the specimens as the shell was deflected first by the cornice and then by hitting the metal rims of both table-cases. Had this not happened, specimens would have been 'seriously injured'.

6 OCTOBER 1917 Frederick Edwards, the Entomology assistant and conscientious objector who has been working on a fruit farm in Letchworth has been informed by his employer that there is now insufficient work for him. He moves to a nearby farm where he works as an agricultural labourer, digging, sorting, bagging and hoisting sacks of potatoes. Edwards has not abandoned his study of the Diptera. He is spending his free time collecting specimens for the Museum in the countryside of Hertfordshire and the neighbouring counties of Cambridgeshire and Bedfordshire.

9 OCTOBER 1917 Dr Harmer suggests to the Director that some action should be taken to protect the Museum during air raids. 'I

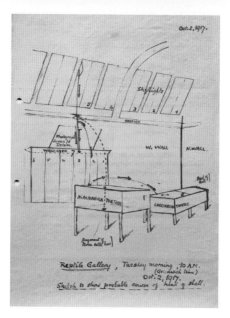

Dr Harmer drew this precise sketch of the probable trajectory of the shell cap that fell into the Reptile Gallery during the air raid on 1 October 1917.

hardly think we can take any effective measure against bombs', he writes, but 'the question is rather different in the case of shrapnel'. He suggests some form of wire netting beneath skylights. It would be very expensive to treat the whole Museum, 'and I offer no opinion as to its desirability,' but he thinks it might be practicable to protect skylights that are immediately above important specimens.

12 OCTOBER 1917 The supply of spirit for zoological specimens is still critical. The Museum receives a letter from the Director of Propellant Supplies, Explosives Department of the Ministry of Munitions, stating that there is no objection to the Museum purchasing small quantities of spirit as may be required to preserve specimens. However, in view of 'the urgent requirements' of spirit for war and medical purposes, 'every economy may be exercised by the Museum in the use of any spirit supplied'.

13 OCTOBER 1917 Charles Fagan writes to all the Keepers. 'I regret that I must warn you that owing to the exigencies created by war conditions, the Office of Works are compelled to cut off heat from the Museum for 14 hours out of the 24 daily, and it will therefore be impossible to maintain anything like adequate warmth in the galleries and elsewhere throughout the Museum'. He adds that the Museum 'is not the only sufferer'; this will apply to all public buildings in the area.

15 OCTOBER 1917 A letter is received from the Home Office suggesting that in the event of air raids at night or on Sundays, the Museum (and other public buildings) should be opened to offer shelter to the public. The Trustees agree and inform the Home Secretary that part of the front basement underneath the main entrance doors will be available. A notice that shelter may be found at the Museum is placed at the outer gates. The space is 'amply sufficient' for about 500 people. Charles Fagan has noted in pencil, 'Mem. Lavatory accom. necessary'. In August an air raid warning resulted in 150 visitors taking shelter in the basement.

16 OCTOBER 1917 Dr Harmer's suggestion that skylights be protected with wire-netting receives a prompt reply from Charles Fagan – that it is not to be. 'I am informed', Fagan writes, 'that it is not practicable for the reason that neither wire-netting nor labour is available'. However, Dr Harmer has been looking at other possibilities for protecting cases with valuable specimens, and that is to move them away from windows and skylights, wherever possible. This is done at once.

23 OCTOBER 1917 Dr Gahan, Entomology Keeper, reports to the Trustees on progress to date with the map showing the distribution of the malaria-carrying *Anopheles* mosquito in the British Isles.

Hugh Scott, the Cambridge entomologist loaned for a few hours each week to the department, has almost completed his work researching published records on the occurrence of the species and contacting those with some knowledge of the subject. To widen the search, the Local Government Board has been asked to issue a notice to all Medical Officers of Health to send specimens of mosquitoes to the Museum for identification. The Public Schools' Association of Science Masters has also notified its members to send specimens. The Museum asks for them to be sent either in small glass tubes or between layers of tissue paper enclosed in a box packed loosely with cotton wool, so as to avoid crushing or other damage.

As a result, 'a considerable number' of mosquitoes are now arriving in the department. To help cope with the huge task of identifying them all, William Dickson Lang, an assistant in Geology, has been loaned to Entomology. Although new to the work, within a few weeks Dr Gahan reports that he has made 'such good progress that the determination of any British species...presents little difficulty for him'.

24 OCTOBER 1917 Dr Arthur Smith Woodward, Geology Keeper, reports to the Trustees on the extra-official war work of his Assistant Keeper, Dr Francis Bather. This includes his allotment work, Red Cross activities, and propaganda work at the War Office. Now he has another government task. In August the Prime Minister, David Lloyd George, set up a new Ministry of Reconstruction, concerned with post-war economic and social planning. It has established a range of committees, one of which, the Committee on Adult Education, has asked Dr Bather to report on the educational work of local natural history societies and similar bodies. Dr Smith Woodward recommends to the Trustees that Dr Bather should be given permission to continue all this work only on condition 'he does not absent himself from duty at the Museum without previously notifying the Keeper'. It is scarcely surprising that, after the war, this extraordinarily able, energetic and, for many, inspirational man, never fully recovers from these years of exhausting activity.

27 OCTOBER 1917 At their committee meeting, the Trustees are told of the latest casualties. Zoology assistant Captain [John] Guy Dollman is recovering after being injured by a hand grenade. He is a divisional bombing officer and is in charge of a brigade bombing school based in England. Captain TJ Dudley, packer of publications, who was suffering from shell shock, is returning to the front. Private Thomas Douglas, who is on the cleaning staff, was sent to France in June 1917. On 22 September he was severely wounded by shrapnel in the thigh. He is now in hospital in Woking, Surrey.

31 OCTOBER 1917 At 11. 45pm, the Natural History Museum receives notice of an impending air raid. From the surrounding streets, 30 members of the public take refuge in the Museum's basement. According to the *Pall Mall Gazette*, 'determined and repeated attacks' are being attempted on London. There are 30 hostile aircraft in seven groups. Anti-aircraft fire is heard and many of the planes turn back. Three penetrate the air defences. Initial casualties are given as eight killed and 21 injured.

At the Museum, a shell-case penetrates the roof of the Botanical Gallery and considerable damage is done, both to wall- and to table-cases. As the Keeper of Botany, Dr Rendle, reports, once again 'the shell-case was from one of our own guns'. A number of specimens are damaged or destroyed, but 'as the specimens exhibited do not belong to the study series, the damage is not irremediable'.

1 NOVEMBER 1917 Throughout the autumn, the Government has warned that food economy is imperative. *The Daily Mirror* reports there will be no further warnings. 'Unless the people practise immediate and drastic economy in the consumption of food-stuffs, there is every reason to believe that a system of food rationing will be undertaken by the Government'.

5 NOVEMBER 1917 The Secretary of the Royal Society, William Hardy, writes to Dr Harmer regarding an enquiry by the Institution of Civil Engineers into the corrosion of cement, metals and wood in seawater. The proposed monograph will be in two sections, one on 'the ravages of animals' and the other on 'the ravages of plants, including, of course, bacteria'. Hardy asks Harmer if he can recommend a zoologist with the requisite knowledge.

Harmer replies at once. 'I presume the principle enemies to contend with will be found among mollusca and crustacea:- namely the Ship-worm and other boring Lammelli-branchs [bivalves such as clams and oysters] and the 'Gribble' [a tiny, wood-boring crustacean] and other destructive crustacea'. The most suitable person is the Museum's crustacean expert, Dr William Calman, but the consent of the Trustees is required.

6 NOVEMBER 1917 HM Office of Works writes to the Museum stating that the need to save fuel 'is more urgent than ever'. Coal rationing is being considered for Government departments. Meanwhile, fires are no longer to be lit early in the morning, but only when a room's occupants come on duty. If a room has a radiator that heats up to 60 degrees Fahrenheit, 'in no circumstances' can fires also be lit. The Office of Works is confident, Charles Fagan tells the Keepers, that every civil servant will 'loyally co-operate… and cheerfully accept the discomforts involved'.

In Belgium, the village of Passchendaele is taken by the Canadians. Four days later, a battle that has lasted 103 days with a total of well over half a million casualties on both sides, comes to an end.

8 NOVEMBER 1917 Charles Fagan has been tireless in publicising and sending out the Museum's economic pamphlets, posters and leaflets to civilians and the military at home and abroad. He sends Captain W Thomas of the Royal Army Medical Corps, 66th Field Ambulance, in Salonika, a complete set which he asks him to circulate among all medical officers serving with the Salonika forces as 'We desire to make them known as widely as possible'. It is a constant battle to contain the huge incidence of malaria and dysentery there. Hygiene is crucial. A few weeks later, at the request of John Ramsbottom, the Botany assistant who is serving as a protozoologist in Salonika, he sends two parcels of the pamphlets and posters to Lt Col Nathanial Rutherford of the 48th General Hospital, Salonika, 'in the hope that they may be of use to you and others of the British Expeditionary Force in Salonika'.

13 NOVEMBER 1917 The Government announces a new scale of voluntary food rations, giving greater amounts to those engaged in manual labour than those with sedentary occupations. Sir Arthur Yapp, Director of Food Economy, says, 'No one must take more food than his share, and there must be no hoarding'. *The Times* reports his appeal that 'obedience to this new scale of rations' will set free tonnage 'to convey more and more soldiers across the Atlantic to the battlefields of the Western front, where the vital decision would be fought out'. He appeals to all to adopt as simple a style of living as possible, avoid expensive meals, 'and not be afraid of wearing faded or frayed clothes'.

15 NOVEMBER 1917 Special leave of three days is granted to Charles Tate Regan, the 39 year-old Museum zoologist in charge of the fish collection. This is to enable him to visit a proposed eel farm in Hampshire with the government-appointed Freshwater Fish Committee of which he is a member. The Committee is considering

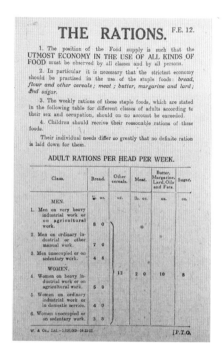

The League of National Safety issued this table of adult rations per week to encourage the 'UTMOST ECONOMY' in the use of all kinds of food.

possible measures to secure a greater output of eels from UK waters for home consumption. Food shortages mean all possible ways of increasing the food supply are being considered. Compulsory rationing with 'food cards' has not been ruled out.

Frederick Edwards, the Entomology assistant and conscientious objector, has had to change jobs again. He is now one of about 20 men and boys employed as labourers on a large farm in Letchworth. His colleague and friend at the Museum, the entomologist Norman Denbigh Riley, notes in his obituary in the journal *Nature* that Edwards never uttered 'a word of complaint or hint of bitterness'.

17 NOVEMBER 1917 The Keeper of Zoology, Dr Sidney Harmer, recommends to the Trustees that a pamphlet dealing with the dangers posed by rats and mice should be prepared. 'These small rodents', he reports, 'are responsible, by their ravages, for the loss of thousands of tons of valuable food-material, as well as for the dissemination of disease'. He believes a 'short treatise' on the subject will be particularly useful and suggests that it should be prepared by Martin Alister Campbell Hinton, the unofficial scientific worker who is an expert on both rodents and whales.

20 NOVEMBER 1917 Dr George Thurland Prior, Keeper of Mineralogy, reports to the Trustees that his department has just assisted the Government in the identification of rock fragments used in German fortifications in Flanders, which are built of concrete aggregate. These 'pillboxes' are equipped with machine guns from which the Germans, protected by thick concrete walls, can fire on the advancing Allies. Specimens of the rock have been brought to the department by the Geological Survey and, on comparison with the series of German rocks in the collection, are identified as coming from 'the neighbourhood of the Rhine'. *The Times* reports in October that the British Government has demanded from the Dutch 'a complete cessation' of the transit of sand and gravel through Holland from Germany to Belgium. The question at issue is whether the sand and gravel is for civil or military purposes. Through its tests on the aggregate, Dr Prior's department shows it is being used for the latter.

21 NOVEMBER 1917 Frederick John Bean, a boy attendant in Geology, reaches military age – 18 – and is called up. He joins the 24th (County of London) Battalion (The Queens) and is sent for training. His colleague, 18-year-old George Pagnoni, also a boy attendant in Geology, died of wounds in 1916.

Dr Rendle, Keeper of Botany, recommends that a selection of the Museum guide-books should be sent to John Ramsbottom in

Martin Hinton (1883–1961) at work in the Museum's mammal room in 1924. An expert on rodents and whales, he only joined the Museum staff in 1921. He became Zoology Keeper in 1936.

Salonika. They are for 'judicious distribution' among the soldiers in hospital there. Ramsbottom has been giving talks to the men on scientific topics and has told Dr Rendle of 'the great enthusiasm' with which the men listen to him. He has also said that 'there is a great dearth' of anything to interest the men.

23 NOVEMBER 1917 Felix Gilbert Wiltshear, a private in the King's Royal Rifle Corps, dies in France from wounds received in action. Wiltshear enlisted in June 1916 and is buried in the Rocquigny-Equancourt Road British Cemetery, Manancourt. In 1896 he joined the Botany department as a 14-year-old boy attendant and in 1905 he was appointed Departmental Librarian. The Keeper, Dr Rendle writes that he was 'an admirable Librarian; he was quiet and methodical, very accurate, and had a good memory and plenty of common-sense'. He leaves a widow, Ellen, and one surviving son. Wiltshear was 35 years old.

24 NOVEMBER 1917 The Trustees are informed that Charles Hill, an attendant in Entomology, has been wounded near Ypres. He is a Lance Sergeant in the (Prince of Wales' Own Civil Service Rifles) 15th Battalion, London Regiment. He has been brought back to England and is receiving treatment in hospital. He joined the Museum as a boy attendant in the insect section of the Zoology department in 1903, and was promoted to attendant in 1910. In 1913 the insect section was separated from Zoology, becoming the Entomology department, and Hill went with it. John Cecil Vickery, a private in the 1st City of London Royal Fusiliers, has also been wounded. He joined the Museum in 1897 as a boy attendant in Zoology, becoming an attendant in 1901. Mineralogy assistant, Captain Walter Campbell Smith, who was awarded the Military Cross in 1916, has been promoted to Major. He is attached to the Special Brigade, Royal Engineers. Captain Ernest Edward Austen, an assistant in Entomology, is also promoted to Major. He is attached to the Royal Army Medical Corps, Sanitary Corps.

Private Felix Gilbert Wiltshear, the Botany department librarian, died in France on 23 November 1917 from wounds received in action.

30 NOVEMBER 1917 The Director of Food Economy, Sir Arthur Yapp, writes to the Director, Sir Lazarus Fletcher. He tells him that he has been asked by the Prime Minister to undertake a National Campaign to bring home to the nation the paramount importance of food economy at this critical moment of the war. 'I find that wherever I go', Yapp writes, 'that one class holds back on the ground that it believes that another class is not "playing the game"'. Yapp feels sure that this is 'erroneous' and that everyone who is willing to practise economy will be willing to show his intention. To that end, he has instituted a League of National Safety, 'with a little badge – an anchor, which persons of all classes are asked to wear'. He hopes that this will make everyone realise that people of every class are willing to practise economy, 'and that the mutual suspicion between classes will be destroyed'. He concludes by asking Sir Lazarus to become a member of the League and circulate this request through the Museum, which the Director does. Forms for enrolment and a leaflet on rations are distributed to the staff.

5 DECEMBER 1917 The Home Office proposes once again to suspend the protection of gulls' eggs, to make them available for food 'in the present emergency' and asks for the Museum's observations on the matter. Last year restrictions were suspended until 21 June. Dr Harmer's advice is that gull, coot and waterhen eggs should not be taken after 1 June, though guillemot, razor-bill and puffin eggs might be collected until 21 June. Plovers' eggs should not be collected after 15 April, and systematic collection of those of wild ducks should be discouraged as the bird itself has considerable food value. However, Dr Harmer asks whether steps have been taken to divert the supply of eggs used in 'unessential manufacturing processes to the food-market'. He also asks whether eggs collected could be immediately 'preserved or used for egg powders, etc'. His report is sent to the Home Office.

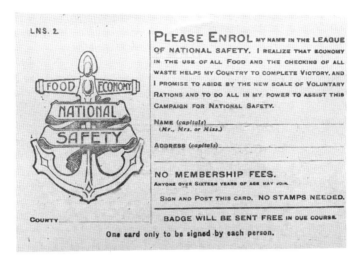

LNS. 2.

FOOD ECONOMY

NATIONAL

SAFETY

PLEASE ENROL MY NAME IN THE LEAGUE OF NATIONAL SAFETY. I REALIZE THAT ECONOMY IN THE USE OF ALL FOOD AND THE CHECKING OF ALL WASTE HELPS MY COUNTRY TO COMPLETE VICTORY, AND I PROMISE TO ABIDE BY THE NEW SCALE OF VOLUNTARY RATIONS AND TO DO ALL IN MY POWER TO ASSIST THIS CAMPAIGN FOR NATIONAL SAFETY.

NAME (capitals)
(Mr., Mrs. or Miss.)

ADDRESS (capitals)

NO MEMBERSHIP FEES.
ANYONE OVER SIXTEEN YEARS OF AGE MAY JOIN.

SIGN AND POST THIS CARD. NO STAMPS NEEDED.

COUNTY

BADGE WILL BE SENT FREE IN DUE COURSE.

One card only to be signed by each person.

The League of National Safety enrolment form. It was sent to the Director, Sir Lazarus Fletcher on 30 November 1917, who had it distributed to the staff. The League's aim was to encourage economy in 'every class'.

6 DECEMBER 1917 About 25 enemy aircraft approach London in the early hours and, at 5am, five or six get through the air defences. They drop so many incendiary bombs that *The Times* suggests the Germans want to burn London 'rather than smash it'. Seven people are killed and 25 injured. Three of the incendiary bombs fall in the Museum's Eastern Gardens and close by in the Cromwell Road. No damage is reported.

7 DECEMBER 1917 Incendiary bombs falling so close to the Museum is the first time the building has come so near disaster and it shocks everyone. Charles Fagan asks all Keepers to give their 'immediate attention' to ensuring as far as possible the protection of all type or irreplaceable specimens by storing them in safer places.

12 DECEMBER 1917 The Museum receives a threat from another quarter. It is in a letter from Sir Arthur Durrant, Secretary to the Cabinet Committee on Accommodation. There is a proposal, he informs Sir Lazarus Fletcher, to allocate the greater part of the Museum's galleries and studies for occupation by two Government departments.

An urgent meeting of all the Keepers is called at once and, a few days later, Charles Fagan replies to Sir Arthur. He tells him his letter will be put before the Trustees at their next meeting in January. In the meantime, 'I am to point out that this Museum has been kept open to the public with the express sanction of the Government and the House of Commons as fulfilling a national want'. The packing and removal of the collections would take at least a year, Fagan writes, nor does Durrant indicate where the collections, their cases and cabinets are to be moved to. Furthermore, 'you do not state where the functional and research work, much of it directly bearing on the successful prosecution of the war, or of the highest economic importance, is to be carried out'. And he ends, 'The proposal would appear to be wholly impracticable'.

17 DECEMBER 1917 Dr Harmer, Zoology Keeper, reports to the Trustees on his proposals to safeguard the collections. The study collection of birds, eggs, and the collection of shells are to be transferred from their present very unsafe positions, 'which have no more effective a protection than a skylight or thin roof, to the Bird Gallery, which is protected by two concrete floors and a roof'. He points out the great difficulties, risks and delay involved in the removal of these collections to an outside locality. He advocates the removal of the study collection of small mammals and the type specimens of other mammals, which occupy an exposed position at the top of the building, to the Royal Albert Memorial Museum in

Exeter, Devon, which has placed accommodation for this purpose at the disposal of the Trustees.

Lord Rothschild expresses his readiness to provide accommodation at his Museum at Tring for certain key specimens in the Museum's collections. A few days later, Charles Fagan catches the 11 o'clock train to Tring to inspect the proposed accommodation.

19 DECEMBER 1917 Charles Fagan writes to Museum Trustee and politician, Viscount Harcourt, about 'the outrageous proposal' of the Cabinet Committee on Accommodation to take over most of the Museum for two Government departments. He has just heard from the Office of Works that it is possible the War Cabinet will give its approval 'without demur, in total ignorance of what it means without waiting to hear the views of the Trustees'.

Fagan tells Lord Harcourt, 'it is of the utmost importance' that Sir Alfred Mond, Chairman of the Committee, 'should fully realize the impracticability of the proposal'. What seems to offend Fagan particularly is 'what would be said in the country when it became known that the National Museum of Natural History was to be dismantled to find room for the Registry of Friendly Societies & the Department of Woods & Forests!' And this is happening, Fagan writes, just when 'much is being written about the importance of scientific research to the future of the country. If Sir Alfred Mond knew all the facts, I feel sure he would withdraw the proposal, the carrying out of which means the ruin of the Natural History Museum for many years'. He hopes that as a Trustee, Lord Harcourt would be able to make this clear to Mond and perhaps suggest that he might visit the Museum.

Fagan has to deal not just with the threat to the Museum's future from the Government, but also from hostile aircraft. The danger from air raids is so severe that he arranges for an official to sleep in the Upper Mammal Gallery during periods when attack seems most probable. To take care of those sheltering in the Museum basement, a nurse from the St John's Ambulance Brigade has volunteered and Fagan writes to thank her. She is the Hon Katharine Thring, who lives close to the Museum. Miss Thring is available for four nights a week and another nurse, Mrs Dennistoun, volunteers for the remaining three.

This evening, about five enemy aircraft reach London, bombing the capital between 7 and 8pm. *The Times* reports that 10 people are killed and 70 injured. This time the Museum is undamaged.

20 DECEMBER 1917 The newspapers have been reporting, with mounting alarm, the 'chaos' in Russia and the rise of the Bolsheviks. Charles Fagan informs the Keepers that a letter has been received from the Foreign Office, stating that 'it would not seem to be advisable to enter into official correspondence with Government departments in Russia or to propose arrangements for the exchange of publications until conditions in that country become more settled'.

Fagan also writes to the Department of the Director of Food Economy, Sir Arthur Yapp. He has asked whether the Museum will arrange an exhibit 'illustrating from the natural history side the food values etc of certain articles of food'. Sir Arthur is anxious that Museums should take a prominent part in his campaign for Food Economy. John Leonard, the Museum's well-known and popular official guide, is to prepare the exhibit and details, Fagan tells Sir Arthur's office, should be discussed with him.

With the threat of closure hanging over the Museum, Dr Harmer writes a 12 page report on the work of a practical and economic nature that the Zoology department has undertaken in the last few years. There are 16 items directly related to the war where invaluable assistance has been given to Government departments, and numerous others of an economic nature. He highlights exhibits

> *Department of Zoology,*
> *Dec. 20, 1917.*
>
> Memorandum relating to work of a practical or
> Economic nature undertaken by the Department
> within the last few years. — — —
>
> I. The War.
> (a) Protective coloration in Nature, in its bearing on the
> concealment of gun-stations and other posts or objects
> of Naval or military importance. A model illustrat-
> ing this subject was prepared for use at Aldershot;
> and many parties of Officers and men have attend-
> ed demonstrations in the Galleries of the Museum.
>
> (l) Horse, structure of. Facilities for study given to
> representatives of the Army.
> (m) Human skull. Facilities given for study of certain
> points, in connexion with bullet-wounds.

With the threat of closure hanging over the Museum, Dr Harmer wrote a 12-page report on the economic and practical work of the Zoology department during the war.

in the public galleries and publications, both popular and technical, which contain an immense amount of information indispensable to those studying particular problems concerned with economic zoology. And of course he writes extensively on whales, 'of fundamental importance during the War, owing to the utilization of [whale-oil] in the manufacture of explosives'.

21 DECEMBER 1917 The Institution of Civil Engineers has been in touch with Dr Calman regarding their enquiry into the deterioration of structures exposed to sea action. Dr Harmer tells them that as at least some of the work would have to be done in Dr Calman's own time, 'he would naturally expect to receive some remuneration'. They reply that they do not think there will be any difficulty with this.

28 DECEMBER 1917 Dr Prior, Keeper of Mineralogy, reports to the Trustees on his proposals to safeguard the collection. 'A removal involving the whole Mineral Collection', he writes, 'is quite impracticable within the limited time, even if material for packing cases could be provided. The number of specimens in the Collection, including Rock specimens, is roughly 200,000'. When packed into cases they would occupy about 10,000 cubic feet. Prior itemises the enormous quantities of packing materials needed and says the task would take about a year. The most precious specimens, such as cut gemstones, are already in the safe in the Keeper's room. Other moderate-sized and valuable specimens could be put in the safe, although 'putting all the eggs into one basket' gives him an uneasy feeling. He proposes to transfer the safe to a corner of the basement under one of the towers and cover and surround it with sandbags. As for other specimens, he considers minerals and meteorites as at less risk in the Museum than if transferred somewhere where they could not be properly safeguarded from dust and decay. However, they might be moved to new cases in the Rock room in the basement, and could be covered and protected with sandbags. It is impossible to move cases in the Mineral gallery, he writes, as they are secured to the floor and any attempt to move them would damage specimens, the cases and the locks.

Chapter 11
January-April 1918

In early 1918, the Museum mounts a
fierce fightback against closure and warns the
British public of the dangers of malaria-carrying
mosquitoes. The threat of air raids means precious
specimens are evacuated, and the Museum tries
to interest the nation in the nutritious qualities of
whale meat. As food queues lengthen, compulsory
rationing is introduced. Pigs and chickens now thrive
in the Museum's grounds and the Museum itself is
camouflaged. The Mineralogy department is asked
for the loan of three of its tourmaline crystals for
experiments of great importance. In France, the
British Army is driven back under the onslaught of
the great German offensive and suffers horrendous
casualties, including three men associated with
the Museum. In fighting near Jerusalem, another
Museum man dies from wounds received in
action. The need for more men to enlist is
critical and the maximum age for
military service is raised to 55.

Charles Fagan's telegram of 2 January 1918 to Trustee and zoologist
Lord Rothschild regarding the Government threat to close the Museum.

2 JANUARY 1918 Charles Fagan begins the new year with a
telegram to Lord Rothschild, Museum Trustee and eminent
zoologist. 'Serious news of threatened dismantlement of Natural
History Museum. This must be stopped. Fagan.'

4 JANUARY 1918 There is vigorous protest in the columns and letter
pages of the newspapers against the proposal. The distinguished
zoologist and Vice-Chancellor of Cambridge University, Dr Arthur
Everett Shipley, writes to *The Times,* 'Very sinister rumours are
beginning to spread about the country with reference to a piece of
incredible folly on the part of a certain Government Department
which, it is alleged, has the intention of taking over the British
Museum (Natural History)…to house an army of clerks'. Shipley
mounts a robust defence of the Museum and emphasises the
importance of its war work. Another eminent scientist calls the
proposal 'Utterly ruthless and barbarous'.

Dr Harmer is most active in marshalling support, writing to eminent scientists and politicians with details of the disastrous effect the requisitioning of the Museum would have.

7 JANUARY 1918 The Royal Seed Establishment writes to *The Times* in support of the Museum, describing the 'immense value' of its research, especially regarding problems affecting the country's food supplies. Of particular importance is 'the unremitting toil and labour of the staff' in their work on 'the fertility of the soil and for safeguarding the crops upon which we depend from the ravages of insect pests and fungoid diseases'. This work, the letter concludes, 'should be allowed to proceed unfettered and unhindered'.

The Times also carries an anonymous article headed 'Science and War', summarising the vital work the Natural History Museum has undertaken on behalf of Government departments during the war.

The Linnean Society of London summons a special meeting and unanimously adopts a resolution excoriating the Government's proposed action. It records their 'dismay', 'profound astonishment and alarm', 'emphatic protest', and emphasises 'the disgrace which must accrue to the Nation in the eyes of the world', by the Government's evident inability to appreciate the essential value of the scientific assistance rendered by the Museum to the country.

Charles Fagan sends a memo to the Keepers. 'Sir Alfred Mond, First Commissioner of Works, is coming to the Museum tomorrow (Tuesday) at 3 o'clock. It is desirable that you should be in the Museum during his visit. This is in addition to the visit of the Office of Works' representatives at 12'. These are crucial meetings that will determine the Museum's future.

8 JANUARY 1918 The politician and industrialist Sir Alfred Mond, is the Chairman of the Cabinet Committee on Accommodation. At 3pm he has an interview with Charles Fagan, who points out the unsuitability of the building for office purposes, the great difficulties and expense involved in removing the collections, and of course, the Museum's vital contributions to the war effort. The Office of Works representatives examine the galleries and rooms the Government proposes to requisition.

9 JANUARY 1918 Dr Rendle, Botany Keeper, writes a summary of recent enquiries his department has investigated or dealt with on matters of national importance. None of them, he points out, could have been answered without access to the collections and libraries. They have dealt with an enquiry about a fungus that was destroying army tents on Malta and costing the Government thousands of pounds. Careful study of the growth of the fungus on canvas treated in various ways led to discovery of a complete remedy. The Army's Special Works School has enquired about camouflaging guns in winter by use of seaweed. 'Very helpful suggestions' were made. They have received enquiries from several sources, including government departments, regarding the use of sphagnum moss for surgical dressings – and sources of supply. They have also been asked about seaweed and fungi as sources of food, seaweed as a source of potash for manure and other uses, and of iodine and medical purposes. Government departments have enquired about sources of supply of various timbers, including special timbers, and of damage to timber by diseases. Local bodies have asked about the cause of 'ropey' bread, which was due to a fungus. They have also dealt with numerous enquiries regarding attacks of mould and disease in garden allotments, and the first indication of potato disease last year was diagnosed in the Department. Dr Rendle marks his report 'Strictly Confidential'.

This afternoon comes the news the Museum has hoped for. The Government has listened. In Parliament Earl Curzon, Lord President of the Council, announces that after detailed examination, it has been found that the Natural History Museum is no longer needed for the two Government departments. The difficulties in converting it to office use are too great. The British Museum, which was similarly threatened, is also reprieved. There are cheers in the House of Lords.

Whether Fagan also cheered is not recorded. To Edwin Ernest Lowe, Secretary of the Museums Association which had been campaigning vigorously on behalf of the Museum, Fagan sends 'the best thanks' of the Trustees. 'I may add', he ends, 'that we owe you, personally, a debt of gratitude for the prompt manner in which you dealt with the situation at a period when it was most serious and threatening'. Dr Harmer writes in a similar vein to those who have supported the Museum. 'It is a great satisfaction to have come well out of the conflict', he tells one, 'I hope the Museum is now safe from interference during the remainder of the War'.

10 JANUARY 1918 The Museum receives a circular letter from the Ministry of National Service regarding those exempted from military service. It expresses the hope that 'every effort' will continue to be made to release any men of military age 'who may cease to be indispensable'. The Ministry requires a full report of the staff currently employed in the Museum. The Government says there is a need for a further 420,000–450,000 men in the armed forces.

16 JANUARY 1918 The Home Office has replied to Dr Harmer's report on the use of gulls' eggs for food. It states that 'in view of the importance of increasing the food supply', it proposes taking eggs of certain species 'under proper safeguards' in bird sanctuaries. What the Home Office would like to know is in which sanctuaries are eggs sufficiently numerous to make it worthwhile suspending the existing orders. Dr Harmer reports that, according to William Ogilvie-Grant who is in charge of the Museum's bird collections, there are only four localities. Collecting in other sanctuaries would 'not materially increase the amount of food, and would result in the destruction of other species which it is specially desirable to protect'.

Charles Fagan writes to the General Officer Commanding, British Expeditionary Force, Basrah, Persian Gulf. He informs him that two parcels of collecting materials have been dispatched to Major Cuthbert Christy, RAMC, a naturalist, explorer and prolific collector for the Museum who left England for Mesopotamia in November. 'Mesopotamia is a region from which the Museum is badly in need of specimens', Fagan writes, 'and it is hoped that Major Christy may have occasional opportunity to profit by his long experience in obtaining valuable material for us'. He also names three more officers whom he hopes will be able to collect and writes that 'any facilities that may be properly granted' to any of them will be gratefully appreciated by the Trustees.

21 JANUARY 1918 Charles Fagan writes again to the Permanent Secretary to the Admiralty, Sir Oswyn Murray, regarding the possible use of seagulls to detect submarines. He sends a report summarising the idea and encloses a letter from Dr Pentz, whose 'original suggestion' was sent to Fagan by the Director of the American Museum of Natural History, Dr Lucas. He includes a sketch by Pentz 'of a mechanical device with which friendly submarines should be equipped to train seagulls, also some pen-pictures showing some of the steps of training'.

Fagan also encloses some remarks by Dr Harmer which include, 'A gull cannot be expected to pay attention to the nationality of a submarine. There thus arises the obvious preliminary question whether the balance would be in our favour if all enemy submarines were revealed to us, and all our own submarines were made visible to the enemy'. It could be, Harmer suggests, that gulls already follow submarines out of curiosity 'in the hope of getting food from them, without having had any special training to do so'. There have been

The original suggestion comes from Dr. Pentz, who
forwards a sketch of a mechanical device with which friendly
submarines should be equipped to train sea-gulls, also some
pen-pictures showing some of the steps of the training.

Dr. Harmer, Keeper of the Department of Zoology, in
a report to the Trustees of the British Museum, makes the
following remarks on the subject :-

"A gull cannot be expected to pay any attention to
"the nationality of a submarine. There thus arises the
"obvious preliminary question whether the balance would be
"in our favour if all enemy submarines were revealed to us,
"and all our own submarines were made visible to the enemy.
"It may, moreover, prove to be the case that gulls already
"follow submarines, out of curiosity or in the hope of
"getting food from them, without having had any special
"training to do so. But these are questions for the
"Admiralty, and the Museum need take no responsibility for
"them.

Charles Fagan wrote to the Admiralty in January 1918 about the
possible use of seagulls to detect submarines. He enclosed some
remarks by Dr Harmer, which included: 'a gull cannot be expected
to pay any attention to the nationality of a submarine'.

a number of newspaper stories to this effect, including one widely
reported in January 1916 of a sailor who related how 'we have always
a lot of seagulls following us about…I was at a 12-pounder gun after
dinner…when I was startled to see them all circling round an object
which proved to be the periscope of a German submarine, and I can
assure you, if it had not been for the seagulls we should have been
in Davy Jones's locker'.

Harmer has consulted other naturalists and concludes that the 'general consensus' is that it is one of those ideas worth looking into, 'even though it might prove, on trial, useless as a practical measure'. Its use would in any event be limited, as seagulls do not, Harmer writes, 'wander over the Oceans generally'. They are 'practically limited' to the continental shelf, so while that would include the English Channel and much of the North Sea, 'gulls could not be expected to give much assistance over most of the Atlantic'.

22 JANUARY 1918 Dr George Thurland Prior, Mineralogy Keeper, reports to the Trustees that Sir Joseph John Thomson, physicist, Nobel laureate and President of the Royal Society, has requested the loan of three sections of large tourmaline crystals for experiments related to issues 'of great importance' to the Admiralty. Dr Prior writes that the experiments 'will involve some risk of damage', but he recommends 'that this risk be incurred'. The work is of 'great national importance and has a direct bearing on the war, and the specimens, although intrinsically valuable, are not unique'. The Trustees instruct the Director, Sir Lazarus Fletcher – who is a mineralogist – to ask Sir Joseph for further information, including how the tourmalines are to be treated. The Trustees will authorise the loan, if the matter is urgent, but Thomson is to be asked if he would be satisfied with two of them.

Thomson had been on the Board of Invention and Research, which has now become part of the Department of Scientific Research and Experiment. The Board's main work was in antisubmarine warfare – notably the development of underwater listening devices, for which crystals, particularly with the unique electric properties of tourmaline, are key. Tourmalines are also invaluable in measuring the force of gun explosions, with the aim of improving gun design. After the war, as *Popular Science Monthly* reports in September 1919, Sir Joseph tells the Royal Institution, 'tourmaline crystal, properly encased, would be exposed to the explosive pressures to be measured...Knowing exactly what goes on within a gun or a gas engine makes possible designing them for maximum efficiency'. In 1918, Thomson's work is urgent and top secret. He does not say for which use the Museum's tourmalines are required.

26 JANUARY 1918 The Trustees are informed about the arrangements for the removal of part of the collections to places of greater safety both within the Museum and outside London. Dr Harmer's plans to send the more valuable and irreplaceable specimens of the study collection of small mammals to the Exeter Museum, now include the curator of mammals, Michael Oldfield Thomas, accompanying them to Devon, together with the department's articulator, William Robert Sherrin. The Entomology collections are comparatively safe in the basement and, as Dr Gahan points out, any stoppage of work which a removal would involve 'would be a very serious matter for the country, and the certainty of damage to specimens in travelling'.

Lord Rothschild's offer to house parts of the Botany collections at his Museum at Tring is accepted. Dr Rendle recommends that the precious and important Sloane Herbarium and other historic collections of plants, original drawings, books and manuscripts should be sent there. As it is impracticable to remove the whole of the collections, the staff are now selecting the type specimens, 'preservation of which is of the utmost importance'. The Keepers of Geology and Mineralogy prefer to keep their collections in the Museum because of risk of damage if they are moved.

As an additional safeguard against fire should incendiary bombs fall on the upper two floors which contain the highly inflammable upper mammal gallery and the herbarium, it is recommended that Treasury sanction should be obtained to employ two night watchmen to be stationed in these galleries whenever there is an air raid warning.

Dr Harmer also reports on the precautions he has taken to safeguard the Spirit collection. The larger bottles of specimens, which have been standing on top of the smaller cases through lack of space in cupboards, are now in the basement of the Spirit Building. Some of these bottles are four feet in height and many contain several gallons of spirit. He points out that it is scarcely practicable to move the collection to an outside locality: the expense would be enormous, it would take far too long, it would stop all economic and other work on the specimens, and they could well be damaged in a move. He also reports to the Trustees that he agrees with the Office of Works' proposal to spread a nine-inch layer of sand, either in bags or in wooden boxes, on the roof of the Spirit Building because of the 'exceptionally dangerous nature' of its contents, and the work should proceed without delay.

The Trustees sanction a request from the Director of the Wellcome Tropical Research Laboratories in Khartoum to translate the Museum's highly successful posters on 'The Fly Danger' and the 'Mosquito Danger' into Arabic. He tells the Museum that they will be 'placed in every dispensary, office and school in the Sudan'. The Egyptian government has made a similar request and is also given permission. They consider the posters are of 'great interest and importance' to the Egyptian people.

28 JANUARY 1918 London is again attacked from the air at night. Skylights in the Museum are broken but no damage is done to specimens or cases. A shell from an anti-aircraft gun falls in the east garden. About 50 people take refuge in the basement of the Museum, as they do during the air raid the following night.

1 FEBRUARY 1918 The Museum's opening hours are extended by an hour until 5pm. This follows an appeal from the International Young Men's Christian Association Hospitality League. A later time is not possible at this time of year because of police regulations restricting lights. Part of the League's activities is taking overseas soldiers on leave in London to places of 'wholesome interest'. The Natural History Museum – and other museums – is high on the list.

4 FEBRUARY 1918 Dr Rendle, Botany Keeper, reports that assistance has been given 'to an official connected with the Air Board in connection with the recognition of timbers used for aeroplane construction and the diseases to which they are subject'.

6 FEBRUARY 1918 The Representation of the People Act is given Royal Assent. The franchise is extended to all men over 21, those in the military over 19, and – for the first time – women, but only those over 30 and with a property qualification. There are 8.5 million of them. The following year, the Speaker of the House of Commons tells Parliament that the age limit was put in 'because had it not been...the number of women voters would have been far in excess of the men. It was thought desirable that women and men should be somewhere about on a parity,' and 30 was the nearest age 'we could get to'.

It will take another 10 years before women are given parity in voting age with men, and access to the same careers. Parity in pay is still work in progress. In 1918 there are just 12 women working in the Museum: clerks, typists, illustrators, model-makers, and four who are unofficial scientific workers. One is the eminent botanist Annie Lorrain Smith who has been made a temporary scientific assistant as so many men are now in the military or employed on other war work. Dorothea Bate, the pioneering palaeontologist and courageous explorer, has been associated with the Museum since 1898 and is now working as a preparator in Geology. In 1924, four years before women are permitted to apply for staff scientific posts, she is appointed curator of fossil mammals and birds, even though

Dorothea Minola Alice Bate (1878–1951), fossil hunter, palaeontologist and unofficial scientific worker in Geology, one of just 12 women working in various capacities in the Museum in 1918.

she is (and will always remain), a temporary member of staff. In Entomology, Emily Mary Bowdler-Sharpe, daughter of the late Curator of Birds, Richard Bowdler-Sharpe, and Miss GM Shepherd, are both temporarily employed preparing and mounting insects.

Major Manners Howe of the Cromwell Gardens Barracks, whose men are tending allotments in the Museum's grounds, has applied for permission to keep fowls as well. Charles Fagan tells him, 'In view of the necessity of maintaining a sufficient food supply, there seems to be no objection'. He will be allowed to erect a shed for the birds.

7 FEBRUARY 1918 As requested in January, Charles Fagan sends the particulars of staff currently employed in the Museum to the Ministry of National Service. He tells them there are now 106 men employed. Of these, 87 are over military age. Since the beginning of the war 68 men have been released for military service. The number of women working in the Museum has increased from nine in 1914 to 12. All of them, like the majority of the men, earn less than £200. Only 35 men are paid more than that, including nine members of the senior staff who earn more than £500.

8 FEBRUARY 1918 George Reavell of the Office of Works – who has been concerned about the Spirit Building since 1914 – writes that he has received instructions to proceed with the sand covering to the Spirit Building roof. He is planning to put down an under-layer of sand with a top-layer of shingle. This provides an even better protection than sand, and should prevent the sand blowing about in dry weather.

The Museum has sent out more slides to the army in France, illustrating the protective coloration of animals as applied to war. Explanatory notes for the military lecturers are also sent. For the slide of fish (*Phyllopteryx*) the notes state: 'Mimicry of seaweed – the waving strands of which are imitated by the shape, texture and colour of the fish & especially of its fins'. For the black grouse: 'Note coloration of hen & chicks – harmonising with the herbage-shadows & dead bracken & heather. They seek protection chiefly from birds of prey'. For the green spider on a fern leaf: 'Note colour to harmonise with surroundings (fir leaves)'. For two slides of ruffed lemur: 'These are two remarkable slides. The animal adopts the rare device of breaking its outline up by its black & white colour pattern so that at a distance it does not appear like an animal at all. In one slide the background is light; in the other it is dark; but the resulting concealment effect is the same, in complementary fashion'. There are notes for 12 slides in all, highlighting the key camouflage points.

9 FEBRUARY 1918 Charles Fagan receives a letter from Captain Forster Delafield Arnold-Forster, who is on the staff of the Director of the Anti-Submarine Division, in response to the information he sent to the Admiralty on seagulls detecting submarines. Arnold-Forster thanks him for his letter, but 'I am to inform you that the suggestions contained therein have already been fully considered by the Board of Invention and Research and the Admiralty and,

Slides illustrating protective coloration in animals were sent to the army in France to assist with camouflage techniques. Among them was a slide of a ruffed lemur, and the explanatory note that 'the animal adopts the rare device of breaking its outline up by its black & white colour pattern so that at a distance it does not appear like an animal at all'.

after preliminary investigation, it has been decided not to proceed further with the matter'.

In 1917 serious, though ultimately unproductive, research and trials were being carried out into seagulls and submarines, even while Fagan and Harmer were investigating the theoretical possibilities of the scheme, unaware of what was taking place. The Admiralty and the Board of Invention and Research also began experiments with sealions for the same purpose – and these too were abandoned.

The Museum has to take further air raid precautions. The General Headquarters, Home Forces, advises that the skylights should be distempered 'in some dull colour'. The Colonel Commandant of the Special Works School, Kensington Gardens [which specialises in camouflage techniques], writes twice to state that the Central Hall roof is visible in moonlight from the air, and the glass reflects light. He suggests that the skylights should be camouflaged, painted in 'irregular patches of dark green or khaki "Greenscreen" paint'. This will transmit light but give a dull surface and prevent reflection. The Office of Works is asked to carry out these suggestions as quickly as possible.

16 FEBRUARY 1918 Dr Harmer, in a report, is persevering with trying to promote whale meat as an important, but neglected, source of food. He quotes a number of instances in which the flesh of cetaceans has been used for food. He writes that on 27 December 1917, *Nature* reported that meat from the Californian grey whale, both fresh and canned, 'has already been placed on the market'. A single individual of this species 'yields about twelve tons of most succulent "beef"'.

The Museum, he continues, has recently had the opportunity to put cetacea meat to a practical test. The head and shoulders of a white-beaked dolphin stranded in Aldeburgh were sent to the Museum. Portions of the meat not wanted for research and in fresh condition, were taken home by some of the Museum staff, and cooked. 'The general verdict', he writes, 'was very favourable.' Dr Harmer, who tried it, considers the meat 'to be fully equal to the best quality beefsteak which it most resembles in appearance and taste'. Small pieces of blubber were boiled down and produced 'a quart of oil with very little trouble'. The oil has proved most useful to taxidermists for dressing skins.

Dr Harmer suggests that with the present 'notorious shortage' of meat and fat, it might be advisable to reopen one or more of the whaling stations in West Ireland, Scotland or the Shetland Isles, 'if operations would not be too much interfered with by hostile submarines'. He also suggests that the Ministry of Food should be informed about the possibility of using cetacea meat and oil that could be obtained in this country, particularly from smaller specimens which are frequently captured in the nets of fishing boats and often thrown overboard.

Charles Fagan subsequently sends Harmer's report to the Board of Trade, the Ministry of Food, the Natural Products Committee of the Royal Society, and the Board of Agriculture and Fisheries. He tells them that whale meat was the principal article of food at a luncheon recently given in New York by the AMNH to demonstrate the possibilities of whale meat.

It is not just to cetacea that Harmer is looking as possible food. He writes to a colleague in Scotland, 'Have you any suggestion as to the best way of cooking Puffin? I expect they would be a little fishy unless they were treated in a proper way'.

16–18 FEBRUARY 1918 Air-raids hit London on each of these nights. The only damage to the Museum is, again, to skylights. Over the three nights, more than 200 people take refuge in the Museum's basement shelter. The St John's Ambulance Brigade nurse, Miss Thring, is in attendance on all three nights.

21 FEBRUARY 1918 Dr Prior reports to the Trustees that the President of the Royal Society, Sir Joseph Thomson, has obtained suitable specimens of tourmaline 'elsewhere', and therefore no longer requires the Museum's.

22 FEBRUARY 1918 Isaac James Frederick Kingsbury, a private in the 15th Battalion, London Regiment (Prince of Wales' Own Civil Service Rifles), dies of wounds received in action near Jerusalem the previous day. He was appointed a boy attendant in the Zoology department in 1908 and was promoted to attendant in August 1914.

Private Isaac James Frederick Kingsbury, an attendant in Zoology, died on 22 February 1918 from wounds received in battle near Jerusalem.

He enlisted in February 1916 and saw service in France, Salonika, Egypt and Palestine. Georges Boulenger, the Museum's expert on reptiles, recalls his 'bright intelligence', his 'excellent character and the painstaking manner in which he discharged the duties entrusted to him'. For Boulenger personally, Kingsbury was 'a valued helper, who had become so efficient in his knowledge of the collection of Reptiles and Fishes as to be of great service. Such men are not easily replaced'. As a memorial, Boulenger names a new species of frog after him: *Allobates kingsburyi*, Kingsbury's Rocket Frog. Kingsbury is buried in the Jerusalem Military Cemetery. He was 24 years old.

23 FEBRUARY 1918 The Director calls the attention of the Trustees to the fact that there is no senior officer in residence at the Museum. He suggests that it might be advisable (with Treasury sanction) that one of them in turn should stay at a hotel in the Cromwell Road 'during the period of the month when air-raids may be expected' [generally when it is full moon], in order to be on the spot if a bomb should strike the Museum.

The Director also reports that Captain M Coplans, Royal Army Medical Corps (Sanitation) of the Italian Expeditionary Force, has requested a supply of the economic pamphlets and leaflets for the use of the troops. Several hundred copies have been sent to him. These are so successful that Captain Coplans asks for a further supply, and several hundred more are sent.

25 FEBRUARY 1918 This is what the newspapers call 'Ration Day'. The scarcity of so many essential foods, and what *The Times* describes as 'the scandal of food queues', has 'swept away opposition'. *The Times* reports that 'after three years and a half of war, compulsory rationing of food comes into operation in an area which includes London and the Home Counties, and has a population of over 10,000,000 people'. In a month's time, meat rationing will apply to the whole country, and a month after that, there will be a rationing scheme that can be applied 'as the necessity arises to any staple foodstuffs'. Just as the introduction of conscription was resisted until 1916, so it is with rationing, until there is no possible alternative.

5 MARCH 1918 The Stationery Office informs the Museum that it will no longer be possible to supply Government departments with 'such large quantities of Wire Paper Clips and Pins as have been issued hitherto'. This is in view of the 'urgent necessity for the utmost economy in the use of wire for civil purposes'. Paperclips and pins should be used sparingly, never thrown away, and kept safe for further use. There should be no orders for further supplies at present.

7–8 MARCH 1918 London is attacked by another air raid and shrapnel again hits the Museum. Windows in the passage between the Bird and Reptile Galleries, the Shell Gallery and the Whale Room are slightly damaged. Seventy-six people take refuge in the Museum shelter. Across London at least 11 people are reported killed and 46 injured.

8 MARCH 1918 A memorandum is sent to the Treasury regarding the measures necessary for the safety of the collections. All the plans are detailed, from the removal of valuable specimens to Tring and Exeter, to senior officers staying overnight near the Museum, with reasons given for each proposal. The two night watchmen, for example, are essential in the event of an incendiary bomb falling in the upper galleries. The bomb could set fire to all the cases and their contents before the two Museum firemen on duty or on patrol could reach the spot. The Trustees have been advised that 'an incendiary bomb can be quite readily rendered harmless if attacked at once.' The night watchmen would be available to come on duty as soon as the warning is received and would remain at their posts until the 'all clear' is received.

11 MARCH 1918 Charles Fagan writes to all the Keepers. At the end of February a new Registration Act came into force, whereby employers are required to see the registration certificates of all males between 15 and 65 in their employment. If a certificate is not produced within seven days, the Local Registration Authority has to be notified. 'Lads and men' discharged from the Forces are now liable to register themselves and must do so before 28 March. The Keepers are asked to certify that all men have the required certificate and any who do not must be reported to Fagan.

Dr Rendle reports that his department has dealt with various enquiries from Government departments. These include examining and reporting on rotting timbers from the Postal censor's office, and reporting on three separate cases of rotting stored army potatoes.

12 MARCH 1918 Charles Fagan sends a parcel of Government propaganda literature to the former Governor of the Bahamas, Sir William Grey-Wilson, who is now chairman of the Central Committee for National Patriotic Organisations. He sends 'Subject nationalities of the German Alliance' – a leaflet and map; the poster, 'A Reminder from France; and the map, 'What Germany Wants'. Fagan offers to send more, 'if you can make use of them'. One of the functions of Grey-Wilson's Committee is the dissemination of propaganda to Britain and the Empire.

20 MARCH 1918 Dr Prior is changing his mind about not moving any of the Mineralogy collections. He proposes that a large part of the meteorite collection – about 900 selected specimens – should be moved to rooms in the South East basement under the tower, after the windows have been sandbagged. He also suggests, 'if it should be considered advisable', that a further selection of unique specimens, especially meteorites, might be moved out of London.

21 MARCH 1918 Private John Henry Smitheringale of the 2nd (City of London) Royal Fusiliers, is killed in action in France. He was on the contractors' staff of the Museum. He was 39 years old.

Following on from the chickens now kept in the Museum grounds, Major Manners Howe of the Royal Defence Corps in Cromwell Gardens Barracks requests permission to keep a few pigs as well. The Chief Sanitary Inspector of Kensington Borough and the Acting Medical Officer of Health are consulted and raise no objection on sanitary or public health grounds. Charles Fagan writes to Major Manners Howe to tell him his request to keep a few pigs – Fagan's emphasis – has been granted. 'I should be glad, however, if you would kindly see that no nuisance is caused by way of smell etc to the Department of the Food Controller, which will shortly be located in the New Science Museum'.

25 MARCH 1918 Six members of staff have failed to produce registration certificates. Charles Fagan writes to the local registration authorities of the men concerned to inform them of this. Another man is unsure whether he needs to have one and is making enquries. He is 46 years old and a Naval pensioner. He has to report periodically and is liable to be recalled to the Navy.

26 MARCH 1918 The Treasury agrees to the proposals for air raid precautions. They sanction lodging allowances to those members of staff who have moved out of London, the engagement of two night watchmen and a subsistence allowance to the officer in residence at a hotel near the Museum.

30 MARCH 1918 Dr Harmer writes in great haste to a correspondent, telling him 'I am just off to France for a few days'. He does not say why. He is away from the Museum for five days. On his return he writes to the Curator of Mammals, Michael Oldfield Thomas, who is in Exeter. 'My dear Thomas, I have several letters of yours to answer, but you will understand the reason for my delay in doing so when I tell you that my son was dangerously wounded at the beginning of the great offensive, and I have been over to France to see him. I am thankful to say I found him making excellent progress and I believe there is no further reason for anxiety as to life or limb, though he may perhaps be permanently lame'. Captain Russell Harmer, Royal Engineers, is 21 years old. Two weeks after this, Harmer tells Oldfield Thomas that Russell is now in hospital in London, 'I rejoice to say that he is making excellent progress'.

Russell Harmer was severely injured, but he is fortunate. He is just one of more than 150,000 soldiers in the British Army who, in that critical week of the great German offensive, were killed, injured or captured in northern France. The onslaught continues into April. The Prime Minister addresses a packed House of Commons, impressing on it as forcefully as he can the gravity of this military crisis. In France, Field-Marshal Sir Douglas Haig's rallying call to the troops is printed in many newspapers with the headline: 'Our Backs

M E M O R A N D U M.

Safety of the Natural History Collections against
destruction by hostile air-craft.

The Trustees have given their anxious consideration
to the question of the safety of the collections at the
Natural History Museum against damage by hostile air-raids.

1. They have accepted an offer from the Corporation
Committee of the Royal Albert Memorial Museum, Exeter, to
provide accommodation for the type specimens and other
irreplaceable specimens in the study collection of small
mammals. The series is of exceptional scientific value,
including as it does a large number of type specimens and
others of historical interest, which to a very large extent
form the basis of the world's knowledge of this branch of
zoological science. The cabinets occupied an exposed
position at the top of the building, protected by a single
roof only.

2. Portions of the botanical collections, including
Sir Hans Sloane's Herbarium and other historical specimens,
which were in an equally exposed position in a gallery at
the top of the Museum, have been transferred to Lord
Rothschild's Museum at Tring.

3. The removal to Exeter and Tring has been carried
out by His Majesty's Office of Works, and the collections

                    are

Part of the memorandum sent to the Treasury in March 1918 detailing
measures necessary for the safety of the collections.

to the Wall'. The message is stark, the danger to the country all too clear. 'There is no other course open to us but to fight it out. Every position must be held to the last man; there must be no retirement. With our backs to the wall, and believing in the justice of our cause, each one of us must fight to the end. The safety of our homes and the freedom of mankind depend alike upon the conduct of each one of us at this critical moment'.

Manpower is critical. Under a new Military Service Act, the military age is to be raised to 50, even 55 in the case of 'medical men'. All civil servants under 25 who are fit are to be called up. There are none in the Museum. Even munitions and mine workers are no longer exempt – 150,000 men are needed from these two essential industries. This process is referred to as 'combing out'.

5 APRIL 1918 Captain Arthur Knyvett Totton, an assistant in Zoology, is discharged from the army. In September 1916 he was severely wounded in an action for which he was awarded the Military Cross. There are now nine men in the Museum, who have been invalided out of the Army – about a sixth of those who enlisted.

For the first time, an officer of the Museum is on night duty. He is based at the Vandyke Hotel on Cromwell Road, opposite the Museum. At the first warning of an impending air raid he will either be telephoned or summoned personally by the police, and will go to the Museum as soon as the sound warning is heard and the gates open to admit the public to the basement shelter. He will remain on duty until the 'all clear' signal is received. Fittingly, the first officer tonight – who will be on duty for the whole week – is Charles Fagan.

24 APRIL 1918 Dr Prior, Mineralogy Keeper, reports to the Trustees that it has been possible to obtain material for sandbagging the windows of the basement rooms and he proposes to move the unique and most valuable specimens there, 'where they will

The map showing the distribution in England and Wales of the malarial mosquito *Anopheles maculipennis*. Dr Gahan, Entomology Keeper, recommended that 2,000 copies should be printed.

be under his own supervision'. Although he is still reluctant to move anything out of the Museum, he reports that Lord Rothschild has offered space at his Museum at Tring. The offer is accepted with thanks.

25 APRIL 1918 *The Times* carries an article in which the correspondent notes that 'the malarial mosquito' has been noticed along riverbanks in this country. 'It may be,' he writes, 'that they or their eggs came over in transports that serve our eastern fronts. We must never allow these frail, graceful, busy insects to become established in England'.

Dr Gahan, Keeper of Entomology, responds to correct this immediately, his letter appearing in the newspaper two days later. 'It is quite time,' he writes, 'that your Correspondent, in common with the public, should know that the malarial mosquito, *Anopheles maculipennis*, is a species endemic to England' and quite common in river valleys and other low-lying areas. He describes the map that William Lang is preparing, which will show that 'the dreaded mosquito is very widely established in this country'. It is not the mosquito itself that is the source of malaria, Gahan informs readers of *The Times*, but it is 'the agent by which the disease is transmitted from one person to another'. As long as there were 'few or no malaria patients in the country, there was little or no danger to be apprehended from its presence'. However, as 'so many malaria patients from abroad' have arrived during the war, 'the danger of infection by mosquito bites has become acute. It is well that the public should thoroughly understand this', Gahan concludes, 'and be on their guard'.

27 APRIL 1918 At the Trustees meeting, Dr Gahan reports that William Lang has completed the text to accompany his mosquito distribution map. Gahan recommends that 2,000 copies of the map and 500 of the text be printed. The Local Government Board wishes to purchase 600 copies of the map.

The Trustees are also told that more than 2,000 of all of the Museum's economic pamphlets, leaflets and posters advising of the danger from insects and vermin have been sent to Salonika for distribution among the medical officers and troops there. More men die or are incapacitated from malaria and gastrointestinal diseases than are killed or wounded in battle in the Salonika campaign. In May nearly 6,000 men contract malaria, in June the figure is more than 7,500.

The Trustees also consider the use of whale flesh as a source of food. Letters on the nutritional possibilities of whales 'in the present emergency' have been received from the Ministry of Food and the Board of Agriculture in response to Dr Harmer's report. The Board thinks that 'owing to transport and other difficulties', little can be done. The Ministry of Food, however, suggests that if it is possible to 'utilise' cetacea in home waters, then the proposition deserves further consideration, 'especially from the point of view of obtaining oils'.

The Trustees are informed that Captain TJ Dudley, packer of publications, has been shot in the left arm. After recovering from shell shock, he had returned to the front in the autumn of 1917. They are also informed that PH Chamberlain, a Museum labourer, has enlisted as a private in the Royal Marine Engineers. He originally volunteered in 1915 and served in the Army Service Corps until May 1916 when he was discharged on medical grounds. He was given permission to volunteer again and has now passed the medical test.

Chapter 12
May–November 1918

Gradually, in summer and early autumn,
the tide of war begins to turn – at a cost of
nearly 400,000 British casualties. An influenza
pandemic sweeps across the world, taking the lives
of many millions. It arrives in Britain in early
summer. There is another attempt to enlist Charles
Tate Regan, and the eligibility of all exempt scientists
of military age at the Museum is investigated.
Museum Trustee Lord Rothschild shares his office
with meteorites. Senior staff ask for more pay.
Dolphin meat is on the menu for the Archbishop
of Canterbury and the Lord Mayor of London,
protection for the whimbrel is guaranteed, and the
Government threatens a leak enquiry. The Museum
assists Naval intelligence in establishing the age of
a wreck – of key operational importance. Two more
Museum men are killed in action in France and
another is killed in a tragic accident during training.
By October there is talk of victory and peace.
Belgium is liberated. Turkey, then Austria, are
out of the war. In the first week of November
there is a great British and allied advance.
On 9 November, Germany is given
48 hours to accept the armistice.

7 MAY 1918 Charles Fagan sends more details to the Ministry of Food of Dr Harmer's report on the utilisation of whale flesh as food. These discuss the feasibility of re-opening whaling stations in home waters and give numbers and species of whales caught there in previous years. The report also refers to the possibilities presented by stranded whales, though the supply, Dr Harmer writes, is very uncertain. He also recognises that as there might be difficulties 'in inducing people to eat them, it might be best to arrange for their utilisation as preserved meat, or perhaps with an even better prospect of success, they might be made at once into sausages'.

9 MAY 1918 A large van, provided by the Office of Works, leaves the Museum, heading for Lord Rothschild's museum at Tring in Hertfordshire. It carries four cases of precious meteorites from the Mineralogy collections. There are 148 specimens from 129 meteorites in the cases. Travelling with them is Mineralogy clerk, Thomas Frederick Vincent. When they arrive at Tring, they are 'placed in Lord Rothschild's study which will be kept locked when not occupied by him'.

In the Museum, a further 204 specimens from 117 meteorites – 'the unique and most valuable specimens' – are removed from the Mineralogy Gallery to a strong room in the basement.

10 MAY 1918 Lance Sergeant Charles Hill, in civilian life an attendant in Entomology, is accidentally killed in training during a machine-gun demonstration on Wimbledon Common, London. He was 28. At the outbreak of war Hill was already enrolled in the 15th Battalion, London Regiment (Prince of Wales' Own Civil Service Rifles), and was sent to France with the 1st Battalion. In September 1917 he was wounded while fighting near Ypres and was invalided home. Charles Fagan writes to his father, telling him, 'It is with great sorrow that I have heard this morning of the death under tragic

Lance Sergeant Charles Hill, a 28-year-old attendant in Entomology, was accidentally killed in training during a machine gun demonstration on Wimbledon Common on 10 May.

circumstances of your son Charles'. He tells him how much he was respected in the Museum, and particularly by Major Ernest Edward Austen, the assistant in Entomology for whom Hill worked. Writing for the Museum's *War Memorial Record*, Major Austen records that Hill joined the Museum in 1903 'as a little boy straight from school'. He was 'always careful, neat and precise, attentive to detail, and possessing in a marked degree that capacity for appreciating small differences which is essential in Museum work'. For Austen, his death is not only a 'personal loss', he is also a loss to the Museum.

17 MAY 1918 The senior staff of both the British Museum and the Natural History Museum whose salaries exceed £500, write to the Treasury. They respectfully request that the war bonus now paid to all civil servants whose salaries are less than £500 should also be paid to them. Since the beginning of the war, prices – and taxes – have risen enormously, but 'our incomes have remained stationary in amount and have seriously diminished in purchasing power, despite the more strenuous conditions under which we have been called upon to perform our official duties. In brief the War, whilst increasing our duties and responsibilities, has materially decreased the monetary value of our official positions'. Senior civil servants in other Government departments are making similar requests. Some estimates give the rise in the cost of living at 60 percent or more.

19 MAY 1918 It is the Whitsun Bank Holiday weekend. Dr Rendle, Keeper of Botany, is the senior officer on air-raid duty. At 11pm he receives the first warning. Five minutes later comes the 'take cover' notice. Sixty-eight people seek refuge in the Museum's basement shelter. It is a huge air attack – about 30 Gotha aeroplanes converge on London. Dr Rendle notes that 'the sound of our anti-aircraft guns is very much deadened in the Museum basement'. So too is the sound of bombs smashing into London across a wide area. At 1.20am the 'all clear' is given, but just 15 minutes later, there is a second warning. This time 46 people take shelter in the Museum. Dr Rendle writes that there was no untoward event or damage during the raid. Across London, however, 44 people are reported killed and 179 injured. At least five of the German planes are destroyed. What no one then knows is that this is the last air raid to reach London in this war. There is, however, no respite from fear.

14 JUNE 1918 On 8 May, a bottlenose dolphin, *Tursiops truncatus*, was stranded in the Thames near Battersea Bridge, on the Surrey side. It was '10 feet 7 inches in length' and weighed about half a ton. It was sent to the Museum the following day, and work began on it immediately to turn it into food. Zoology assistant and cetacea expert William Pycraft, writes about his work on the dolphin in his regular column in *The Illustrated London News*. He and a colleague 'spent three laborious days in cutting up the carcase. It produced 'several hundred pounds of meat'. Every day for a week, he writes, 'we rewarded ourselves with a steak for lunch, fried with onions; and the savour of those meals I shall not soon forget'. He recounts that various methods of cooking the meat were reported to him, including 'fried,

Attempts have been made for some time past, on the part of the Museum, to interest the proper authorities in the salvage of the valuable materials derivable from the bodies of stranded Whales. An increased amount of success was obtained in this particular case, as some of its flesh was used as food, and some of the blubber was purchased by a firm of Soap Manufacturers (Messrs John Knight). In view of the extreme age of the specimen Dr Harmer felt that it was not a very

Parts of the blubber were retained in the Museum for the preparation of oil needed in the taxidermists' room. Another part was given to Mr E. Sinkinson, of the Imperial College of Science and Technology, who kindly undertook to make a chemical analysis. The remainder was taken by Messrs John Knight, as already explained. The skeleton was retained for the Museum, and the condition of the bones when cleaned ought to show whether the animal

Part of Dr Harmer's report on the bottlenose dolphin stranded in the Thames near Battersea Bridge. He discusses the mammal itself – and the use that was made of it.

grilled, stewed, curried, or cooked en casserole with mushrooms'. All were agreed, he writes, 'that it was tender and delicious'.

To test its palatability, the Museum sends out portions of the meat – together with hints on cooking. Among those to receive it are the Local Government Board, the Board of Agriculture, the Board of Trade, the Ministry of Food, the Lord Mayor of London, two of the Trustees – the Archbishop of Canterbury and the Speaker of the House of Commons – and several members of the Museum staff.

Today Dr Harmer reports to the Trustees on how the whale meat was received. Almost without exception, he states, the reports are 'favourable and even enthusiastic'. He has kept many of them: 'I wish we could get it regularly'; 'a real royal dish…somewhat like tender beef with a slight taste of liver'; 'palatable'; 'excellent'. The response from Mr Proctor of the Ministry of Food however, is 'unattractive in appearance', 'tender but somewhat lacking in flavour' though that may be through 'par-boiling for too long a time'. However, 'in times of great meat shortage', Proctor concedes, 'this might prove a serviceable food'. Part of the blubber is retained by the Museum for the preparation of oil, and the remainder is purchased by a soap works in Silvertown, East London. With the agreement of the Board of Trade, the sum paid is to go to HM Exchequer.

The Port of London Authority has written to the Museum, stating that it 'will have much pleasure' in complying with the Museum's request to be informed of any cetacea strandings in the Thames.

The Trustees are also informed of a letter from Roy Chapman Andrews, an explorer and zoologist at the American Museum of Natural History, whose adventures and discoveries of dinosaur and mammal fossils in Central Asia in the 1920s are to bring him great fame. He has written to say that the utilisation of whale meat as food 'has been taken up energetically' in America. There are now five whaling stations with cold storage or canning plants to prepare the meat for human consumption. Analysis of the protein value of the canned product shows that it is about 34 per cent, 'while ordinary beef is only 13 or 14%'.

15 JUNE 1918 Basil Soulsby in the Director's Office writes to the Office of Works about complaints, reported by the police, that women clerks in the Eastern Pay Command Office in the Museum's grounds have been trespassing on the military allotments. The Colonel Commandant of the Cromwell Gardens Barracks has asked that the lavatory windows be fastened up so they cannot climb out,

364

NATURAL HISTORY MUSEUM, LONDON, S.W.

UTILIZATION OF WHALE FLESH AS HUMAN FOOD.

Whale meat has a certain oily taste which is not disagreeable, and would not be so to any one who cares for gamey meat. This can largely be eliminated by soaking the meat in boiling water to which a teaspoonful of soda has been added, or by parboiling it for a short time. The canning process largely eliminates the oily taste and the meat is excellent.

The American Museum of Natural History has had several analyses of whale meat made, and they find that the protein value of the canned product is about 34%, while ordinary beef is only 13 or 14%. Of course the protein of the fresh meat is not so high because in the canned a great deal of the water has been eliminated.

On the last occasion of eating whale flesh by some of the members of the staff of the Natural History Museum, at South Kensington, the meat was treated like beefsteak and proved excellent. The addition of some onions is probably a recommendation.

To test the palatability of cetacea meat, portions of the stranded dolphin were sent to a number of people, including the Lord Mayor of London and the Archbishop of Canterbury – a Museum Trustee. Charles Fagan enclosed these hints on how to cook it.

even though Soulsby has mentioned the possibilities of fire. 'In view of the value of the crops on the allotments', Soulsby writes, 'I am to request that the alteration be put in hand at the earliest possible moment'.

18 JUNE 1918 Dr Harmer reports that Dr Knud Andersen, a temporary worker in the Mammal Room, has disappeared and 'there is considerable reason for anxiety as to his fate'. Andersen, who is a Danish citizen, has been at the Museum since 1906 and is an expert on bats. For the last two years he has also been working part time as a translator in the Military Intelligence Department of the War Office. The first indication that there was anything wrong was a letter in May from Lieutenant Colonel Wake – whose section has been redesignated MI7(d) – enclosing a letter from Dr Andersen announcing his resignation. On 17 May Dr Andersen came to the Museum – when he should have been at the War Office. No definite information has been heard of him since then, apart from a confidential letter he sent to the Curator of Mammals, Michael Oldfield Thomas, from which 'there can be little doubt that serious domestic troubles furnished the motive for his disappearance'. Enclosed with his letter is his Museum diary, written up to 14 May. The letter, Dr Harmer reports, makes it 'quite clear that this was the last communication he intended to make to anyone representing the Museum'. Nothing more has been heard of him. For Harmer, 'the loss of his great knowledge is a serious blow'.

19 JUNE 1918 Botany Keeper Dr Rendle, in his report for the next meeting of the Trustees, notes that John Ramsbottom, the fungi expert who is working as a protozoologist in Salonika, has had time to collect specimens for the Museum. It is 'a small but useful collection of plants', Rendle writes, and it contains two new species.

Ramsbottom, who has been serving as a civilian with the Royal Army Medical Corps, now holds a temporary commission as 2nd lieutenant. Before the end of the war he will be promoted to Captain and mentioned three times in dispatches.

22 JUNE 1918 At their regular meeting, the Trustees are informed by Dr Harmer that the issue of Zoology assistant and fish expert Charles Tate Regan's exemption from military service has again arisen. In 1917 he was granted exemption conditional on his continuing membership of the Freshwater Fish Committee of the Board of Agriculture and Fisheries – work of national importance. However, despite this, his local Military Tribunal has now withdrawn the exemption 'which renders him liable for military service on July 10'. Dr Harmer urges 'very strongly' all the reasons against Mr Regan's 'absorption into the Army'. He submits an account of his work of economic importance as a fish expert at the Museum and on the Committee. The Trustees direct that application should again be made to the Ministry of National Service for an exemption certificate, and that the Board of Agriculture and Fisheries should be asked to support the application.

The Trustees also consider some of the consequences of the relaxation of rules governing the shooting of migratory wild birds for food. The question of permitting the whimbrel, a migratory wading bird, to be shot after 31 March in order to increase the food supply has been referred to the Museum by the Home Office. Both Lord Rothschild, an expert on birds, and Miss Gardiner, secretary of the Royal Society for the Protection of Birds, are agreed that any relaxation of the existing orders 'would certainly lead to unfortunate results'. It would be impossible, in practise, to distinguish between the whimbrel and the curlew, 'which is not good to eat until the autumn'. The Home Office is advised that it is 'undesirable' to alter the existing regulations for the protection of the whimbrel.

24 JUNE 1918 The Keeper of Entomology, Dr Gahan, deals with an urgent request for a new edition of 'The Fly Danger' poster. Fewer than 5,000 copies are left from the 40,000 that were printed less than a year ago, and to meet the demands of summer and autumn, a further supply is required. The Director recommends that 10,000 copies be printed as soon as Dr Gahan has had the poster revised. There is still great demand for the leaflets and posters on the dangers from flies and mosquitoes – and the mosquito map – particularly for the numerous child welfare exhibitions taking place throughout the country.

Dr Gahan also proposes a poster leaflet calling attention to the danger of disease from the louse, and setting out the most approved methods of prevention. It will be similar in style to those on the housefly and the mosquito, He recommends that 10,000 copies should be printed. The subject, he notes, 'is very pertinent just now'. Research by Major William Byam, RAMC, of the War Office Trench Fever Committee, has demonstrated by experiment – he used volunteers – the part the louse plays in the transmission of trench fever.

27 JUNE 1918 Charles Fagan applies to the Ministry of National Service for a certificate of exemption from military service for Charles Tate Regan. The application is made on the grounds of the 'national importance' of Regan's work. Fagan informs the Ministry that Regan is a scientific man of great value, who 'has an expert's knowledge of a group of questions of great practical importance'. He summarises some of the issues Regan has dealt with. Fagan also tells the Ministry that he is a member of the Board of Agriculture and Fisheries' Freshwater Fish Committee, the aim of which is to increase the food supply.

29 JUNE 1918 Private Edward Albert Bateman, 1st Battalion Norfolk Regiment, dies in northern France from wounds inflicted by a gas-shell. He was a boy attendant in the Imperial Bureau of Entomology

– based in the Entomology department – which he joined in 1914 straight from school. He enlisted in 1917. He is buried in Terlincthun British Cemetery near Boulogne. He was 18 years old.

2 JULY 1918 Charles Fagan sends the Ministry of National Service a list of members of staff whose age now brings them within the upper age limit of 50 (55 for medical men) under the 1918 Military Service Act. They are 15 essential members of staff – permanent and temporary. Fagan asks for certificates of exemption for each of them. Within a few days, all are granted the certificates. They are, however, marked 'conditional on the exigencies of the military situation'.

Dr Harmer writes to the unofficial scientific worker, Martin Hinton, who is preparing an economic booklet on the dangers of rats and mice. 'I am becoming very seriously concerned about the want of progress in the "Rats" Guide', Harmer tells him. 'I cannot imagine why we have not been able to get a Rat and a Mouse by now. If the Guide is not presented to the Meeting of the Trustees on July 27, there is no doubt that the efficiency of the Department will be severely criticised'. That is clearly of great concern to Harmer. He tells Hinton, 'we are making special efforts to have a Rat and a Mouse here tomorrow. If we

On 29 June, Private Edward Albert Bateman, a boy attendant in the Imperial Bureau of Entomology based in the Entomology department, died in France from wounds inflicted by a gas shell.

BRITISH MUSEUM (NATURAL HISTORY), CROMWELL ROAD, LONDON, S.W.

Date   June 13, 1918.

From   MEMORANDUM.   To

S.F.Harmer   The Director

          I understand that a question has arisen whether the intro-
duction of living Rats into the Museum is attended with any risk
of communicating Plague to persons working here. The question arises
from the fact that we have recently received two Black Rats from the
Port of London Authority, in order to have drawings made for Mr Hinton's Economic Guide on Rats and Mice. It is obvious that a responsible body which is fully alive to the importance of suppressing
Plague in this country would not distribute animals to which the
slightest risk was attached. But perhaps the best answer to the objection which has been made is that the Rats have been here some
days and they would have been dead of Plague, and might have communicated the disease to persons here, before now if they had been in-

The guide to rats and mice that Martin Hinton wrote met unexpected
obstacles. There was a question that the living rats needed for
illustrations might communicate the plague to 'persons working here'.
Dr Harmer briskly dismissed the concerns.

succeed I want these drawings approved by you as quickly as possible.'
Everything must be ready for the printers 'at a moment's notice…The
matter is really urgent, and we have not a day to spare'.

3 JULY 1918 An influenza epidemic is sweeping the country. A
report by the Office of Works Sanitary Adviser is issued to all the
Keepers and senior staff. All workers who 'feel ill from headache,
sore throat, running of the eyes, feverishness, pains in the back or
limbs or other symptoms of influenza', should report at once to their
departmental heads for permission to go home. There they should
remain. If absent for more than two days, a medical certificate
is required. It is recommended in the current warm weather,
windows at home and work should be kept open as fully as possible.
Ventilation 'is the best general preventative of disease transmission'.

Since May the papers have been reporting a flu epidemic in Spain. By June 'Spanish influenza' has reached Britain. *The Daily Mirror* reports that there are 300 cases in just one London hospital. The Royal Small Arms Factory in Enfield has 500 cases, and emergency temporary hospitals are set up to try to cope. One doctor in Birmingham arrives at his surgery to find nearly 200 patients waiting to see him. There are rumours that it can kill in a day. Those most affected are between 25 and 40 years old. In army depots in Britain, cases of flu leap from under 5,000 in May to more than 31,000 in June. The army in France is similarly affected.

4 JULY 1918 In accordance with a directive from the Office of Works, the American flag and the Union Jack are flown side by side at the Museum and other Government buildings. On 14 July, the Union Jack will be flown similarly with the French flag.

9 JULY 1918 The Special Works School in Kensington Gardens, which trains the military in camouflage techniques, has asked if it may make a copy of the case containing the disappearing birds exhibited in the Central Hall. Permission is granted.

10 JULY 1918 Mrs Cottam, who runs the Museum's public Refreshment Room, is facing considerable difficulties through food restrictions and too few staff. The Trustees give her permission to close the Refreshment Room on Sundays in August and September.

16 JULY 1918 Dr Harmer writes his report for the Trustees' meeting to be held on the 27th, with no hint of his anxiety over the delay in the 'Rat' guide. He writes that he is proposing a small exhibit of general interest to illustrate the transmission of disease by rodents and possibly other small mammals. The new guide, *Rats and Mice as Enemies of Mankind* by Martin Hinton, seems to be back on track. Two thousand copies are being printed. The guide explains the habits and breeding of these 'noxious' animals, the impact they have on public health and food, and measures by which they can be controlled 'if not exterminated'.

Harmer is also proposing an exhibit of 'Boring Animals and their operations'. This is in connection with the work that Dr Calman is

Illustrations of the black rat, *Rattus rattus*, and the brown rat, *Rattus norvegicus*, from Hinton's *Rats and Mice as Enemies of Mankind*. The rodents were drawn from life. No incidence of plague was reported.

doing with the Institution of Civil Engineers on the deterioration of structures exposed to sea-action. The exhibit will include ship worms, which damage submerged timber 'on a very large scale' at 'immense' cost. It will also illustrate the 'Gribble' and another crustacean very destructive to timber; certain bivalves and sponges which bore into stone; and fish, crustacea and molluscs which damage telegraph cables.

17 JULY 1918 The Ministry of National Service writes to inform the Museum that it is to be investigated by representatives of the Military Service Committee. The Military Service (No 2) Act 1918 provides for the cancellation of any exemption from military service granted on occupational grounds. In the first instance, 20 members of staff under the age of 41 (the upper limit for military service under the 1916 Military Service Act) will be investigated. The Museum is asked to nominate two representatives on the Committee and to appoint a Museum official as secretary. An immediate reply is required. The Ministry is told that two Trustees will serve, with Charles Fagan as secretary. The Museum is informed that it is not intended, at present, to call up civil servants over the age of 42.

19 JULY 1918 The Ministry of National Service informs the Director that Charles Tate Regan's application for exemption from military service should come before the Military Service Committee in their investigation of the Museum staff.

24 JULY 1918 Charles Fagan sends a memo to the Keepers marked <u>SECRET AND VERY IMPORTANT</u>. It is underlined twice in red. It is headed 'Leakage of Information'. The War Cabinet has sent an instruction to all civil servants holding positions giving them access to confidential information, to the effect that there have been several recent cases of leakage of such information. The next occasion of a leak – in the press or otherwise, 'powers would be exercised under the Defence of the Realm Regulations to trace the leakage to its source'.

27 JULY 1918 The Director, Sir Lazarus Fletcher, reports that a number of economic pamphlets and posters have recently been distributed to the military. These include the anopheline mosquito map to the Army Medical Service, New Zealand Expeditionary Force; the fly-danger poster to the Wool Military Hospital, Dorset and also to the Specialist Sanitary Officer, Harwich Garrison, who also asked for the mosquito-danger poster.

3 AUGUST 1918 London County Council's Public Health Committee estimates that between 15 June and today, influenza has caused the death of about 1,700 Londoners.

7 AUGUST 1918 The Board Room, 10.30am. It is the day of the Military Service Committee meeting. A list of 20 members of staff who, by their ages, come under the Military Service Act 1916, is before them. So too is the tribunal and military history and other particulars for each man. Of these 20, only two are in categories that call for consideration by the Committee. Both are Zoology assistants. Arthur Hirst is 34 and has been assessed Grade 1 for military service. Charles Tate Regan, 40, is grade Bi. All the other cases are men who have been either discharged from the Army, rejected as unfit, or in the lower categories of fitness. In view of the highly technical nature of their duties, and of the national importance of their work, the Committee decides that absolute exemption should be granted to Hirst and Regan. All those in the lower medical categories should also be retained in the Museum.

9 AUGUST 1918 Dr Harmer receives a letter from Commander Guybon Chesney Castell Damant, an Admiralty Salvage Officer based in Dover. Damant sends in a small piece of tin with a barnacle and a small mollusc shell growing on it. He writes that it was in a wreck at a depth of 18 fathoms in the English Channel. He wishes to know the approximate date the wreck was sunk, 'or rather the shortest time in which the 2 shells could have grown to their present size'. He ends: 'I may say that the matter is of serious importance'.

Dr Harmer gives the tin fragment to the department's invertebrate specialist, Randolph Kirkpatrick, to analyse. He gives the barnacle to crustacean expert, Dr William Calman. Damant does not reveal what type of wreck the tin is from, but Kirkpatrick suspects it may be a German U-boat. Kirkpatrick hoped to be able to give Damant an answer within a couple of days, but he has now found that there are about 10 different organisms growing on the tin's surface and he will need to consult three scientists who are not in London. 'It is essential', Kirkpatrick writes to Damant, 'to make the utmost use of every scrap of evidence'.

By the time the analysis is finished, no fewer than 19 different organisms are shown to be growing on the fragment. Kirkpatrick consults seven different specialists. He also visits several tinplate and lacquer firms to get information regarding 'a crust on the "upper" exposed surface of the metal – a matter of some relevance as the organisms were growing on this peculiar crust'.

The consensus of opinion is that, apart from the barnacle (for which Calman writes a separate report), all the specimens seem to have settled on the tin since February or March. The barnacle however, probably 'cannot be much less than six, and may be as much as eighteen months old', but the problem all the scientists found is how little is known about the growth rate of all the organisms. Kirkpatrick suggests that 'the probability of reaching a sound and definite conclusion' would be greatly increased if specimens obtained from the wreck could be preserved in alcohol 'at the time of capture'. He also suggests that much valuable information might be obtained by acquiring 'pieces of organism-encrusted wreckage' from other ships, the dates of whose sinking are known.

Commander Damant sends his 'best thanks' for the reports. 'I had in effect to decide whether the craft was sunk before June of this year, and the line to be taken in very extensive operations depended on the decision'. From the reports, particularly of the barnacle, he writes that it must have been earlier than June. He tells Kirkpatrick that he will try to get more specimens and preserve them in formalin or spirit. 'I am constantly diving and supervising work in depths up to twenty five fathoms and if there is any way in which I could get information or specimens that might be wanted by your specialists I would be very glad'.

He also writes that 'Admiral Keyes and the Director of Naval Intelligence have been greatly interested in this matter'. Keyes is vice admiral at Dover and since 1917 has been concerned with how to limit U-boat movements in the Dover Strait, operations involving considerable danger but which have been increasingly effective. Keyes thanks Charles Fagan for the reports, which 'have proved most valuable and interesting'. Nearly two years later, in June 1920, the fragment of tin is exhibited in the Museum's Boardroom. It is labelled: 'Fragment of a German submarine sunk in 18 fathoms in the English Channel'.

22 AUGUST 1918 After the horrendous losses of the spring in northern France, the British and allied armies at last seem to be making real advances. Near Albert, the British advance two miles – and are then driven back 500 yards. There is an enemy air attack and Private Frederick John Bean, a boy attendant in Geology, who is on the British lines near Albert, is killed. He joined the Museum in November 1913 when he was 14 and was attendant to the Keeper, Dr Arthur Smith Woodward at the entrance to the department. In 1916, Smith Woodward noted that 'his conduct is in all respects admirable'. In November 1917, Bean joined the 24th (County of London) Battalion (The Queen's). Frederick Bean is buried in the British Cemetery, Bray-sur-Somme, France. He was 18 years old.

The Government has determined that no one should be employed in any Government office during the war who is 'not the child of natural-born subjects of this country or an Allied country', unless there is 'a definite National reason for such employment'. Charles Fagan today asks the Keepers to send him the names of anyone of this description currently working in their departments, whether permanent or temporary staff. It leads to some awkward communications. The 37-year-old taxidermist Percy Stammwitz has worked in the Museum since 1902. He is currently a lieutenant in the 1st County of London Yeomanry. In February 1917 his battalion was sent to Egypt. Dr Harmer has now to write to his father: 'I am extremely sorry to trouble you about this matter, but it is necessary for me to ask whether you and your wife are both natural born subjects of this country or of an Allied country. I am almost prepared to answer this question in the affirmative but I have not really sufficient information to justify me in doing so. Please excuse me for writing to ask you to confirm my impression. I should be glad if you would state the nationality in each case'.

His impression is confirmed. Both parents are British, born in London. Percy Stammwitz survives the war and he and his son Stuart become indispensable to the Museum as taxidermists and preparators through much of the 20th century, until Stuart's retirement in 1969.

30 AUGUST 1918 There is just one man in the Natural History Museum who is not the child of natural-born subjects of Britain or of an allied country. He is Henrik Grönvold, a 59-year old Dane who has been resident in Britain since 1892. He is not naturalised. Charles Fagan today notes that he is an artist 'with highly technical skill for scientific work'. His work is of 'National importance for the Museum and other Government departments'. His special skills mean that it would not be possible to replace him and it is thus 'very desirable to retain his services'. An application is made to the Government committee dealing with these cases to retain his services.

Lt John Ramsbottom asks for more than 1,000 insect and vermin pamphlets and posters to be sent to Salonika, for use by the Sanitation Officers of the British Expeditionary Force. He tells Charles Fagan that he is arranging a plant-collecting competition for officers and men with the aim of obtaining a representative collection of Macedonian plants for the Museum.

3 SEPTEMBER 1918 Charles Fagan writes to the Coal Controller on a matter of urgency. It is regarding the 'very valuable collections' evacuated to Lord Rothschild's Museum at Tring. 'It is of the utmost importance', Fagan writes, 'for the preservation of these collections that they should be kept in rooms of uniform temperature. A low temperature would certainly cause grave damage to irreplaceable specimens.' He therefore states, 'on national grounds', that an adequate amount of fuel should be supplied to the Tring museum so the correct temperature for these 'unique objects, the property of the nation', can be maintained.

9 SEPTEMBER 1918 The Treasury sends out a circular letter to all Government departments. Under the Defence of the Realm Act, everyone serving in an established capacity in the civil service must take the oath of allegiance before 1 November. Charles Fagan will administer the oath to officers and assistants, who are requested to call on him up to and including Saturday, 19 October. Basil Soulsby will administer the oath to the museum clerks and hall clerks within the same timeframe.

21 SEPTEMBER 1918 The Belgian Ministry of Science and Art asks for duplicate specimens and books for use by soldier-students on the Belgian front for whom it is proposed to arrange natural history lectures. The Museum selects publications, about 100 zoological specimens, 100 fossils and about 50 minerals to present to the Ministry.

OCTOBER 1918 A new, even more virulent strain of influenza appears. For many it leads to septic pneumonia. In one week in Britain, it is reported to have caused nearly 2,000 deaths. This is a preliminary estimate. Schools and factories close, public services are badly hit, people are taken ill in the street. There are calls for improvements in hygiene and a Ministry of Health.

2 OCTOBER 1918 Charles Fagan receives letters from the Museum's bookbinders, WH Smith & Sons, and the printers, Messrs W Clowes. As a consequence of the substantial rise in wages for both men and women, WH Smith have no alternative but to increase their prices by a further 17½ percent. This is a 100 percent increase in their prices since January 1916. Clowes are increasing their prices by another 15 percent, through 'the further heavy increase in wages' and 'the continued advance in the cost of all materials'. The Trustees have no choice but to accept the increase.

6 OCTOBER 1918 Captain Arthur Knyvett Totton, holder of the Military Cross and Zoology assistant who was severely wounded in 1916, is about to leave hospital after a further operation. He has been on sick leave since resigning his commission in April. As that is now six months, under Treasury regulations he will be placed on half pay, as of today.

7 OCTOBER 1918 Dr Rendle notes the work for Government departments undertaken recently by the Botany Department. It includes investigating the contents of a poultry mixture, presumed poisonous; the name and nature of timbers and their diseases; the use of beech mast as a source of oil, and the economic use of British algae, especially the possibilities of collecting carrageen on British coasts. They have also been studying soil fungi and other causes of plant diseases.

12 OCTOBER 1918 Dr Harmer reports that he has granted Mr John Robert Pannell of the Aeronautics Division of the National Physical Laboratory permission to take pencil tracings of certain fish and cetaceans. This is in connection with the design of airship hulls. Pannell is working on the design of the R38, a huge airship more than 200 metres long. It is intended for long-range sea-patrols, but it is not built until after the war ends. In 1921, Pannell is on board the R38 on a test flight over the Humber. Stresses on the fuselage are too great. The airship breaks apart and explodes. There are 49 crew and engineers on board and only five survive. Pannell is not one of them.

21 OCTOBER 1918 Dr Harmer receives an enquiry regarding the extermination of land-leeches in the tropics. He is asked for information on their life history and 'mode of life'. Dr Harmer learns that the Board of Agriculture and Fisheries has been experimenting with chlorine gas for the destruction in the open of injurious insects. 'The experiments are said to have been

Aeronautics Division COM. 26 OCT. 1918

THE NATIONAL PHYSICAL LABORATORY,

ALL COMMUNICATIONS
TO BE ADDRESSED TO
THE DIRECTOR.

Aero/JRP TEDDINGTON, MIDDLESEX,

7th October 1918.

The Secretary,
  British Museum of Natural History,
  Cromwell Road,
  S.W.7.

BRITISH MUSEUM
NATURAL HISTORY

2132

P

8 OCT 1918

Dear Sir,

      In connection with the design of
airship hulls we are interested to see the
outlines tails of certain fish. I should be much
obliged if you could arrange for me to call
at the Museum and take pencil tracings of
some of the fastest swimmers. I should
particularly be glad to have the outline of
the porpoise. The official at the Board
of Agriculture and Fisheries informed me
that Mr. Tate-Regan would be the proper
person to see and I should be glad to know
if he could spare a little time on Tuesday,
October 8th, as I shall be in town and
could call soon after 2 o'clock.

      I am also rather interested in the
outline of whales on account of their size
and should be glad to have some tracings
of these also.

      I will endeavour to telephone you
to-morrow to know if you can made arrangements for my visit.

                    Yours faithfully,

SFH.

W 7540 6M 5-18 W 14835 5M 7-18 W FP

John Robert Pannell of the Aeronautics Division of the National
Physical Laboratory asked permission in October 1918 to make 'pencil
tracings' of fast swimming fish, the porpoise and of whales. His work
was designing airships hulls.

very encouraging'. After the first effect of the gas has passed, its use 'has resulted in an improved growth of the plants treated and better crops'. Dr Harmer thinks this method might be used against leeches and, in view of the importance of the subject, he suggests 'that the War Office should be asked whether the use of war-methods is at present permissible for experiments having for their object the extermination of Land-leeches in India and the Tropics'.

Charles Fagan writes to the War Office, describing the leeches as 'a formidable obstacle to travel in forest regions, where they lie in wait for passers-by and show a blood-thirstiness which may well be termed ferocious. Their large number make their occurrence a serious matter'. The Trustees, he writes, would be glad to be assured that there is no objection on the part of the War Office to the use of this "War method" at the present time'. Chlorine gas was first used by the Germans in 1915.

25 OCTOBER 1918 The Librarian of the Polish Library and School at the Aliens' Detention Camp on the Isle of Man applies to the Museum for natural history books, especially botanical, for educational purposes. The condition does not matter, even 'shop-soiled specimens in whatever state of dilapidation'. There is no objection from the Government's Civilian Internment Camp Committee and the material is sent.

28 OCTOBER 1918 The influenza epidemic continues to rage. It affects the Speaker of the House of Commons, a Museum Trustee. He recovers, but his illness means he is not present in the House when, for the first time in history, women are permitted to sit in the Strangers' Gallery with men. In this week the Registrar-General gives influenza deaths in London as 2,458. The epidemic does not abate until December. It returns in early 1919.

29 OCTOBER 1918 Permission is given to some temporary members of staff to leave their bicycles in the Museum's bicycle shed. Since August there have been strikes – or threats of them – involving the police, the tube, firemen, cotton spinners, aircraft workers, railways, omnibuses and municipal workers. Increased pay and union recognition is a principal cause – and women demanding equal pay for equal work.

3 NOVEMBER 1918 Austria-Hungary surrenders to the allies. Turkey did so three days ago. Germany, as *The Times* reports, 'now stands alone'. In the next few days, a great allied offensive makes 'splendid progress'.

7 NOVEMBER 1918 A German delegation leaves Berlin for the Western Front. Its object is to obtain an armistice. *The Times* reports 'events are moving fast indeed'.

9 NOVEMBER 1918 Arthur Totton is at last recovering and considering returning to work. Charles Fagan tells him 'I don't think you could do better service to the country at the present time…than resuming duty here. We shall be very glad to have you'. He ends his letter: 'The War looks likely to end in a debacle for Germany as well as for Austria'. Germany has been given two days to accept the terms of the armistice.

11 NOVEMBER 1918 At 5am, the armistice is signed. Hostilities will cease on all fronts at 11am. The Prime Minister, David Lloyd George, appears at the door of 10 Downing Street. 'At 11 o'clock this morning', he tells a huge, cheering crowd, 'the war will be over. We have won a great victory and we are entitled to a bit of shouting'. A moment or two later, *The Times* reports, 'the maroons crashed out their message of peace and, as if by magic, every office in Whitehall

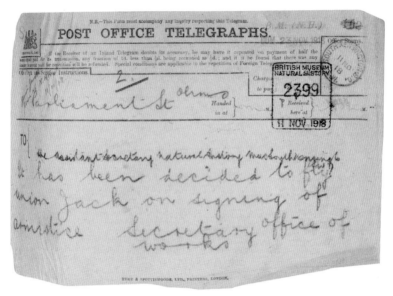

The Museum was informed by telegram on 11 November 1918 that
the signing of the armistice was to be marked by flying the Union Jack.

emptied itself'. The Union Jack flies on the Museum, as it does on all
public buildings. At Buckingham Palace, crowds appear from every
direction, cheering, shouting, singing, crying. The rain falls. No one
cares. The transition from war to peace begins.

Postscript

After nearly four and a half years of war, it is hard to believe it really is over. Air raid duty for the senior staff at the Vandyke Hotel ceases on 14 November. The Office of Works is asked to remove sandbags and sand. But a week after the armistice is signed, Dr Harmer writes to Michael Oldfield Thomas in Devon: 'I suppose we shall have to consider before long the question of your return from Exeter, but nothing has been decided at present, and I imagine it will be best to wait until the Armistice turns definitely into peace'.

The overwhelming priority for the Museum is 'To commence restoration at once', as Charles Fagan notes. On 16 November, he begins applying for the release of staff from the military and those attached to other Government departments. The Office of Works is contacted to begin the arrangements to return the evacuated specimens from Tring and Exeter. Precious specimens moved to secure places within the Museum are returned to galleries and collections. On 16 December, the whole Museum is open once again to the public, and can remain open until 5pm – after dark. The relief for staff no longer having to work in the gloom of dimly-lit studies is immense. It will be some time, however, before there is sufficient coal for the temperature in their chilly rooms to begin to approach pre-war days.

Early in December 1918, Charles Fagan writes to Dr Lucas of the American Museum of Natural History. 'I am writing to express to you,' he begins, 'our hearty felicitations on the glorious victory of the Allies over the common enemy. It is hardly necessary for me to assure

50.

B.M. (N.H.)

COM. 25 JAN 1919

AMERICAN MUSEUM OF NATURAL HISTORY
NEW YORK

BRITISH MUSEUM
NATURAL HISTORY

66

P -

8 JAN 1919

December 23, 1918.

Dear Mr. Fagan:

    Your kind letter of December 2nd was
received just in time to be presented at the meeting of our Executive Committee whose members highly
appreciate your cordial greeting. We have unbounded
admiration for the indomitable spirit and tenacity
of purpose that has enabled you to carry on your
scientific work with the enemy at your very door
and we heartily re-echo your hope that in the near
future you may prosecute your work under more
favorable conditions.

    Meantime, on behalf of the President and
staff of this Museum, I send sincere congratulations
for what your great institution has done in the past
and best wishes for the future.

    Believe me,

        Sincerely yours,

                F.A.Lucas,
                    Director.

Mr. C. E. Fagan,
British Museum, Cromwell Road, London.

A letter from the Director of the American Museum of Natural History,
who wrote of his 'unbounded admiration' for the way in which the
Museum pursued its scientific work 'with the enemy at your very door'.

you of our sense of the splendid aid rendered by the United States in effecting this great result'. To the Belgian Minister of Science and Art, Fagan offers 'our respectful and sincere congratulations on the glorious termination of the devastating war'. The Museum receives similar letters from its many international correspondents. One of these, from the National Museum of Natural Science in Madrid, is 'not a mere formula of courtesy', but an expression of 'sincere feelings of sympathy' towards Britain. It reads: 'Please let us congratulate very warmly your Museum on the end of the great war, so glorious an end for your country and for the cause of universal freedom and peace'. The Museum is so struck by the tone of this letter, that it sends it to *The Times*, which reprints it on 8 January 1919.

For weeks after the war ends the Museum is still sending out Government propaganda to its international correspondents. On 29 November *The Times* carries a report headlined: 'Germany still lying to neutrals. Need for British propaganda', and stating that 'the German propaganda service has never been more active'. On 3 December, Charles Fagan writes directly to the head of the Propaganda department, Colonel Buchan – John Buchan, the novelist. He asks Buchan if he has seen the report in *The Times*, and suggests that, 'There would seem to be strong reason for continuing this British propaganda work abroad in face of the unceasing efforts and insidious methods of Germany to create an atmosphere favourable to herself during the peace conference.' Fagan has done an extraordinary job throughout the war in utilising the Museum's contacts to send Government propaganda round the world to where it can do most good. He does not stop now. The Museum continues to send out this material until well into 1919, by which time it has a new Director and much deserved promotion for Charles Fagan.

The Museum's Director since 1909, Sir Lazarus Fletcher, has long suffered from poor health. He lets it be known in December 1918

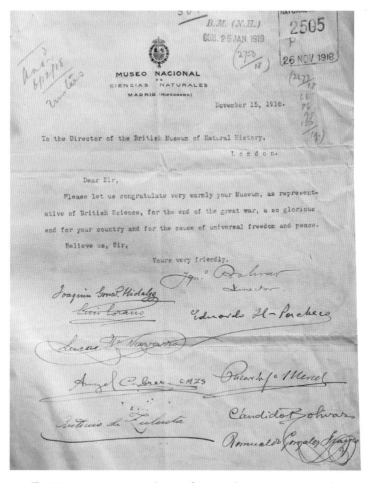

The Museum receives many letters of congratulations. It was so struck
by this one from the National Museum of Natural Science in Madrid
that it was sent to *The Times* who reprinted it on 8 January 1919.

that he will retire on his 60th birthday in March 1919. The Trustees'
first thought to succeed him is the man who has carried the
administrative burden of the Museum for the past 20 years, not only

for Fletcher, but also for his predecessor, Sir William Flower. Charles Fagan is a man whose abilities are legion, and who commands almost universal respect. He is however, an administrator, not an eminent scientist. When his name emerges as a possible successor, there is uproar from the scientific community. Twenty fellows of the Royal Society – including many who know of Fagan's tireless work for the Museum in the war, sign a letter that appears in *The Times* on 1 March 1919, deploring his appointment. There are 'at least two of the present Keepers' and several eminent men not on the staff who are eligible, the fellows write. 'To pass over these…in favour of one of the ordinary office staff would be an affront to scientific men and of grave detriment to science'.

There are many for whom this description of Fagan is an equal affront, one of whom is Dr Harmer. He writes to *Nature* on 13 March, in defence of Fagan, arguing that his work 'has been essentially scientific, and that his services in rendering the national museum a scientific institution have been exceptionally great'. But *Nature* is also against Fagan, and the Trustees, in the face of such a weight of scientific opinion, cannot proceed. Fagan is due to retire in two years, and his appointment as Director would therefore have been short, but long enough to mastermind the reconstruction of the Museum after the war. It would also have given him a much-deserved increase to both his salary and pension.

What is decided instead is that Fagan's title will become Secretary (rather than Assistant Secretary), with increased salary and pension. He will be in a position to carry through the difficult transition from war to peace. The Director is to be Dr Sidney Harmer, the distinguished Keeper of Zoology, an appointment that is much deserved. While every department – most particularly Entomology – has carried its share of war work, it is Harmer and Fagan whose work is outstanding. Harmer's exceptional abilities have been evident from his first arrival at the Museum from Cambridge in 1907.

For nearly two years they run the Museum together, but in December 1920, Fagan becomes ill. On 30 January 1921, two months before he is due to retire, Charles Fagan dies. Sidney Harmer has lost a great friend and esteemed colleague. In the journal *Nature* Harmer writes, 'It is impossible to speak too highly of the services Mr Fagan rendered to the Natural History Museum'. He touches on his tact and 'remarkable insight', and his 'extraordinary capacity for forming a correct judgment on a difficult question'. It was Fagan, Harmer writes, who 'thoroughly realised' that as well as its role as a 'treasure-house' of natural history, there was 'the importance of making it a centre of research, and there can be no question that his initiative was responsible for many new departures which have materially assisted in the advancement of knowledge'. That the consultative functions of the Museum have been increasingly appreciated in recent years, and particularly during the war, is 'a result largely due to his influence'. Charles Fagan's career, Harmer wrote, 'was one long record of single-minded service, strenuously and successfully performed'.

Without Fagan's exceptional combination of passion for his institution and its staff, his clarity of thought and his selfless duty, the Natural History Museum's path through the vicissitudes of the Great War might have been very, very different. Sidney Harmer's grief

Thomas Douglas (left), a member of the cleaning staff, is the Museum's last military death in this war. He died on 13 March 1919 in Belgium from bronco-pneumonia.

The Museum's War Memorial in the Hintze Hall honours the dead from World War I (opposite).

IN MEMORY
1914 -1918

DIED FOR KING AND COUNTRY

EDWARD A. BATEMAN
FREDERICK J. BEAN
THOMAS DOUGLAS
JOHN GABRIEL
E. GEORGE GENTRY
DUNCAN H. GOTCH
CHARLES HILL
H. FREDERICK KINGSERY
GEORGE PIGOTT
JOHN H. SUTHERLAND
ROBERT J. SWIFT
STANLEY T. WELLS
R. GILBERT WILTSHEAR

BRITISH MUSEUM (NATURAL HISTORY)

for his colleague is unconcealed. He closes his obituary with this: 'He is deeply mourned by his many friends, and particularly by his colleagues who recognised his lovable qualities and the great value of his services to the Museum and to science'.

In the spring of 1919 there was one more military death for the Museum to absorb. Thomas Douglas, a 29 year-old member of the cleaning staff, died on 13 March. He enlisted in February 1916 and saw service in France. He was severely wounded in 1917 but in April 1918 he returned to France where he survived the German 'great offensive'. In October he was transferred to Belgium. In March he contracted bronco-pneumonia and it was that which killed him. He was buried at Tournai.

*

Sixty-eight men went to war and 13 of them died. Their sacrifice is commemorated in the simple bronze plaque placed in the Central Hall in 1921. There is no physical memorial to those men – and women – who were left, and who kept the spirit of the Natural History Museum alive through four and a half years of war. Yet it was their dedication and effort, working in gloomy and often bitterly cold rooms, which nurtured, maintained and preserved the priceless collections for their successors. It is not possible to quantify how many lives were saved by the Museum's wartime researches. What is undoubtedly true is that many lives were improved through the scientists' tireless work to transform public health, fight insect and bacteria-born infections, their many and varied contributions to the military effort, and the hundreds of thousands of visitors who found respite from war in the galleries of the Museum – in spite of repeated attempts by Government to close it.

The endeavours of them all should be honoured.

Further reading

This a small selection of the publications I consulted and found most useful:
Bather, Francis A, 1914–18, *Museums Journal*.
Charman, Terry, 2015, T*he First World War on the Home Front*, London: Andre Deutsch and Imperial War Museum.
Haller, JS, 1990, 'Trench foot – a study in military-medical responsiveness in the Great War, 1914–1918', *Western Journal of Medicine*, 152(6).
Macleod, RM & Andrews E Kay, 1971, 'Scientific Advice in the War at Sea, 1915–17: The Board of Invention and Research', *Jnl of Contemporary History*, 6(2).
MacPherson, Maj-Gen Sir WG, 1921, 'Medical Services General History', *History of the Great War Based on Official Documents vols I–IV*, London: HMSO.
MacPherson, Maj-Gen Sir WG et al, eds., 1922–23, 'Medical Services Diseases of the War', *History of the Great War Based on Official Documents*, London: HMSO.
Pattison, Michael, 1983, 'Scientists, Inventors and the Military in Britain, 1915–19: The Munitions Inventions Department', *Social Studies of Science*, 13(4).
Stearn, William T, 1998, *The Natural History Museum at South Kensington*, London: Natural History Museum.
Thayer, Abbott H, 1896, 'The Law Which Underlies Protective Coloration', *The Auk*, 13(2)
Thayer, Gerald H, 1909, *Concealing Coloration in the Animal Kingdom*, New York: The Macmillan Co.
War Office Committee of Enquiry into 'Shell Shock', 1922, Cmd. 1734, London: HMSO.
White, Jerry, 2015, *Zeppelin Nights, London in the First World War*, London: Vintage.

Index

Sources

The main source for this book has been the correspondence, papers and publications held in the Library and Archives of the Natural History Museum. The Imperial War Museum's WWI galleries and online resources have been invaluable, as have many other online resources including Ancestry.co.uk, Archive.org., the British Library, the British Newspaper Archive, Forces War Records, *Hansard*, The National Archives, *Obituary Notices of Fellows of the Royal Society*, *Oxford Dictionary of National Biography*, Redcross.org.uk and *The Times*.

Acknowledgements

This book could not have been written without the help, patience and support of the staff of the Library and Archives of the Natural History Museum. My thanks particularly to Andrea Hart, Laura Brown and Hellen Pethers. For the last four years, I have been writing a quarterly 'diary' of WWI for the Museum's magazine *Evolve* – 'Snapshot of War'. That has formed the basic structure of this book, and I am very grateful to *Evolve's* editor, Helen Sturge, for her support and enthusiasm for the project.

Across the Museum – and outside it – I also offer sincere thanks for their help and knowledge to Ruth Benny, Paul Martyn Cooper, James Downs, Adrian Jackson, Adrian Lister, Geoff Martin, Ben Nathan, Katie Ormerod, Lorraine Portch, Sarah Sworder, John Tennent and Kate Tyte. Apologies to those I do not have space to acknowledge here. My thanks to all at NHM Publishing, particularly Trudy Brannan and Colin Ziegler. And thanks, as ever, to Henry Kelly for his editorial pencil at various stages of this book.

Picture credits